New Perspectives on

Microsoft® Office PowerPoint® 2003

CourseCard Edition

Introductory

Beverly B. Zimmerman

Brigham Young University

S. Scott Zimmerman

Brigham Young University

THOMSON

COURSE TECHNOLOGY

Australia • Canada • Mexico • Singapore • Spain • United Kingdom • United States

THOMSON

COURSE TECHNOLOGY

New Perspectives on Microsoft® Office PowerPoint® 2003—Introductory, CourseCard Edition
is published by Course Technology.

Senior Managing Editor:
Rachel Goldberg

Senior Product Managers:
Kathy Finnegan, Karen Stevens

Senior Technology Product Manager:
Amanda Young Shelton

Product Manager:
Brianna Hawes

Associate Product Manager:
Emilie Perreault

Editorial Assistant:
Shana Rosenthal

Marketing Manager:
Joy Stark

Developmental Editor:
Katherine T. Pinard

Production Editors:
Jennifer Goguen, Kelly Robinson

Composition:
GEX Publishing Services

Text Designer:
Steve Deschene

Cover Designer:
Nancy Goulet

Cover Artist:
Ed Carpenter
www.edcarpenter.net

Preface

Real, Thought-Provoking, Engaging, Dynamic, Interactive—these are just a few of the words that are used to describe the New Perspectives Series' approach to learning and building computer skills.

Without our critical-thinking and problem-solving methodology, computer skills could be learned but not retained. By teaching with a case-based approach, the New Perspectives Series challenges students to apply what they've learned to real-life situations.

Our ever-growing community of users understands why they're learning what they're learning. Now you can too!

See what instructors and students are saying about the best-selling New Perspectives Series:

"The New Perspectives layout is thoughtfully designed and organized. It is very easy to locate concepts and step-by-step instructions. The Case Problems provide different scenarios that cover material in the tutorial with plenty of exercises."
— Shui-lien Huang, Mt. San Antonio College

...and about New Perspectives on Microsoft Office PowerPoint 2003:

"Helpful tips and hints for delivering effective presentations are offered throughout the book. The authors truly emphasize the fact that the PowerPoint software is a tool to use and a presentation is only as interesting as its presenter."
— Candice Spangler, Columbus State Community College

"New Perspectives PowerPoint 2003 is an excellent text for helping students master the skills necessary for developing dynamic presentations. Step-by-step examples integrated with tips for effective presentations are reinforced with exercises and cases relevant to today's world."
— Kathleen Bent, Cape Cod Community College

www.course.com/NewPerspectives

Review

Apply

Reference Window

Task Reference

Why *New Perspectives* will work for you

Context
Each tutorial begins with a problem presented in a "real-world" case that is meaningful to students. The case sets the scene to help students understand what they will do in the tutorial.

Hands-on Approach
Each tutorial is divided into manageable sessions that combine reading and hands-on, step-by-step work. Screenshots—now 20% larger for enhanced readability—help guide students through the steps. **Trouble?** tips anticipate common mistakes or problems to help students stay on track and continue with the tutorial.

Review
In New Perspectives, retention is a key component to learning. At the end of each session, a series of Quick Check questions helps students test their understanding of the concepts before moving on. And now each tutorial contains an end-of-tutorial summary and a list of key terms for further reinforcement.

Assessment
Engaging and challenging Review Assignments and Case Problems have always been a hallmark feature of the New Perspectives Series. Now we've added new features to make them more accessible! Colorful icons and brief descriptions accompany the exercises, making it easy to understand, at a glance, both the goal and level of challenge a particular assignment holds.

Reference
While contextual learning is excellent for retention, there are times when students will want a high-level understanding of how to accomplish a task. Within each tutorial, Reference Windows appear before a set of steps to provide a succinct summary and preview of how to perform a task. In addition, a complete Task Reference at the back of the book provides quick access to information on how to carry out common tasks. Finally, each book includes a combination Glossary/Index to promote easy reference of material.

Student Online Companion
This book has an accompanying online companion Web site designed to enhance learning. This Web site includes:
- Internet Assignments and Lab Assignments for selected tutorials
- Student Data Files and PowerPoint presentations
- Microsoft Office Specialist Certification Grids

www.course.com/NewPerspectives

New Perspectives offers an entire system of instruction

The New Perspectives Series is more than just a handful of books. It's a complete system of offerings:

New Perspectives catalog

Our online catalog is never out of date! Go to the catalog link on our Web site to check out our available titles, request a desk copy, download a book preview, or locate online files.

Coverage to meet your needs!

Whether you're looking for just a small amount of coverage or enough to fill a semester-long class, we can provide you with a textbook that meets your needs.

- Brief books typically cover the essential skills in just 2 to 4 tutorials.
- Introductory books build and expand on those skills and contain an average of 5 to 8 tutorials.
- Comprehensive books are great for a full-semester class, and contain 9 to 12+ tutorials.
- Power Users or Advanced books are perfect for a highly accelerated introductory class or a second course in a given topic.

So if the book you're holding does not provide the right amount of coverage for you, there's probably another offering available. Go to our Web site or contact your Course Technology sales representative to find out what else we offer.

Instructor Resources

We offer more than just a book. We have all the tools you need to enhance your lectures, check students' work, and generate exams in a new, easier-to-use and completely revised package. This book's Instructor's Manual, ExamView testbank, PowerPoint presentations, data files, solution files, figure files, and a sample syllabus are all available on a single CD-ROM or for downloading at www.course.com.p

How will your students master Microsoft Office?

SAM (Skills Assessment Manager) 2003 helps you energize your class exams and training assignments by allowing students to learn and test important computer skills in an active, hands-on environment. With SAM 2003, you create powerful interactive exams on critical Microsoft Office 2003 applications, including Word, Excel, Access, and PowerPoint. The exams simulate the application environment, allowing your students to demonstrate their knowledge and to think through the skills by performing real-world tasks. Designed to be used with the New Perspectives Series, SAM 2003 includes built-in page references so students can create study guides that match the New Perspectives textbooks you use in class. Powerful administrative options allow you to schedule exams and assignments, secure your tests, and run reports with almost limitless flexibility. Find out more about SAM 2003 by going to www.course.com or speaking with your Course Technology sales representative.

Distance Learning

Enhance your course with any of our online learning platforms. Go to www.course.com or speak with your Course Technology sales representative to find the platform or the content that's right for you.

www.course.com/NewPerspectives

About This Book

This book is ideal for an introductory course on Microsoft PowerPoint 2003, covering topics ranging from planning and creating a presentation to presenting a slide show and integrating PowerPoint with other programs.

- New! Now includes a free, tear-off PowerPoint 2003 CourseCard that provides students with a great way to have PowerPoint skills at their fingertips
- Updated for the new software! This book includes coverage of new PowerPoint 2003 features, including using the new Research task pane and saving a presentation to a CD.
- For PowerPoint 2003, there is increased emphasis on understanding graphics—including tables, diagrams, shapes, and clip art images—and how to use them effectively in a presentation.
- Many of the Reference Windows contain helpful tips for how to use PowerPoint slide components, including text, graphics, transitions, and special effects, to create and deliver professional-looking and successful presentations.

Features of the New Perspectives series include:

- Large screenshots offer improved readability.
- Sequential page numbering makes it easier to refer to specific pages in the book.
- The Tutorial Summary and Key Terms sections at the end of each tutorial provide additional conceptual review for students.
- Meaningful labels and descriptions for the end-of-tutorial exercises make it easy for you to select the right exercises for your students.

Acknowledgments

The authors would like to thank the following reviewers for their valuable feedback on this project: Kathleen Bent, Cape Cod Community College; Michael Feiler, Merritt College; Shui-lien Huang, Mt. San Antonio College; Glen Johansson, Spokane Community College; Mary Logan, Delgado Community College; Candice Spangler, Columbus State Community College, and Kathy Winters, The University of Tennessee at Chattanooga. Also we give special thanks to Rachel Goldberg, Senior Managing Editor; Kathy Finnegan and Karen Stevens, Senior Product Managers; Kelly Robinson and Jennifer Goguen, Production Editors; Emilie Perreault, Associate Product Manager; Shana Rosenthal, Editorial Assistant; John Bosco and John Freitas, Quality Assurance Managers; Harris Bierhoff and Susan Whalen, Quality Assurance Testers; Steven Freund, Dave Nuschera, and Rebekah Tidwell for their work on the Instructors Resources; and the staff at GEX. Thank you all for your expertise, enthusiasm, and vision for this book. Finally, we would like to thank Katherine T. Pinard, our Developmental Editor, for her shepherding this project to completion. Her experience, knowledge, and attention to detail have been invaluable in helping bring this project to fruition. She has been a delight to work with.

Beverly B. Zimmerman
S. Scott Zimmerman

www.course.com/NewPerspectives

Table of Contents

New Perspectives on

Using Common Features of Microsoft® Office 2003

Preparing Promotional Materials   OFF 3

Read This Before You Begin

To the Student

Data Files

To complete the Using Common Features of Microsoft Office 2003 tutorial, you need the starting student Data Files. Your instructor will either provide you with these Data Files or ask you to obtain them yourself.

The Using Common Features of Microsoft Office 2003 tutorial requires the folder named "OFF" to complete the Tutorial, Review Assignments, and Case Problems. You will need to copy this folder from a file server, a stand-alone computer, or the Web to the drive and folder where you will be storing your Data Files. Your instructor will tell you which computer, drive letter, and folder(s) contain the files you need. You can also download the files by going to www.course.com; see the inside back or front cover for

more information on downloading the files, or ask your instructor or technical support person for assistance.

If you are storing your Data Files on floppy disks, you will need one blank, formatted, high-density disk for this tutorial. Label your disk as shown, and place on it the folder indicated.

▼ **Common Features of Office: Data Disk**

  OFF folder

When you begin this tutorial, refer to the Student Data Files section at the bottom of the tutorial opener page, which indicates which folders and files you need for the tutorial. Each end-of-tutorial exercise also indicates the files you need to complete that exercise.

To the Instructor

The Data Files are available on the Instructor Resources CD for this title. Follow the instructions in the Help file on the CD to install the programs to your network or standalone computer. See the "To the Student" section above for information on how to set up the Data Files that accompany this text.

You are granted a license to copy the Data Files to any computer or computer network used by students who have purchased this book.

System Requirements

If you are going to work through this book using your own computer, you need:

• **Computer System** Microsoft Windows 2000 or Windows XP Professional or higher must be installed on your computer. This tutorial assumes a typical installation of Microsoft Office 2003. Additionally, to

complete the steps for accessing Microsoft's Online Help for Office, an Internet connection and a Web browser are required.

• **Data Files** You will not be able to complete the tutorals or exercises in this book using your own computer until you have the necessary starting Data Files.

www.course.com/NewPerspectives

Objectives

- Explore the programs that comprise Microsoft Office
- Start programs and switch between them
- Explore common window elements
- Minimize, maximize, and restore windows
- Use personalized menus and toolbars
- Work with task panes
- Create, save, close, and open a file
- Use the Help system
- Print a file
- Exit programs

Using Common Features of Microsoft Office 2003

Preparing Promotional Materials

Case

Delmar Office Supplies

Delmar Office Supplies, a company in Wisconsin founded by Jake Alexander in 1996, sells recycled office supplies to businesses and home-based offices around the world. The demand for quality recycled papers, reconditioned toner cartridges, and renovated office furniture has been growing each year. Jake and all his employees use Microsoft Office 2003, which provides everyone in the company the power and flexibility to store a variety of information, create consistent files, and share data. In this tutorial, you'll review how the company's employees use Microsoft Office 2003.

Student Data Files

▼**OFF folder**

▽ **Tutorial folder**　　　　　　▽ **Review folder**

(no starting Data Files)　　　Finances.xls
　　　　　　　　　　　　　　　Letter.doc

Exploring Microsoft Office 2003

Microsoft Office 2003, or simply **Office**, is a collection of the most popular Microsoft programs: Word, Excel, PowerPoint, Access, and Outlook. Each Office program contains valuable tools to help you accomplish many tasks, such as composing reports, analyzing data, preparing presentations, compiling information, sending e-mail, and planning schedules.

Microsoft Word 2003, or simply **Word**, is a word-processing program you use to create text documents. The files you create in Word are called **documents**. Word offers many special features that help you compose and update all types of documents, ranging from letters and newsletters to reports, brochures, faxes, and even books—all in attractive and readable formats. You can also use Word to create, insert, and position figures, tables, and other graphics to enhance the look of your documents. The Delmar Office Supplies sales representatives create their business letters using Word.

Microsoft Excel 2003, or simply **Excel**, is a spreadsheet program you use to display, organize, and analyze numerical data. You can do some of this in Word with tables, but Excel provides many more tools for recording and formatting numbers as well as performing calculations. The graphics capabilities in Excel also enable you to display data visually. You might, for example, generate a pie chart or a bar chart to help readers quickly see the significance of and the connections between information. The files you create in Excel are called **workbooks**. The Delmar Office Supplies operations department uses a line chart in an Excel workbook to visually track the company's financial performance.

Microsoft Access 2003, or simply **Access**, is a database program you use to enter, organize, display, and retrieve related information. The files you create in Access are called **databases**. With Access you can create data entry forms to make data entry easier, and you can create professional reports to improve the readability of your data. The Delmar Office Supplies operations department tracks the company's inventory in a table in an Access database.

Microsoft PowerPoint 2003, or simply **PowerPoint**, is a presentation graphics program you use to create a collection of slides that can contain text, charts, pictures, and so on. The files you create in PowerPoint are called **presentations**. You can show these presentations on your computer monitor, project them onto a screen as a slide show, print them, share them over the Internet, or display them on the World Wide Web. You can also use PowerPoint to generate presentation-related documents such as audience handouts, outlines, and speakers' notes. The Delmar Office Supplies sales department has created an effective slide presentation with PowerPoint to promote the company's latest product line.

Microsoft Outlook 2003, or simply **Outlook**, is an information management program you use to send, receive, and organize e-mail; plan your schedule; arrange meetings; organize contacts; create a to-do list; and jot down notes. You can also use Outlook to print schedules, task lists, phone directories, and other documents. Jake Alexander uses Outlook to send and receive e-mail, plan his schedule, and create a to-do list.

Although each Office program individually is a strong tool, their potential is even greater when used together.

Integrating Office Programs

One of the main advantages of Office is **integration**, the ability to share information between programs. Integration ensures consistency and accuracy, and it saves time because you don't have to re-enter the same information in several Office programs. The staff at Delmar Office Supplies uses the integration features of Office daily, including the following examples:

- The accounting department created an Excel bar chart on the previous two years' fourth-quarter results, which they inserted into the quarterly financial report created in Word. They included a hyperlink in the Word report that employees can click to open the Excel workbook and view the original data.
- The operations department included an Excel pie chart of sales percentages by divisions of Delmar Office Supplies on a PowerPoint slide, which is part of a presentation to stockholders.
- The marketing department produced a mailing to promote the company's newest products by combining a form letter created in Word with an Access database that stores the names and addresses of customers.
- A sales representative wrote a letter in Word about a sales incentive program and merged the letter with an Outlook contact list containing the names and addresses of his customers.

These are just a few examples of how you can take information from one Office program and integrate it into another.

Starting Office Programs

You can start any Office program by clicking the Start button on the Windows taskbar, and then selecting the program you want from the All Programs menu. Once the program starts, you can immediately begin to create new files or work with existing ones. If you or another user has recently used one of the Office programs, then that program might appear on the most frequently used programs list on the left side of the Start menu. You can click the program name to start the program.

Starting Office Programs
Reference Window

- Click the Start button on the taskbar.
- Point to All Programs.
- Point to Microsoft Office.
- Click the name of the program you want to start.
or
- Click the name of the program you want to start on the most frequently used programs list on the left side of the Start menu.

You'll start Excel using the Start button.

To start Excel and open a new, blank workbook:

▶ **1.** Make sure your computer is on and the Windows desktop appears on your screen.

Trouble? If your screen varies slightly from those shown in the figures, then your computer might be set up differently. The figures in this book were created while running Windows XP in its default settings, but how your screen looks depends on a variety of things, including the version of Windows, background settings, and so forth.

▶ **2.** Click the **Start** button on the taskbar, and then point to **All Programs** to display the All Programs menu.

▶ **3.** Point to **Microsoft Office** on the All Programs menu, and then point to **Microsoft Office Excel 2003**. See Figure 1. Depending on how your computer is set up, your desktop and menu might contain different icons and commands.

Figure 1 ▶ **Start menu with All Programs submenu displayed**

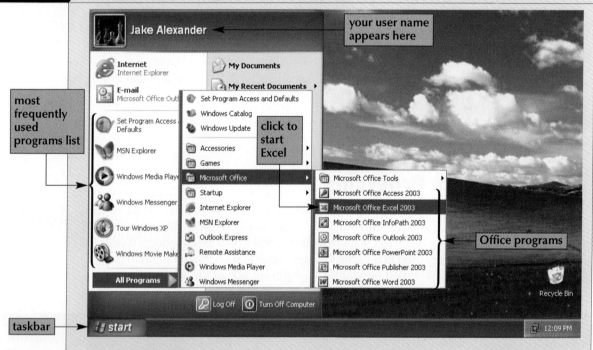

Trouble? If you don't see Microsoft Office on the All Programs menu, point to Microsoft Office Excel 2003. If you still don't see Microsoft Office Excel 2003, ask your instructor or technical support person for help.

▶ **4.** Click **Microsoft Office Excel 2003** to start Excel and open a new, blank workbook. See Figure 2.

New, blank Excel workbook | **Figure 2**

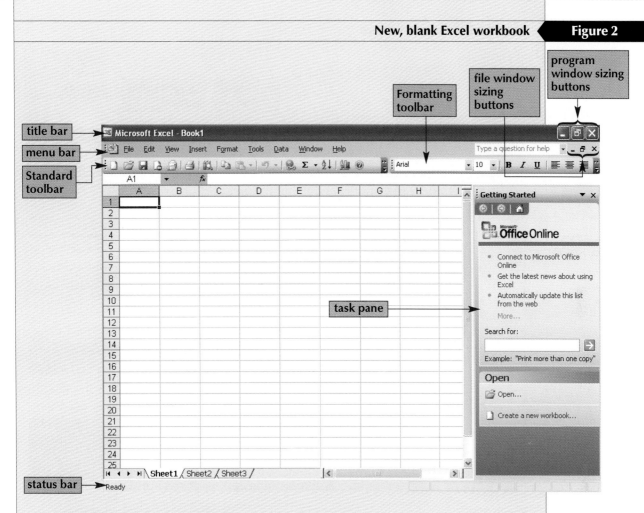

Trouble? If the Excel window doesn't fill your entire screen, the window is not maximized, or expanded to its full size. You'll maximize the window shortly.

You can have more than one Office program open at once. You'll use this same method to start Word and open a new, blank document.

To start Word and open a new, blank document:

▶ **1.** Click the **Start** button on the taskbar.

▶ **2.** Point to **All Programs** to display the All Programs menu.

▶ **3.** Point to **Microsoft Office** on the All Programs menu.

    Trouble? If you don't see Microsoft Office on the All Programs menu, point to Microsoft Office Word 2003. If you still don't see Microsoft Office Word 2003, ask your instructor or technical support person for help.

▶ **4.** Click **Microsoft Office Word 2003**. Word opens with a new, blank document. See Figure 3.

Figure 3 ▶ **New, blank document in Word**

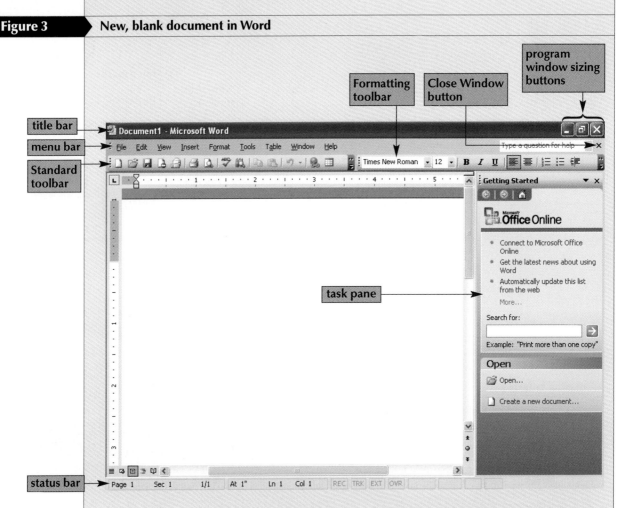

Trouble? If the Word window doesn't fill your entire screen, the window is not maximized. You'll maximize the window shortly.

When you have more than one program or file open at a time, you can switch between them.

Switching Between Open Programs and Files

Two programs are running at the same time—Excel and Word. The taskbar contains buttons for both programs. When you have two or more programs running, or two files within the same program open, you can use the taskbar buttons to switch from one program or file to another. The employees at Delmar Office Supplies often work in several programs at once.

To switch between Word and Excel:

▶ **1.** Click the **Microsoft Excel – Book1** button on the taskbar to switch from Word to Excel. See Figure 4.

Excel and Word programs opened simultaneously   **Figure 4**

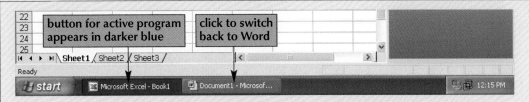

▶ **2.** Click the **Document1 – Microsoft Word** button on the taskbar to return to Word.

As you can see, you can start multiple programs and switch between them in seconds.

Exploring Common Window Elements

The Office programs consist of windows that have many similar features. As you can see in Figures 2 and 3, many of the elements you see in both the Excel program window and the Word program window are the same. In fact, all the Office programs have these same elements. Figure 5 describes some of the most common window elements.

Common window elements   **Figure 5**

Element	Description
Title bar	A bar at the top of the window that contains the filename of the open file, the program name, and the program window sizing buttons
Menu bar	A collection of menus for commonly used commands
Toolbars	Collections of buttons that are shortcuts to commonly used menu commands
Sizing buttons	Buttons that resize and close the program window or the file window
Task pane	A window that provides access to commands for common tasks you'll perform in Office programs
Status bar	An area at the bottom of the program window that contains information about the open file or the current task on which you are working

Because these elements are the same in each program, once you've learned one program, it's easy to learn the others. The next sections explore the primary common features—the window sizing buttons, the menus and toolbars, and the task panes.

Using the Window Sizing Buttons

There are two sets of sizing buttons. The top set controls the program window and the bottom set controls the file window. There are three different sizing buttons. The Minimize button ▭, which is the left button, hides a window so that only its program button is visible on the taskbar. The middle button changes name and function depending on the status of the window—the Maximize button ▭ expands the window to the full screen size or to the program window size, and the Restore button ▭ returns the window to a predefined size. The right button, the Close button ✕, exits the program or closes the file.

Most often you'll want to maximize the program and file windows as you work to take advantage of the full screen size you have available. If you have several files open, you might want to restore the files so that you can see more than one window at a time or you might want to minimize the programs with which you are not working at the moment. You'll try minimizing, maximizing, and restoring windows now.

To resize windows:

1. Click the **Minimize** button on the Word title bar to reduce the Word program window to a taskbar button. The Excel window is visible again.

2. If necessary, click the **Maximize** button on the Excel title bar. The Excel program window expands to fill the screen.

3. Click the **Restore Window** button on the Excel menu bar. The file window, referred to as the workbook window in Excel, resizes smaller than the full program window. See Figure 6.

Figure 6	Resized Excel windows

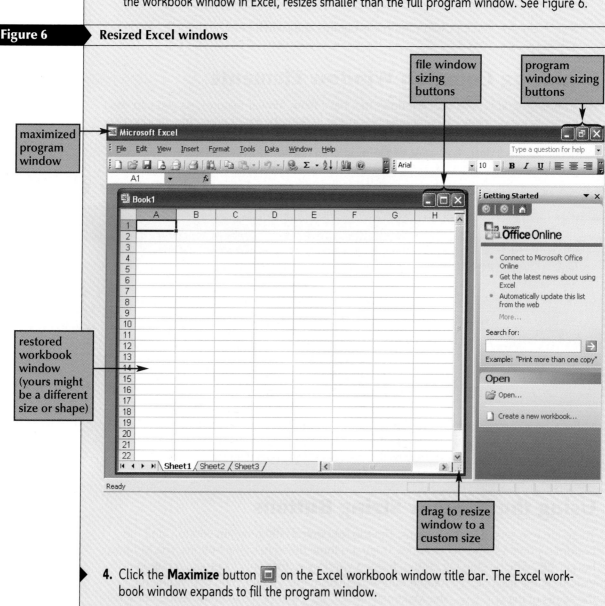

4. Click the **Maximize** button on the Excel workbook window title bar. The Excel workbook window expands to fill the program window.

5. Click the **Document1 - Microsoft Word** button on the taskbar. The Word program window returns to its previous size.

6. If necessary, click the **Maximize** button ▢ on the Word title bar. The Word program window expands to fill the screen.

The sizing buttons give you the flexibility to arrange the program and file windows on your screen to best fit your needs.

Using Menus and Toolbars

In each Office program, you can perform tasks using a menu command, a toolbar button, or a keyboard shortcut. A **menu command** is a word on a menu that you click to execute a task; a **menu** is a group of related commands. For example, the File menu contains commands for managing files, such as the Open command and the Save command. The File, Edit, View, Insert, Format, Tools, Window, and Help menus appear on the menu bar in all the Office programs, although some of the commands they include differ from program to program. Other menus are program specific, such as the Table menu in Word and the Data menu in Excel.

A **toolbar** is a collection of buttons that correspond to commonly used menu commands. For example, the Standard toolbar contains an Open button and a Save button. The Standard and Formatting toolbars (as well as other toolbars) appear in all the Office programs, although some of the buttons they include differ from program to program. The Standard toolbar has buttons related to working with files. The Formatting toolbar has buttons related to changing the appearance of content. Each program also has program-specific toolbars, such as the Tables and Borders toolbar in Word for working with tables and the Chart toolbar in Excel for working with graphs and charts.

A **keyboard shortcut** is a combination of keys you press to perform a command. For example, Ctrl+S is the keyboard shortcut for the Save command (you hold down the Ctrl key while you press the S key). Keyboard shortcuts appear to the right of many menu commands.

Viewing Personalized Menus and Toolbars

When you first use a newly installed Office program, the menus and toolbars display only the basic and most commonly used commands and buttons, streamlining the program window. The other commands and buttons are available, but you have to click an extra button to see them (the Expand button on a menu and the Toolbar Options button on a toolbar). As you select commands and click buttons, the ones you use often are put on the short, personalized menu and on the visible part of the toolbars. The ones you don't use remain available on the full menus and toolbars. This means that the Office menus and toolbars might display different commands and buttons on each person's computer.

To view a personalized and full menu:

1. Click **Insert** on the Word menu bar to display the short, personalized menu. See Figure 7. The Bookmark command, for example, does not appear on the short menu.

Figure 7 | Short, personalized menu

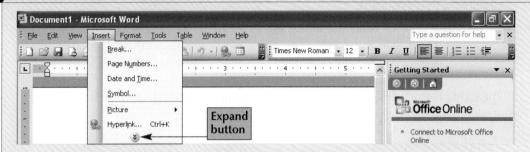

Trouble? If the Insert menu displays different commands than those shown in Figure 7, you need to reset the menus. Click Tools on the menu bar, click Customize (you might need to pause until the full menu appears to see the command), and then click the Options tab in the Customize dialog box. Click the Always show full menus check box to remove the check mark, if necessary, and then click the Show full menus after a short delay check box to insert a check mark, if necessary. Click the Reset menu and toolbar usage data button, and then click the Yes button to confirm that you want to reset the commands. Click the Close button. Repeat Step 1.

You can display the full menu in one of three ways: (1) pause until the full menu appears, which might happen as you read this; (2) click the Expand button at the bottom of the menu; or (3) double-click the menu name on the menu bar.

▶ 2. Pause until the full Insert menu appears, as shown in Figure 8. The Bookmark command and other commands are now visible.

Figure 8 | Full, expanded menu

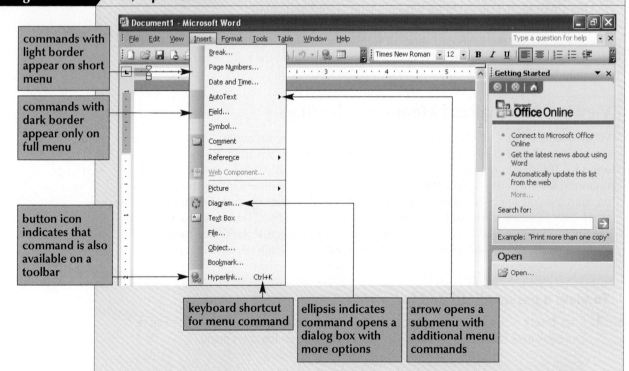

▶ 3. Click the **Bookmark** command. A dialog box opens when you click a command whose name is followed by an ellipsis (...). In this case, the Bookmark dialog box opens.

4. Click the **Cancel** button to close the Bookmark dialog box.

5. Click **Insert** on the menu bar again to display the short, personalized menu. The Bookmark command appears on the short, personalized menu because you have recently used it.

6. Press the **Esc** key on the keyboard twice to close the menu.

As you can see, the menu changed based on your actions. Over time, only the commands you use frequently will appear on the personalized menu. The toolbars work similarly.

To use the personalized toolbars:

1. Observe that the Standard and Formatting toolbars appear side by side below the menu bar.

Trouble? If the toolbars appear on two rows, you need to reset them to their default state. Click Tools on the menu bar, click Customize, and then click the Options tab in the Customize dialog box. Click the Show Standard and Formatting toolbars on two rows check box to remove the check mark. Click the Reset menu and toolbar usage data button, and then click the Yes button to confirm you want to reset the commands. Click the Close button. Repeat Step 1.

2. Click the **Toolbar Options** button ⯆ on the Standard toolbar. See Figure 9.

Toolbar Options palette ◀ **Figure 9**

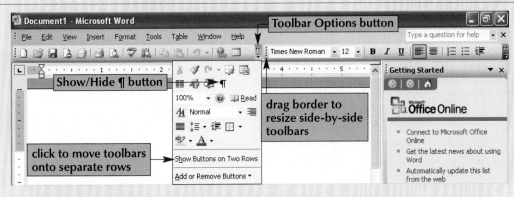

Trouble? If you see different buttons on the Toolbar Options palette, your side-by-side toolbars might be sized differently than the ones shown in Figure 9. Continue with Step 3.

3. Click the **Show/Hide ¶** button ¶ on the Toolbar Options palette to display the nonprinting screen characters. The Show/Hide ¶ button moves to the visible part of the Standard toolbar, and another button may be moved onto the Toolbar Options palette to make room for the new button.

Trouble? If the Show/Hide ¶ button already appears on the Standard toolbar, click another button on the Toolbar Options palette. Then click that same button again in Step 4 to turn off that formatting, if necessary.

Some buttons, like the Show/Hide ¶ button, act as a toggle switch—one click turns on the feature and a second click turns it off.

4. Click the **Show/Hide ¶** button ¶ on the Standard toolbar again to hide the nonprinting screen characters.

Some people like that the menus and toolbars change to meet their work habits. Others prefer to see all the menu commands or to display the default toolbars on two rows so that all the buttons are always visible. You'll change the toolbar setting now.

To turn off the personalized toolbars:

▶ 1. Click the **Toolbar Options** button ▪ on the right side of the Standard toolbar.

▶ 2. Click the **Show Buttons on Two Rows** command. The toolbars move to separate rows (the Standard toolbar on top) and you can see all the buttons on each toolbar.

You can easily access any button on the Standard and Formatting toolbars with one mouse click. The drawback is that when the toolbars are displayed on two rows, they take up more space in the program window, limiting the space you have to work.

Using Task Panes

A **task pane** is a window that provides access to commands for common tasks you'll perform in Office programs. For example, the Getting Started task pane, which opens when you first start any Office program, enables you to create new files and open existing ones. Task panes also help you navigate through more complex, multi-step procedures. All the Office programs include the task panes described in Figure 10. The other available task panes vary by program.

Figure 10	▶ Common task panes

Task pane	Description
Getting Started	The home task pane; allows you to create new files, open existing files, search the online and offline Help system by keyword, and access Office online
Help	Allows you to search the online and offline Help system by keyword or table of contents, and access Microsoft Office Online
Search Results	Displays available Help topics related to entered keyword and enables you to initiate a new search
New	Allows you to create new files; name changes to New Document in Word, New Workbook in Excel, New File in Access, and New Presentation in PowerPoint
Clip Art	Allows you to search for all types of media clips (pictures, sound, video) and insert clips from the results
Clipboard	Allows you to paste some or all of the items that have been cut or copied from any Office program during the current work session
Research	Allows you to search a variety of reference material and other resources from within a file

No matter what their purpose, you use the same processes to open, close, and navigate between the task panes.

Opening and Closing Task Panes

When you first start any Office program, the Getting Started task pane opens by default along the right edge of the program window. You can resize or move the task pane to suit your work habits. You can also close the task pane to display the open file in the full available program window. For example, you might want to close the task pane when you are typing the body of a letter in Word or entering a lot of data in Excel.

You will open and close the task pane.

To open and close the task pane:

1. If necessary, click **View** on the menu bar, and then click **Task Pane**. The most recently viewed task pane opens on the right side of the screen. See Figure 11.

Getting Started task pane ◄ | **Figure 11**

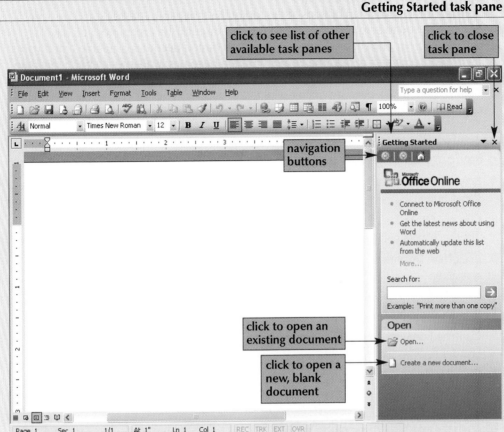

Trouble? If you do not see the task pane, you probably closed the open task pane in Step 1. Repeat Step 1 to reopen the task pane.

Trouble? If a different task pane than the Getting Started task pane opens, then another task pane was the most recently viewed task pane. You'll learn how to open different task panes in the next section; continue with Step 2.

2. Click the **Close** button ☒ on the task pane title bar. The task pane closes, leaving more room on the screen for the open file.

3. Click **View** on the menu bar, and then click **Task Pane**. The task pane reopens.

There are several ways to display different task panes.

Navigating Among Task Panes

Once the task pane is open, you can display different task panes to suit the task you are trying to complete. For example, you can display the New task pane when you want to create a new file from a template. The name of the New task pane varies, depending on the program you are using: Word has the New Document task pane, Excel has the New Workbook task pane, PowerPoint has the New Presentation task pane, and Access has the New File task pane.

One of the quickest ways to display a task pane is to use the Other Task Panes button. When you point to the name of the open task pane in the task pane title bar, it becomes the Other Task Panes button. When you click the Other Task Panes button, all the available task panes for that Office program are listed. Just click the name of the task pane you want to display to switch to that task pane.

There are three navigation buttons at the top of the task pane. The Back and Forward buttons enable you to scroll backward and forward through the task panes you have opened during your current work session. The Back button becomes available when you display two or more task panes. The Forward button becomes available after you click the Back button to return to a previously viewed task pane. The Home button returns you to the Getting Started task pane no matter which task pane is currently displayed.

You'll use each of these methods to navigate among the task panes.

To navigate among task panes:

1. Point to **Getting Started** in the task pane title bar. The title bar becomes the Other Task Panes button.

2. Click the **Other Task Panes** button. A list of the available task panes for Word is displayed. The check mark before Getting Started indicates that this is the currently displayed task pane.

3. Click **New Document**. The New Document task pane appears and the Back button is available.

4. Click the **Back** button ⊕ in the task pane. The Getting Started task pane reappears and the Forward button is available.

5. Click the **Forward** button ⊕ in the task pane. The New Document task pane reappears and the Back button is available.

6. Click the **Home** button 🏠 in the task pane. The Getting Started task pane reappears.

Using the Research Task Pane

The Research task pane allows you to search a variety of reference materials and other resources to find specific information while you are working on a file. You can insert the information you find directly into your open file. The thesaurus and language translation tools are installed with Office and therefore are stored locally on your computer. If you are connected to the Internet, you can also use the Research task pane to access a dictionary, an encyclopedia, research sites, as well as business and financial sources. Some of the sites that appear in the search results are fee-based, meaning that you'll need to pay to access information on that site.

To use the Research task pane, you type a keyword or phrase into the Search for text box and then select whether you want to search all the books, sites, and sources; one category; or a specific source. The search results appear in the Research task pane. Some of the results appear as links, which you can click to open your browser window and display that information. If you are using Internet Explorer 5.01 or later as your Web browser, the Research task pane is tiled (appears side by side) with your document. If you are using another Web browser, you'll need to return to the task pane in your open file to click another link.

The Research task pane functions independently in each file. So you can open multiple files and perform a different search in each. In addition, each Research task pane stores the results of up to 10 searches, so you can quickly return to the results from any of your most recent searches. To move among the saved searches, click the Back and Forward buttons in the task pane.

Using the Research Task Pane

- Type a keyword or phrase into the Search for text box.
- Select a search category, individual source, or all references.
- If necessary, click a link in the search results to display more information.
- Copy and paste selected content from the task pane into your file.

Jake plans to send a copy of the next quarter's sales report to the office in France. You'll use the bilingual dictionaries in the Research task pane to begin entering labels in French into an Excel workbook for the sales report.

To use the bilingual dictionaries in the Research task pane:

1. Click the **Microsoft Excel – Book1** button on the taskbar to switch to the Excel window.

2. Click the **Other Task Panes** button on the Getting Started task pane, and then click **Research**. The Research task pane opens.

3. Click in the **Search for** text box, and then type **paper**.

4. Click the **Search for** list arrow and then click **Translation**. The bilingual dictionary opens in the Research task pane. You can choose from among 12 languages to translate to and from, including Japanese, Russian, Spanish, Dutch, German, and French.

   Trouble? If a dialog box opens stating the translation feature is not installed, click the Yes button to install it.

5. If necessary, click the **To** list arrow, and then click **French (France)**. See Figure 12.

Research task pane   **Figure 12**

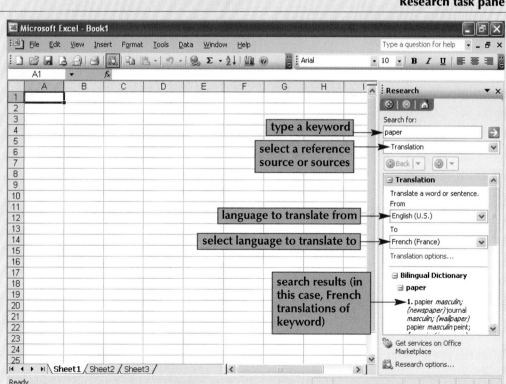

6. Scroll to read the different translations of "paper" in French.

After you locate specific information, you can quickly insert it into your open file. The information can be inserted by copying the selected content you want to insert, and then pasting it in the appropriate location in your file. In some instances, such as MSN Money Stock Quotes, a button appears enabling you to quickly insert the indicated information in your file at the location of the insertion point. Otherwise, you can use the standard Copy and Paste commands.

You'll copy the translation for "paper" into the Excel workbook.

To copy information from the Research task pane into a file:

▶ 1. Select **papier** in the Research task pane. This is the word you want to copy to the workbook.

▶ 2. Right-click the selected text, and then click **Copy** on the shortcut menu. The text is duplicated on the Office Clipboard.

▶ 3. Right-click cell **A1**, and then click **Paste**. The word "papier" is entered into the cell. See Figure 13.

Figure 13 ▶ **Translation copied into Excel**

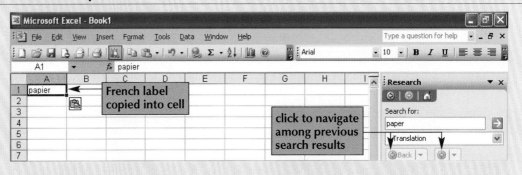

You'll repeat this process to look up the translation for "furniture" and copy it into cell A2.

To translate and copy another word into Excel:

▶ 1. Double-click **paper** in the Search for text box to select the text, type **furniture**, and then click the **Start searching** button in the Research task pane.

▶ 2. Verify that you're translating from English (U.S) to French (France).

▶ 3. Select **meubles** in the translation results, right-click the selected text, and then click **Copy**.

▶ 4. Right-click cell **A2**, and then click **Paste**. The second label appears in the cell.

The Research task pane works similarly in all the Office programs. You'll use other task panes later in this tutorial to perform specific tasks, including opening a file and getting assistance.

Working with Files

The most common tasks you'll perform in any Office program are to create, open, save, and close files. The processes for each of these tasks are the same in all the Office programs. In addition, there are several methods for performing most tasks in Office. This flexibility enables you to use Office in a way that fits how you like to work.

Creating a File

To begin working in a program, you need to create a new file or open an existing file. When you start Word, Excel, or PowerPoint, the program opens along with a blank file—ready for you to begin working on a new document, workbook, or presentation. When you start Access, the Getting Started task pane opens, displaying options for opening a new database or an existing one.

Jake has asked you to start working on the agenda for the stockholder meeting, which he suggests you create using Word. You enter text in a Word document by typing.

To enter text in a document:

1. Click the **Document1 – Microsoft Word** button on the taskbar to activate the Word program window.

2. Type **Delmar Office Supplies**, and then press the **Enter** key. The text you typed appears on one line in the Word document.

   Trouble? If you make a typing error, press the Backspace key to delete the incorrect letters, and then retype the text.

3. Type **Stockholder Meeting Agenda**, and then press the **Enter** key. The text you typed appears on the second line.

Next, you'll save the file.

Saving a File

As you create and modify Office files, your work is stored only in the computer's temporary memory, not on a hard disk. If you were to exit the programs, turn off your computer, or experience a power failure, your work would be lost. To prevent losing work, save your file to a disk frequently—at least every 10 minutes. You can save files to the hard disk located inside your computer or to portable storage disks, such as floppy disks, Zip disks, or read-write CD-ROMs.

The first time you save a file, you need to name it. This name is called a **filename**. When you choose a filename, select a descriptive one that accurately reflects the content of the document, workbook, presentation, or database, such as "Shipping Options Letter" or "Fourth Quarter Financial Analysis." Filenames can include a maximum of 255 letters, numbers, hyphens, and spaces in any combination. Office appends a **file extension** to the filename, which identifies the program in which that file was created. The file extensions are .doc for Word, .xls for Excel, .ppt for PowerPoint, and .mdb for Access. Whether you see file extensions depends on how Windows is set up on your computer.

You also need to decide where to save the file—on which disk and in what folder. A **folder** is a container for your files. Just as you organize paper documents within folders stored in a filing cabinet, you can organize your files within folders stored on your computer's hard disk or a removable disk. Store each file in a logical location that you will remember whenever you want to use the file again.

Reference Window | **Saving a File**

- Click the Save button on the Standard toolbar (*or* click File on the menu bar, and then click Save or Save As).
- In the Save As dialog box, click the Save in list arrow, and then navigate to the location where you want to save the file.
- Type a filename in the File name text box.
- Click the Save button.
- To resave the named file to the same location, click the Save button on the Standard toolbar (*or* click File on the menu bar, and then click Save).

The two lines of text you typed are not yet saved on disk. You'll do that now.

To save a file for the first time:

1. Click the **Save** button 🖫 on the Standard toolbar. The Save As dialog box opens. The first few words of the first line appear in the File name text box, as a suggested filename. You'll replace this with a more descriptive filename.

2. Click the **Save in** list arrow, and then click the location that contains your Data Files.

   Trouble? If you don't have the Common Office Features Data Files, you need to get them before you can proceed. Your instructor will either give you the Data Files or ask you to obtain them from a specified location (such as a network drive). In either case, be sure that you make a backup copy of your Data Files before you start using them, so that the original files will be available on your copied disk in case you need to start over because of an error or problem. If you have any questions about the Data Files, see your instructor or technical support person for assistance.

3. Double-click the **OFF** folder in the list box, and then double-click the **Tutorial** folder. This is the location where you want to save the document. See Figure 14.

4. Type **Stockholder Meeting Agenda** in the File name text box.

Figure 14 ▶ **Completed Save As dialog box**

location where file will be saved;
click list arrow to choose another location

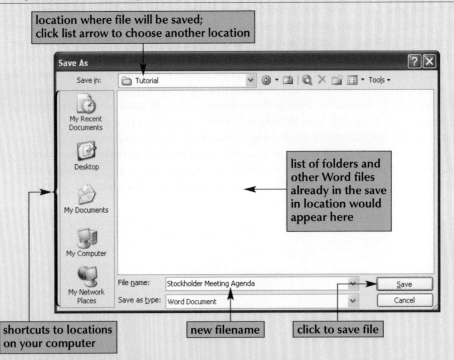

list of folders and other Word files already in the save in location would appear here

shortcuts to locations on your computer

new filename

click to save file

Trouble? If the .doc file extension appears after the filename, then your computer is configured to show file extensions. Continue with Step 5.

5. Click the **Save** button. The Save As dialog box closes, and the name of your file appears in the program window title bar.

The saved file includes everything in the document at the time you last saved it. Any edits or additions you then make to the document exist only in the computer's memory and are not saved in the file on the disk. As you work, remember to save frequently so that the file is updated to reflect the latest content of the document.

Because you already named the document and selected a storage location, the second and subsequent times you save, the Save As dialog box doesn't open. If you wanted to save a copy of the file with a different filename or to a different location, you would reopen the Save As dialog box by clicking File on the menu bar, and then clicking Save As. The previous version of the file remains on your disk as well.

You need to add your name to the agenda. Then you'll save your changes.

To modify and save a file:

1. Type your name, and then press the **Enter** key. The text you typed appears on the next line.
2. Click the **Save** button 🖫 on the Standard toolbar to save your changes.

When you're done with a file, you can close it.

Closing a File

Although you can keep multiple files open at one time, you should close any file you are no longer working on to conserve system resources as well as to ensure that you don't inadvertently make changes to the file. You can close a file by clicking the Close command on the File menu or by clicking the Close Window button in the upper-right corner of the menu bar.

As a standard practice, you should save your file before closing it. If you're unsure whether the file is saved, it cannot hurt to save it again. However, Office has an added safeguard: If you attempt to close a file or exit a program without saving your changes, a dialog box opens asking whether you want to save the file. Click the Yes button to save the changes to the file before closing the file and program. Click the No button to close the file and program without saving changes. Click the Cancel button to return to the program window without saving changes or closing the file and program. This feature helps to ensure that you always save the most current version of any file.

You'll add the date to the agenda. Then, you'll attempt to close the document without saving.

To modify and close a file:

1. Type the date, and then press the **Enter** key. The text you typed appears under your name in the document.
2. Click the **Close Window** button ⊠ on the Word menu bar to close the document. A dialog box opens, asking whether you want to save the changes you made to the document.

3. Click the **Yes** button. The current version of the document is saved to the file, and then the document closes, and Word is still running.

Trouble? If Word is not running, then you closed the program in Step 2. Start Word, click the Close Window button on the menu bar to close the blank document.

Once you have a program open, you can create additional new files for the open program or you can open previously created and saved files.

Opening a File

When you want to open a blank document, workbook, presentation, or database, you create a new file. When you want to work on a previously created file, you must first open it. Opening a file transfers a copy of the file from the storage disk (either a hard disk or a portable disk) to the computer's memory and displays it on your screen. The file is then in your computer's memory and on the disk.

Reference Window | **Opening an Existing or a New File**

- Click the Open button on the Standard toolbar (*or* click File on the menu bar, and then click Open *or* click the More link in the Open section of the Getting Started task pane).
- In the Open dialog box, click the Look in list arrow, and then navigate to the storage location of the file you want to open.
- Click the filename of the file you want to open.
- Click the Open button.

or

- Click the New button on the Standard toolbar (*or* click File on the menu bar, click New, and then (depending on the program) click the Blank document, Blank workbook, Blank presentation, or Blank database link in the New task pane).

Jake asks you to print the agenda. To do that, you'll reopen the file. You'll use the Open button on the Standard toolbar.

To open an existing file:

1. Click the **Open** button 🖼 on the Standard toolbar. The Open dialog box, which works similarly to the Save As dialog box, opens.

2. Click the **Look in** list arrow, and then navigate to the **OFF\Tutorial** folder included with your Data Files. This is the location where you saved the agenda document.

3. Click **Stockholder Meeting Agenda** in the file list. See Figure 15.

Open dialog box | **Figure 15**

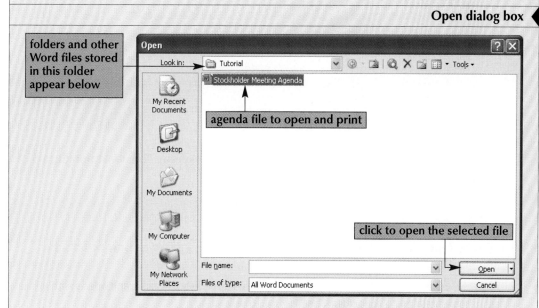

folders and other Word files stored in this folder appear below

agenda file to open and print

click to open the selected file

4. Click the **Open** button. The file containing the agenda opens in the Word program window.

Next, you'll get information about printing files in Word.

Getting Help

If you don't know how to perform a task or want more information about a feature, you can turn to Office itself for information on how to use it. This information, referred to simply as **Help**, is like a huge encyclopedia available from your desktop. You can access Help in a variety of ways, including ScreenTips, the Type a question for help box, the Help task pane, and Microsoft Office Online.

Using ScreenTips

ScreenTips are a fast and simple method you can use to get help about objects you see on the screen. A **ScreenTip** is a yellow box with the button's name. Just position the mouse pointer over a toolbar button to view its ScreenTip.

Using the Type a Question for Help Box

For answers to specific questions, you can use the **Type a question for help box**, located on the menu bar of every Office program, to find information in the Help system. You simply type a question using everyday language about a task you want to perform or a topic you need help with, and then press the Enter key to search the Help system. The Search Results task pane opens with a list of Help topics related to your query. You click a topic to open a Help window with step-by-step instructions that guide you through a specific procedure and explanations of difficult concepts in clear, easy-to-understand language. For example, you might ask how to format a cell in an Excel worksheet; a list of Help topics related to the words you typed will appear.

Getting Help from the Type a Question for Help Box

- Click the Type a question for help box on the menu bar.
- Type your question, and then press the Enter key.
- Click a Help topic in the Search Results task pane.
- Read the information in the Help window. For more information, click other topics or links.
- Click the Close button on the Help window title bar.

You'll use the Type a question for help box to obtain more information about printing a document in Word.

To use the Type a question for help box:

1. Click the **Type a question for help box** on the menu bar, and then type **How do I print a document?**

2. Press the **Enter** key to retrieve a list of topics. The Search Results task pane opens with a list of topics related to your query. See Figure 16.

Figure 16 ▷ Search Results task pane displaying Help topics

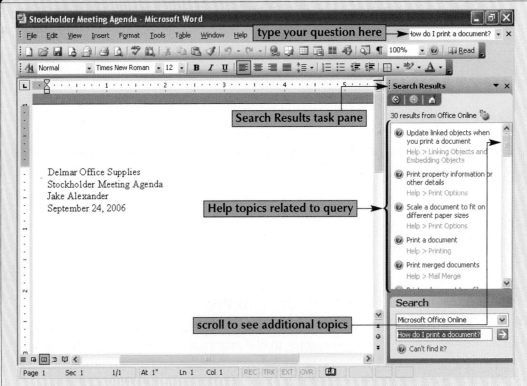

Trouble? If your search results list differs from the one shown in Figure 16, your computer is not connected to the Internet or Microsoft has updated the list of available Help topics since this book was published. Continue with Step 3.

3. Scroll through the list to review the Help topics.

4. Click **Print a document** to open the Help window and learn more about the various ways to print a document. See Figure 17.

Print a document Help window | Figure 17

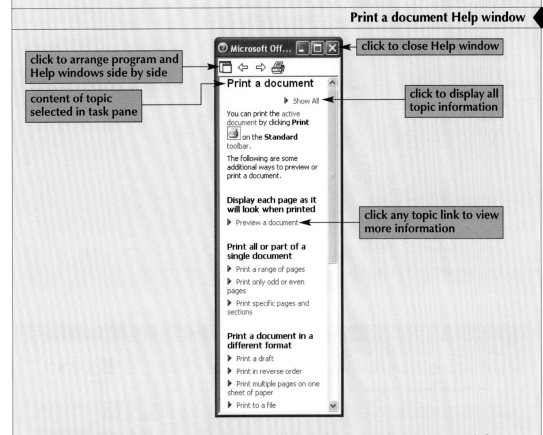

click to arrange program and Help windows side by side

content of topic selected in task pane

click to close Help window

click to display all topic information

click any topic link to view more information

Trouble? If the Word program window and the Help window do not appear side by side, then you need to tile the windows. Click the Auto Tile button on the toolbar in the Help window.

▶ **5.** Read the information, and then when you're done, click the **Close** button ☒ on the Help window title bar to close the Help window.

The Help task pane works similarly.

Using the Help Task Pane

For more in-depth help, you can use the **Help task pane**, a task pane that enables you to search the Help system using keywords or phrases. You type a specific word or phrase in the Search for text box, and then click the Start searching button. The Search Results task pane opens with a list of topics related to the keyword or phrase you entered. If your computer is connected to the Internet, you might see more search results because some Help topics are stored only online and not locally on your computer. The task pane also has a Table of Contents link that organizes the Help system by subjects and topics, like in a book. You click main subject links to display related topic links.

Reference Window

Getting Help from the Help Task Pane

- Click the Other Task Panes button on the task pane title bar, and then click Help (*or* click Help on the menu bar, and then click Microsoft Word/Excel/PowerPoint/Access/Outlook Help).
- Type a keyword or phrase in the Search for text box, and then click the Start searching button.
- Click a Help topic in the Search Results task pane.
- Read the information in the Help window. For more information, click other topics or links.
- Click the Close button on the Help window title bar.

You'll use the Help task pane to obtain more information about getting help in Office.

To use the Help task pane:

▶ 1. Click the **Other Task Panes** button on the task pane title bar, and then click **Help**.

▶ 2. Type **get help** in the Search for text box. See Figure 18.

Figure 18 ▶ **Microsoft Word Help task pane with keyword**

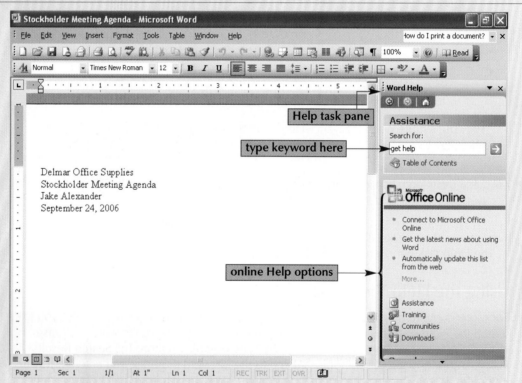

▶ 3. Click the **Start searching** button ➡. The Search Results task pane opens with a list of topics related to your keywords.

▶ 4. Scroll through the list to review the Help topics.

▶ 5. Click **About getting help while you work** to open the Microsoft Word Help window and learn more about the various ways to obtain help in Word. See Figure 19.

About getting help while you work Help window ◄ **Figure 19**

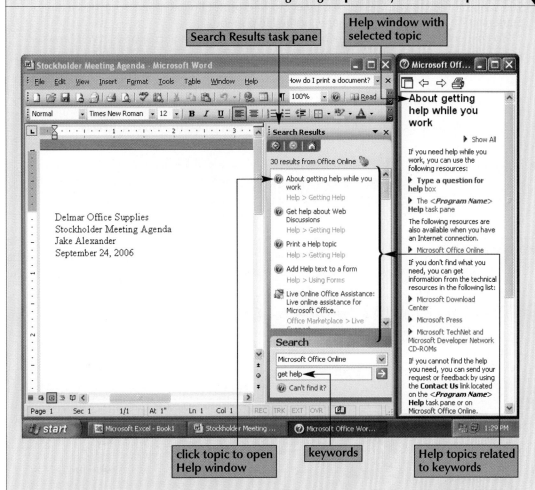

Search Results task pane

Help window with
selected topic

click topic to open
Help window

keywords

Help topics related
to keywords

Trouble? If your search results list differs from the one shown in Figure 19, your computer
is not connected to the Internet or Microsoft has updated the list of available Help topics
since this book was published. Continue with Step 6.

Trouble? If the Word program window and the Help window do not appear side by
side, then you need to tile the windows. Click the Auto Tile button on the toolbar in the
Help window.

6. Click **Microsoft Office Online** in the right pane to display information about that topic.
Read the information.

7. Click the other links about this feature and read the information.

8. When you're done, click the **Close** button ⊠ on the Help window title bar to close the Help
window. The task pane remains open.

   If your computer has a connection to the Internet, you can get more help information
from Microsoft Office Online.

Using Microsoft Office Online

Microsoft Office Online is a Web site maintained by Microsoft that provides access
to additional Help resources. For example, you can access current Help topics, read
how-to articles, and find tips for using Office. You can search all or part of a site to find

information about tasks you want to perform, features you want to use, or anything else you want more help with. You can connect to Microsoft Office Online from the Getting Started task pane, the Help task pane, or the Help menu.

To connect to Microsoft Office Online, you'll need Internet access and a Web browser such as Internet Explorer.

To connect to Microsoft Office Online:

1. Click the **Back** button � in the Search Results task pane. The Word Help task pane reappears.

2. Click the **Connect to Microsoft Office Online** link in the task pane. Internet Explorer starts and the Microsoft Office Online home page opens. See Figure 20. This Web page offers links to Web pages focusing on getting help and for accessing additional Office resources, such as additional galleries of clip art, software downloads, and training opportunities.

Figure 20	Microsoft Office Online home page

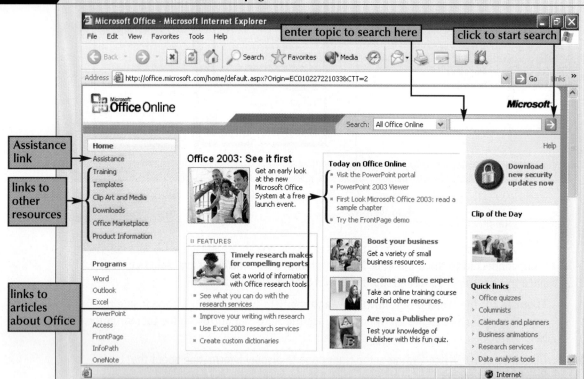

Trouble? If the content you see on the Microsoft Office Online home page differs from the figure, the site has been updated since this book was published. Continue with Step 3.

3. Click the **Assistance** link. The Assistance page opens. From this page, you browse for help in each of the different Office programs. You can also enter a keyword or phrase pertaining to a particular topic you wish to search for information on using the Search box in the upper-right corner of the window.

4. Click the **Close** button ⊠ on the Internet Explorer title bar to close the browser.

The Help features enable the staff at Delmar Office Supplies to get answers to questions they have about any task or procedure when they need it. The more you practice getting information from the Help system, the more effective you will be at using Office to its full potential.

Printing a File

At times, you'll want a paper copy of your Office file. The first time you print during each session at the computer, you should use the Print menu command to open the Print dialog box so you can verify or adjust the printing settings. You can select a printer, the number of copies to print, the portion of the file to print, and so forth; the printing settings vary slightly from program to program. For subsequent print jobs, you can use the Print button to print without opening the dialog box, if you want to use the same default settings.

Reference Window

Printing a File

- Click File on the menu bar, and then click Print.
- Verify the print settings in the Print dialog box.
- Click the OK button.

or

- Click the Print button on the Standard toolbar.

Now that you know how to print, you'll print the agenda for Jake.

To print a file:

1. Make sure your printer is turned on and contains paper.

2. Click **File** on the menu bar, and then click **Print**. The Print dialog box opens. See Figure 21.

Print dialog box | **Figure 21**

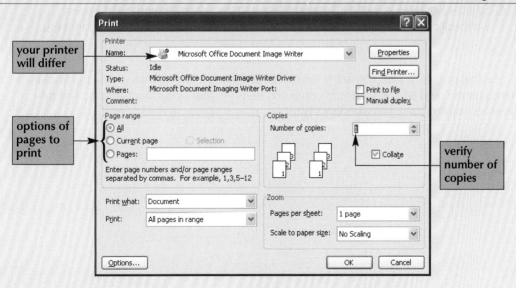

> **3.** Verify that the correct printer appears in the Name list box in the Printer area. If the wrong printer appears, click the **Name** list arrow, and then click the correct printer from the list of available printers.

> **4.** Verify that **1** appears in the Number of copies text box.

> **5.** Click the **OK** button to print the document.

> **Trouble?** If the document does not print, see your instructor or technical support person for help.

Now that you have printed the agenda, you can close Word and Excel.

Exiting Programs

Whenever you finish working with a program, you should exit it. As with many other aspects of Office, you can exit programs with a button or from a menu. You'll use both methods to close Word and Excel. You can use the Exit command to exit a program and close an open file in one step. If you haven't saved the final version of the open file, a dialog box opens, asking whether you want to save your changes. Clicking the Yes button saves the open file, closes the file, and then exits the program.

To exit a program:

> **1.** Click the **Close** button ☒ on the Word title bar to exit Word. The Word document closes and the Word program exits. The Excel window is visible again on your screen.

> **Trouble?** If a dialog box opens, asking whether you want to save the document, you may have inadvertently made a change to the document. Click the No button.

> **2.** Click **File** on the Excel menu bar, and then click **Exit**. A dialog box opens asking whether you want to save the changes you made to the workbook.

> **3.** Click the **Yes** button. The Save As dialog box opens.

> **4.** Save the workbook in the **OFF\Tutorial** folder with the filename **French Sales Report**. The workbook closes, saving a copy to the location you specified, and the Excel program exits.

Exiting programs after you are done using them keeps your Windows desktop unclut-tered for the next person using the computer, frees up your system's resources, and prevents data from being lost accidentally.

Review

Quick Check

1. List the five programs included in Office.
2. How do you start an Office program?
3. Explain the difference between Save As and Save.
4. What is one method for opening an existing Office file?
5. What happens if you attempt to close a file or exit a program without saving the current version of the open file?
6. What are four ways to get help?

Review

Tutorial Summary

You have learned how to use features common to all the programs included in Microsoft Office 2003, including starting and exiting programs; resizing windows; using menus and toolbars; working with task panes; saving, opening, closing, and printing files; and getting help.

Key Terms

Access	menu	Outlook
database	menu bar	PowerPoint
document	menu command	presentation
Excel	Microsoft Access 2003	ScreenTip
file extension	Microsoft Excel 2003	task pane
filename	Microsoft Office 2003	toolbar
folder	Microsoft Office Online	Type a question for help box
Help	Microsoft Outlook 2003	Word
Help task pane	Microsoft PowerPoint 2003	workbook
integration	Microsoft Word 2003	
keyboard shortcut	Office	

Practice

Practice the skills you learned in the tutorial using the same case scenario.

Review Assignments

Data Files needed for the Review Assignments: Finances.xls, Letter.doc

Before the stockholders meeting at Delmar Office Supplies, you'll open and print documents for the upcoming presentation. Complete the following steps:

1. Start PowerPoint.
2. Use the Help task pane to learn how to change the toolbar buttons from small to large, and then do it. Use the same procedure to change the buttons back to regular size. Close the Help window when you're done.
3. Start Excel.
4. Switch to the PowerPoint window using the taskbar, and then close the presentation but leave open the PowerPoint program. (*Hint:* Click the Close Window button on the menu bar.)
5. Open a new, blank PowerPoint presentation from the Getting Started task pane. (*Hint:* Click Create a new presentation in the Open section of the Getting Started task pane.)
6. Close the PowerPoint presentation and program using the Close button on the PowerPoint title bar; do not save changes if asked.

7. Open the **Finances** workbook located in the **OFF\Review** folder included with your Data Files using the Open button on the Standard toolbar in Excel.

8. Use the Save As command to save the workbook as **Delmar Finances** in the **OFF\Review** folder.

9. Type your name, press the Enter key to insert your name at the top of the worksheet, and then save the workbook.

10. Print one copy of the worksheet using the Print command on the File menu.

11. Exit Excel using the File menu.

12. Start Word, and then use the Getting Started task pane to open the **Letter** document located in the **OFF\Review** folder included with your Data Files. (*Hint:* Click the More link in the Getting Started task pane to open the Open dialog box.)

13. Use the Save As command to save the document with the filename **Delmar Letter** in the **OFF\Review** folder.

14. Press and hold the Ctrl key, press the End key, and then release both keys to move the insertion point to the end of the letter, and then type your name.

15. Use the Save button on the Standard toolbar to save the change to the Delmar Letter document.

16. Print one copy of the document, and then close the document.

17. Exit the Word program using the Close button on the title bar.

Assess

SAM Assessment and Training

If you have a SAM user profile, you may have access to hands-on instruction, practice, and assessment of the skills covered in this tutorial. Log in to your SAM account and go to your assignments page to see what your instructor has assigned.

Review

Quick Check Answers

1. Word, Excel, PowerPoint, Access, Outlook
2. Click the Start button on the taskbar, point to All Programs, point to Microsoft Office, and then click the name of the program you want to open.
3. Save As enables you to change the filename and storage location of a file. Save updates a file to reflect its latest contents using its current filename and location.
4. Either click the Open button on the Standard toolbar or click the More link in the Getting Started task pane to open the Open dialog box.
5. A dialog box opens asking whether you want to save the changes to the file.
6. ScreenTips, Type a question for help box, Help task pane, Microsoft Office Online

New Perspectives on
Microsoft® Office PowerPoint® 2003

Read This Before You Begin: Tutorials 1–2

To the Student

Data Files

To complete the Level I PowerPoint Tutorials (Tutorials 1 and 2), you need the starting student Data Files. Your instructor will either provide you with these Data Files or ask you to obtain them yourself.

The Level I PowerPoint Tutorials require the folders shown in the next column to complete the Tutorials, Review Assignments, and Case Problems. You will need to copy these folders from a file server, a standalone computer, or the Web to the drive and folder where you will be storing your Data Files. Your instructor will tell you which computer, drive letter, and folder(s) contain the files you need. You can also download the files by going to www.course.com; see the inside back or front cover for more information on downloading the files, or ask your instructor or technical support person for assistance.

If you are storing your Data Files on floppy disks, you will need **two** blank, formatted, high-density disks for these tutorials. Label your disks as shown, and place on them the folder(s) indicated.

▼**PowerPoint 2003: Data Disk 1**
   Tutorial.01 folder
▼**PowerPoint 2003: Data Disk 2**
   Tutorial.02 folder

When you begin a tutorial, refer to the Student Data Files section at the bottom of the tutorial opener page, which indicates which folders and files you need for the tutorial. Each end-of-tutorial exercise also indicates the files you need to complete that exercise.

To the Instructor

The Data Files are available on the Instructor Resources CD for this title. Follow the instructions in the Help file on the CD to install the programs to your network or standalone computer. See the "To the Student" section above for information on how to set up the Data Files that accompany this text.

You are granted a license to copy the Data Files to any computer or computer network used by students who have purchased this book.

System Requirements

If you are going to work through this book using your own computer, you need:

- **Computer System** Microsoft Windows 2000, Windows XP, or higher must be installed on your computer. These tutorials assume a complete installation of Microsoft Office PowerPoint 2003.

- **Data Files** You will not be able to complete the tutorials or exercises in this book using your own computer until you have the necessary starting Data Files.

www.course.com/NewPerspectives

Objectives

Session 1.1
- Open and view an existing PowerPoint presentation
- Switch views and navigate a presentation
- View a presentation in Slide Show view
- Create a presentation using the AutoContent Wizard

Session 1.2
- Add, move, and delete slides
- Promote and demote text in the Outline tab
- Create speaker notes for slides
- Check the spelling and style in a presentation
- Preview and print slides
- Print outlines, handouts, and speaker notes

Creating a Presentation

Presenting Information About Humanitarian Projects

Case

Global Humanitarian, Austin Office

In 1985, a group of Austin, Texas business leaders established a nonprofit organization called Global Humanitarian. Its goal was to alleviate abject poverty in the third world through public awareness and personal involvement in sustainable self-help initiatives in third-world villages. Today, Global Humanitarian is a large umbrella organization and clearinghouse for national and international humanitarian organizations. Its five major functions are to help provide the following: entrepreneurial support, service expeditions, inventory surplus exchange, funding and grant proposals, and student internships.

The president of Global Humanitarian is Norma Flores, who sits on the board of directors and carries out its policies and procedures. The managing director of the Austin office is Miriam Schwartz, and the managing director in Latin America is Pablo Fuentes, who lives and works in Lima, Peru. Miriam wants you to use PowerPoint to develop a presentation to provide information about Global Humanitarian's current projects to potential donors, expedition participants, and student interns.

In this tutorial, you'll examine a presentation that Miriam created to become familiar with **Microsoft Office PowerPoint 2003** (or simply **PowerPoint**). You'll then create a presentation based on content that PowerPoint suggests by using the AutoContent Wizard. You'll modify the text in the presentation, and you'll add and delete slides. You'll check the spelling and style of the presentation, and then you'll view the completed slide show. Finally, you'll save the slide show and print handouts.

Student Data Files

▼**Tutorial.01**

▽ **Tutorial folder**

Lorena.ppt

▽ **Review folder**

VillageOP.ppt

▽ **Cases folder**

LASIK.ppt
Seafoods.ppt

Session 1.1

What Is PowerPoint?

PowerPoint is a powerful presentation graphics program that provides everything you need to produce an effective presentation in the form of on-screen slides, a slide presentation on a Web site, black-and-white or color overheads, or 35-mm photographic slides. You may have already seen your instructors use PowerPoint presentations to enhance their classroom lectures.

Using PowerPoint, you can prepare each component of a presentation: individual slides, speaker notes, an outline, and audience handouts. The presentation you'll create for Miriam will include slides, notes, and handouts.

To start PowerPoint:

1. Click the **Start** button on the taskbar, point to **All Programs**, point to **Microsoft Office**, and then click **Microsoft Office PowerPoint 2003**. PowerPoint starts and the PowerPoint window opens. See Figure 1-1.

   Trouble? If you don't see the Microsoft Office PowerPoint 2003 option on the Microsoft Office submenu, look for it on a different submenu or as an option on the All Programs menu. If you still cannot find the Microsoft Office PowerPoint 2003 option, ask your instructor or technical support person for help.

Figure 1-1	Blank PowerPoint window

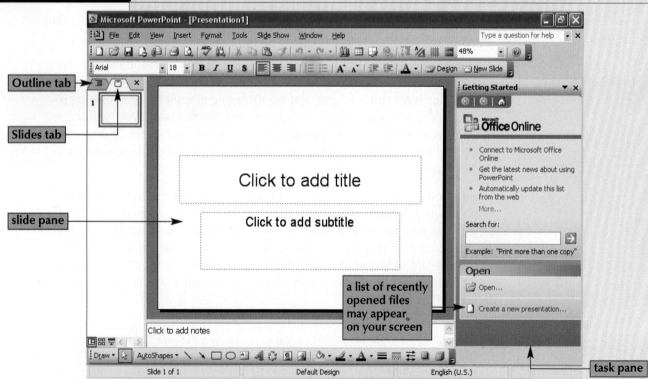

   Trouble? If the PowerPoint program window is not maximized, click the Maximize button on the program window title bar.

   Trouble? If the Office Assistant (an animated icon, usually a paper clip with eyes) opens when you start PowerPoint, right-click the Office Assistant, and then click Hide to close it.

Opening an Existing PowerPoint Presentation

Before you prepare the presentation on Global Humanitarian, Miriam suggests that you view an existing presentation recently prepared under Norma's and Miriam's direction as an example of PowerPoint features. When you examine the presentation, you'll learn about some PowerPoint capabilities that can help make your presentations more interesting and effective. You'll open the presentation now.

To open the existing presentation:

1. Make sure you have access to the Data Files in the Tutorial.01 folder.

   Trouble? If you don't have the PowerPoint Data Files, you need to get them before you can proceed. Your instructor will either give you the Data Files or ask you to obtain them from a specified location (such as a network drive). In either case, be sure that you make a backup copy of your Data Files before you start using them, so that the original files will be available on your copied disk in case you need to start over because of an error or problem. If you have any questions about the Data Files, see your instructor or technical support person for assistance.

2. Click the **Open** link under Open in the Getting Started task pane. The Open dialog box appears on the screen.

   Trouble? If you don't see the Open link, either click More or point to the small triangle at the bottom of the task pane to view additional links.

3. Click the **Look in** list arrow to display the list of disk drives on your computer, and then navigate to the **Tutorial.01\Tutorial** folder included with your Data Files.

4. Click **Lorena** (if necessary), and then click the **Open** button to display Miriam's presentation. The presentation opens in Normal view. See Figure 1-2.

PowerPoint window with presentation open — Figure 1-2

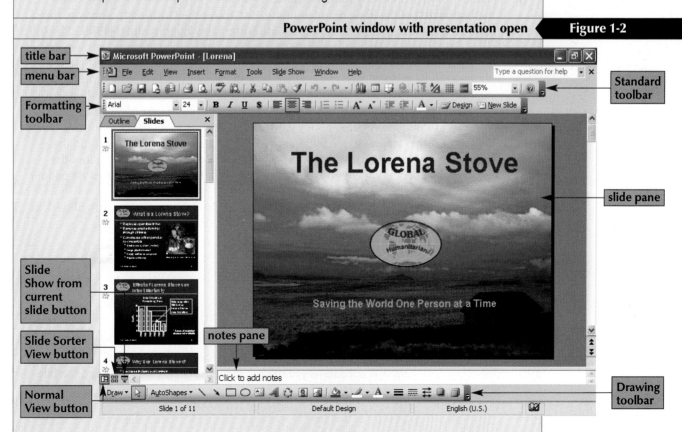

Trouble? If you see filename extensions on your screen (such as ".ppt" appended to "Lorena" in the filename), don't be concerned; they won't affect your work.

Trouble? If your screen doesn't show the Drawing toolbar, click View on the menu bar, point to Toolbars, and then click Drawing.

Trouble? If your screen shows the Standard toolbar and the Formatting toolbar on the same line, click Tools on the menu bar, click Customize, click the Options tab, click the Show Standard and Formatting toolbars on two rows check box to select it, and then click the Close button.

Switching Views and Navigating a Presentation

The PowerPoint window contains features common to all Windows programs, as well as features specific to PowerPoint. One obvious difference between the PowerPoint window and other Office programs is that the PowerPoint window is divided into sections. The section in the center of the screen, to the left of the task pane, is the slide pane. The **slide pane** shows the current slide as it will look during your slide show. Just below the slide pane is the notes pane. The **notes pane** contains notes (also called speaker notes) for the presenter; for example, the notes pane might contain specific points to cover or phrases to say during the presentation. During a slide show, the audience does not see the contents of the notes pane.

Along the left edge of the PowerPoint window, you can see two tabs, the Outline tab and the Slides tab. The **Slides tab** is on top when you first start PowerPoint. It shows a column of numbered slide **thumbnails** (miniature images) so you can see a visual representation of several slides at once. You can use the Slides tab to jump quickly to another slide in the slide pane by clicking the desired slide. The **Outline tab** shows an outline of the titles and text of each slide of your presentation.

At the bottom left of the PowerPoint window, just above the Drawing toolbar, are three view buttons: the Normal View button, the Slide Sorter View button, and the Slide Show from current slide button. These three buttons allow you to change the way you view a slide presentation. PowerPoint is currently in Normal view. Normal view is best for working with the content of the slides. You can see how the text and graphics look on each individual slide, and you can examine the outline of the entire presentation. When you switch to Slide Sorter view, the Slides and Outline tabs disappear from view and all of the slides appears as thumbnails. Slide Sorter view is an easy way to reorder the slides or set special features for your slide show. Slide Show view is the view in which you run the slide show presentation. When you click the Slide Show from current slide button, the presentation starts, beginning with the current slide (the slide currently in the slide pane in Normal view or the selected slide in Slide Sorter view).

Next you'll try switching views. PowerPoint is currently in Normal view with Slide 1 in the slide pane.

To switch views in PowerPoint:

▶ 1. Click the **Slide 2** thumbnail in the Slides tab. Slide 2 appears in the slide pane.

▶ 2. Click the **Next Slide** button ⤓ at the bottom of the vertical scroll bar in the slide pane. Slide 3 appears in the slide pane.

▶ 3. Drag the scroll box in the slide pane vertical scroll bar down to the bottom of the scroll bar. Notice the ScreenTip that appears as you drag. It identifies the slide number and the title of the slide at the current position.

▶ **4.** Click the **Outline** tab. The text outline of the current slide appears in the Outline tab.

▶ **5.** Drag the scroll box in the vertical scroll bar of the Outline tab up to the top of the scroll bar, and then click the **slide icon** ▣ next to Slide 3. Slide 3 again appears in the slide pane.

▶ **6.** Click the **Slides** tab. The Outline tab disappears behind the Slides tab.

▶ **7.** Click the **Slide Sorter View** button ▦. Slide Sorter view appears, and Slide 3 has a colored frame around it to indicate that it is the current slide.

▶ **8.** Position the pointer over the **Slide 2** thumbnail. A thin, colored frame appears around Slide 2.

▶ **9.** Click the **Slide 2** thumbnail to make it the current slide.

▶ **10.** Double-click the **Slide 1** thumbnail. The window switches back to Normal view and Slide 1 appears in the slide pane. You could also have clicked the Normal View button to switch back to Normal view.

Now that you're familiar with the PowerPoint window, you're ready to view Miriam's presentation.

Viewing a Presentation in Slide Show View

Slide Show view is the view you use when you present an on-screen presentation to an audience. When you click the Slide Show from current slide button or click the Slide Show command on the View menu, the slide show starts. If you click the Slide Show from current slide button, the current slide fills the screen, and if you click the Slide Show command on the View menu, the first slide fills the screen. No toolbars or other Windows elements are visible on the screen.

In Slide Show view, you move from one slide to the next by pressing the spacebar, clicking the left mouse button, or pressing the → key. Additionally, PowerPoint provides a method for jumping from one slide to any other slide in the presentation during the slide show: you can right-click anywhere on the screen, point to Go to Slide on the shortcut menu, and then click one of the slide titles in the list that appears to jump to that slide.

When you prepare a slide show, you can add special effects to the show. For example, you can add **slide transitions**, the manner in which a new slide appears on the screen during a slide show. You can also add **animations** to the elements on the slide; that is, each text or graphic object on the slide can appear on the slide in a special way or have a sound effect associated with it. A special type of animation is **progressive disclosure**, a technique in which each element on a slide appears one at a time after the slide background appears. Animations draw the audience's attention to the particular item on the screen.

You can also add a footer on the slides. A **footer** is a word or phrase that appears at the bottom of each slide in the presentation.

You want to see how Miriam's presentation will appear when she shows it in Slide Show view at Global Humanitarian's executive meeting. You'll then have a better understanding of how Miriam used PowerPoint features to make her presentation informative and interesting.

To view the presentation in Slide Show view:

▶ **1.** With Slide 1 in the slide pane, click the **Slide Show from current slide** button 🖵. The slide show begins by filling the entire viewing area of the screen with Slide 1 of Miriam's presentation. Watch as the slide title moves down the slide from the top and the Global Humanitarian logo and motto gradually appear on the screen.

As you view this first slide, you can already see some of the types of elements that PowerPoint allows you to place on a slide: text in different styles, sizes, and colors; graphics; and a background picture. You also saw an example of an animation when you watched the slide title slide down the screen and the logo and motto gradually appear.

▶ **2.** Press the **spacebar**. The slide show goes from Slide 1 to Slide 2. See Figure 1-3. Notice that during the transition from Slide 1 to Slide 2, the presentation displayed Slide 2 by scrolling down from the top of the screen and covering up Slide 1.

Figure 1-3 ▶ **Slide 2 in Slide Show view**

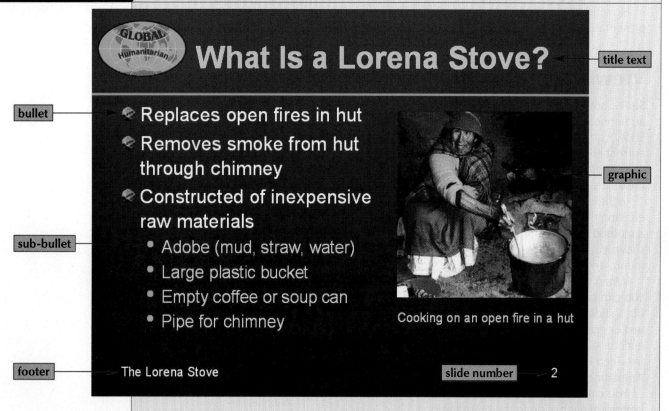

Trouble? If you missed the transition from Slide 1 to Slide 2, or if you want to see it again, press the ← key to redisplay Slide 1, and then press the spacebar to go to Slide 2 again.

Notice in Figure 1-3 that Slide 2 displays: (1) a colored background that varies in color across the slide, (2) Global Humanitarian's logo, (3) a title in large yellow text, (4) a bulleted list (with green textured bullets and white text, or solid cyan bullets with light yellow text), (5) a footer, (6) the slide number (in the lower-right corner of the slide), and (7) a photograph of a villager using an open fire.

▶ **3.** Click the left mouse button to proceed to Slide 3. During the transition from Slide 2 to Slide 3, you again see the slide scroll down onto the screen from the top. Once the slide appears on the screen, you see a chart slowly appear. PowerPoint supports features for creating and customizing this type of chart, as well as graphs, diagrams, tables, and organization charts.

▶ **4.** Press the **spacebar**. The title of Slide 4 appears on screen. What you don't see on the screen is a bulleted list. That's because this slide is designed for progressive disclosure. Additional slide elements will appear on screen after you press the spacebar or click on the screen.

▶ **5.** Press the **spacebar** to reveal the first bulleted item on Slide 4. The item is animated to fly onto the screen from the bottom.

▶ **6.** Press the **spacebar** again to reveal the next bulleted item. As this item appears, the previous item dims. Dimming the previous bulleted items helps focus the audience's attention on the current bulleted item.

▶ **7.** Press the **spacebar** again to cause the last bulleted item to dim.

So far, you've seen important PowerPoint features: slide transitions, progressive disclosure, animations, and graphics (photos and drawings). Now you'll finish the presentation and see custom animations and simple drawings.

To continue viewing the slide show:

▶ **1.** Press the **spacebar** to go to Slide 5, and then press the **spacebar** again. The label "Fuel chamber" and its accompanying arrow appear gradually on the screen. This is another example of an animation.

▶ **2.** Press the **spacebar** three more times, pausing between each to allow the label and arrow to appear gradually on the screen.

▶ **3.** Press the **spacebar** once more. A graphic labeled "smoke" comes into view, and you hear the sound of wind (or a breeze). The smoke object is an example of a user-drawn graphic.

▶ **4.** Press the **spacebar** again to animate the smoke graphic and repeat the sound effect. The smoke graphic travels from the fuel chamber up the stovepipe.

▶ **5.** Go to **Slide 6**. The graphic on this slide is a simple diagram drawn using drawing tools on the Drawing toolbar, which include not only shapes like circles, ovals, squares, and rectangles, but also arrows, boxes, stars, and banners.

▶ **6.** Continue moving through the slide show, looking at all the slides and pausing at each one to read the bulleted items and view the graphics, until you reach Slide 11, the last slide in the slide show.

▶ **7.** Press the **spacebar** to move from Slide 11. A black, nearly blank, screen appears. This signals that the slide show is over, as indicated by the line of text on the screen.

▶ **8.** Press the **spacebar** one more time to return to the view from which you started the slide show, in this case, Normal view.

▶ **9.** Close the current presentation by clicking the **Close Window** button ☒ on the menu bar, and then click the **No** button when asked if you want to save changes.

As you can see from this slide show, PowerPoint has many powerful features. You'll learn how to use many of these features in your own presentations as you work through these tutorials.

You're now ready to create Miriam's presentation on general information about Global Humanitarian's current projects. Before you begin, however, you need to plan the presentation.

Planning a Presentation

Planning a presentation before you create it improves the quality of your presentation, makes your presentation more effective and enjoyable, and, in the long run, saves you time and effort. As you plan your presentation, you should answer several questions: What is my purpose or objective for this presentation? What type of presentation is needed? Who is the audience? What information does that audience need? What is the physical location of my presentation? What is the best format for presenting the information contained in this presentation, given its location?

In planning your presentation, you should determine the following aspects:

- **Purpose of the presentation**: to provide general information about Global Humanitarian
- **Type of presentation**: training (how to become involved with Global Humanitarian)
- **Audience for the presentation**: potential donors, potential participants in humanitarian expeditions, and potential student interns
- **Audience needs**: to understand Global Humanitarian's mission and how to join the effort
- **Location of the presentation**: small conference rooms to large classrooms
- **Format**: oral presentation accompanied by an electronic slide show of 10 to 12 slides

You have carefully planned your presentation. Now you'll use the PowerPoint AutoContent Wizard to create it.

Using the AutoContent Wizard

PowerPoint helps you quickly create effective presentations by using a wizard, a special window that asks you a series of questions about your tasks, and then helps you perform them. The AutoContent Wizard lets you choose a presentation category, such as "Training," "Recommending a Strategy," "Brainstorming Session," or "Selling a Product or Service." After you select the type of presentation you want, the AutoContent Wizard creates a general outline for you to follow and formats the slides using a built-in design template and predesigned layouts. A **design template** is a file that contains the colors and format of the background and the font style of the titles, accents, and other text. Once you start creating a presentation with a given design template, you can change to any other PowerPoint design template or create a custom design template. A **layout** is a predetermined way of organizing the objects on a slide. You can change the layout applied to a slide or you can customize the layout of objects on a screen by moving the objects.

In this tutorial, you'll use the AutoContent Wizard to create a presentation with the goal of training employees, volunteers, and prospective donors on Global Humanitarian's mission. Because "Training" is predefined, you'll use the AutoContent Wizard, which will automatically create a title slide and standard outline that you can then edit to fit Miriam's needs.

To create the presentation with the AutoContent Wizard:

1. Click **File** on the menu bar, and then click **New**. The New Presentation task pane opens on the right side of the PowerPoint window.

2. Click the **From AutoContent wizard** link in the New Presentation task pane. The first dialog box of the AutoContent Wizard opens on top of the PowerPoint program window. The green square on the left side of the window indicates where you are in the wizard.

3. Read the information in the Start dialog box of the AutoContent Wizard, and then click the **Next** button. The next dialog box in the AutoContent Wizard appears. Note that the green square on the left side of the dialog box moved from Start to Presentation type. The Presentation type dialog box allows you to select the type of presentation you want.

▶ **4.** Click the **General** button, if necessary, and then click **Training**. See Figure 1-4.

Selecting the type of presentation in the AutoContent Wizard ◀ **Figure 1-4**

▶ **5.** Click the **Next** button. The Presentation style dialog box opens with the question, "What type of output will you use?" You could also change this option after you create the presentation. As noted in your plan, you want to create an on-screen presentation.

Trouble? If a dialog box opens telling you that PowerPoint can't display the template used in this document because the feature is not currently installed, you must install the Training template before continuing. If you are working on your own computer, click the Yes button. If you are working in a lab, ask your instructor or technical support person for help.

▶ **6.** Click the **On-screen presentation** option button to select it, if necessary, and then click the **Next** button. The Presentation options dialog box opens. In this dialog box, you specify the title and footer (if any) of the presentation.

▶ **7.** Click in the **Presentation title** text box, type **Global Humanitarian**, press the **Tab** key to move the insertion point to the **Footer** text box, and then type **Overview of Global Humanitarian**.

The title will appear on the title slide (the first slide) of the presentation. The footer will appear on every slide (except the title slide) in the presentation. If the other two options are checked, they will appear on either side of the footer on the presentation slides.

▶ **8.** Click the **Date last updated** check box to clear it, and leave the **Slide number** check box checked. You don't want to clutter the screen with information that is not pertinent for the audience. See Figure 1-5.

Selecting information in the AutoContent Wizard ◀ **Figure 1-5**

▶ **9.** Click the **Next** button. The Finish dialog box opens, letting you know that you completed the questions for the AutoContent Wizard.

▶ **10.** Click the **Finish** button. PowerPoint displays the AutoContent outline in the Outline tab and the title slide (Slide 1) in the slide pane. The filename in the title bar "Presentation" followed by a number is a temporary filename. See Figure 1-6.

Figure 1-6 ▶ **Outline and slide after completing the AutoContent Wizard**

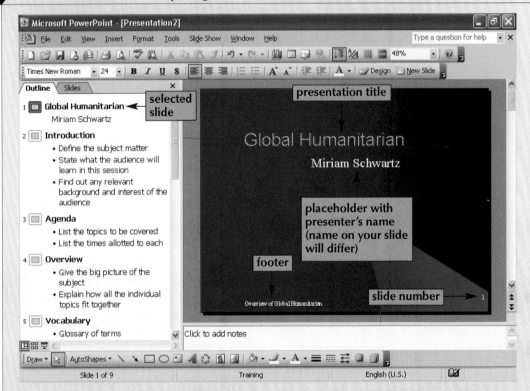

The AutoContent Wizard automatically displays the presenter's name (actually the name of the registered PowerPoint user) below the title in Slide 1. The name that appears on your screen will be different from the one shown in Figure 1-6.

Next, you'll save and name the presentation you created.

To save and name the presentation:

▶ **1.** Click the **Save** button 🖫 on the Standard toolbar. The Save As dialog box opens.

▶ **2.** Click the **Save in** list arrow, and then navigate to the **Tutorial.01\Tutorial** folder included with your Data Files, if necessary.

▶ **3.** Click immediately after Global Humanitarian, the default filename, in the **File name** text box, press the **spacebar**, type **Overview**, and then click the **Save** button. PowerPoint saves the presentation as Global Humanitarian Overview and displays that name in the title bar of the PowerPoint window.

In the next session, you'll edit the text of Miriam's presentation, as well as create notes.

Session 1.1 Quick Check

1. Describe the components of a PowerPoint presentation.
2. Name and describe the two panes and two tabs in the PowerPoint window in Normal view.
3. Define or describe the following:
   a. progressive disclosure
   b. slide transition
   c. design template
   d. layout
4. What are some of the questions that you should answer when planning a presentation?
5. Describe the purpose of the AutoContent Wizard.
6. Describe Slide Show view.

Session 1.2

Modifying a Presentation

Now that you've used the AutoContent Wizard, you're ready to edit some of the words in the presentation to fit Miriam's specific needs. You'll keep the design template, which includes the blue background and the size and color of the text, used by the AutoContent Wizard.

The AutoContent Wizard automatically creates the title slide, as well as other slides, with suggested text located in placeholders. A **placeholder** is a region of a slide, or a location in an outline, reserved for inserting text or graphics. To edit the AutoContent outline to fit Miriam's needs, you must select the placeholders one at a time, and then replace them with other text. Text placeholders are a special kind of **text box**, which is a container for text. You can edit and format text in a text box, or you can manipulate the text box as a whole. When you manipulate the text box as a whole, the text box is treated as an **object**, something that can be manipulated or resized as a unit.

When text is selected, the text box is active and appears as hatched lines around the selected text with sizing handles (small circles) at each corner and on each side of the box. You drag **sizing handles** to make a text box or other object larger or smaller on the slide. When the entire text box is selected as a single object, the text box appears as a dotted outline with sizing handles.

Many of the slides that the AutoContent Wizard created in your presentation for Global Humanitarian contain bulleted lists. A **bulleted list** is a list of paragraphs with a special character (dot, circle, box, star, or other character) to the left of each paragraph. A **bulleted item** is one paragraph in a bulleted list. Bullets can appear at different outline levels. A **first-level bullet** is a main paragraph in a bulleted list; a **second-level bullet**—sometimes called a **sub-bullet**—is a bullet beneath (and indented from) a first-level bullet. Using bulleted lists reminds both the speaker and the audience of the main points of the presentation. In addition to bulleted lists, PowerPoint also supports numbered lists. A **numbered list** is a list of paragraphs that are numbered consecutively within the body text.

When you edit the text on the slides, keep in mind that the bulleted lists aren't meant to be the complete presentation; instead, they should emphasize the key points to the audience and remind the speaker of the points to emphasize. In all your presentations, you should follow the 6 × 6 rule as much as possible: Keep each bulleted item to no more than six words, and don't include more than six bulleted items on a slide.

Creating Effective Text Presentations

- Think of your text presentation as a visual map of your oral presentation. Show your organization by using overviews, making headings larger than subheadings, including bulleted lists to highlight key points, and numbering steps to show sequences.
- Follow the 6 × 6 rule: Use six or fewer items per screen, and use phrases of six or fewer words. Omit unnecessary articles, pronouns, and adjectives.
- Keep phrases parallel.
- Make sure your text is appropriate for your purpose and audience.

Miriam reviewed your plans for your presentation and she has several suggestions for improvement. First, she wants you to replace the text that the AutoContent Wizard inserted with information about Global Humanitarian. She also wants you to delete unnecessary slides, and change the order of the slides in the presentation. You'll start by editing the text on the slides.

Editing Slides

Most of the slides in the presentation contain two placeholder text boxes. The slide **title text** is a text box at the top of the slide that gives the title of the information on that slide; the slide **body text** (also called the **main text**) is a large text box in which you type a bulleted or numbered list. In this presentation, you'll modify or create title text and body text in all but the title slide (Slide 1).

To edit the AutoContent outline to fit Miriam's needs, you must select text in each of the placeholders, and then replace that text with other text. You'll now begin to edit and replace the text to fit Miriam's presentation. The first text you'll change is the presenter's name placeholder.

To edit and replace text in the first slide:

1. If you took a break after the previous session, make sure PowerPoint is running, and then open the presentation **Global Humanitarian Overview** located in the Tutorial.01\Tutorial folder included with your Data Files. Slide 1 appears in the slide pane and the Outline tab is on top.

2. Position the pointer over the presenter's name (currently the registered PowerPoint user's name) in the slide pane so that the pointer changes to I, and then drag it across the text of the presenter's name to select the text. The text box becomes active, as indicated by the hatched lines around the box and the sizing handles at each corner and on each side of the text box, and the text becomes highlighted.

3. Type your first and last name (so your instructor can identify you as the author of this presentation), and then click anywhere else on the slide. As soon as you start to type, the selected text disappears, and the typed text appears in its place. (The figures in this book will show the name Miriam Schwartz.)

   Trouble? If PowerPoint marks your name with a red wavy underline, this indicates that the word is not found in the PowerPoint dictionary. Ignore the wavy line for now, because spelling will be covered later.

You'll now edit Slides 2 through 9 by replacing the placeholder text and adding new text, and by deleting slides that don't apply to your presentation.

To edit the text in the slides:

▶ **1.** Click the **Next Slide** button 🔽 at the bottom of the vertical scroll bar in the slide pane. Slide 2 appears in the slide pane.

▶ **2.** Drag across the word **Introduction** (the title text) to select it. See Figure 1-7.

Selecting title text ◀ **Figure 1-7**

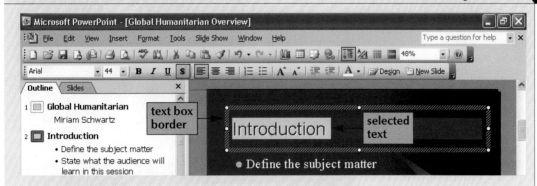

Now you're ready to type the desired title. As you perform the next step, notice not only that the words you type replace the selected text in the slide pane, but also that the slide title on the Outline tab changes.

▶ **3.** Type **Are You Rich?** and then click in a blank space in the slide pane, just outside the edge of the slide, to deselect the text box. The hatched lines and sizing handles disappear. Notice that the slide title changed on the Outline tab as well.

Trouble? If you clicked somewhere on the slide and selected another item, such as the bulleted list, click another place, preferably just outside the edge of the text box, to deselect all items.

Now you're going to edit the text from the Outline tab.

▶ **4.** In the Outline tab, select the text **Define the subject matter**. The text is highlighted by changing to white on black.

▶ **5.** Type **Home has non-dirt floor: top 50%**. Don't include a period at the end of the phrase. This bulleted item is an incomplete sentence, short for "If you live in a home with a non-dirt floor, you're in the top 50% of the wealthiest people on earth."

▶ **6.** Select the text of the second bulleted item in either the Outline tab or the slide pane, and then type **Home has more than one room: top 20%**. Again, don't include a period.

▶ **7.** Select the text of the third bulleted item in the slide pane, and then type **Own more than one pair of shoes: top 5%**.

With the insertion point at the end of the third bulleted item, you're ready to create additional bulleted items.

To create additional bulleted items:

▶ **1.** With the insertion point blinking at the end of the last bulleted item, press the **Enter** key. PowerPoint creates a new bullet and leaves the insertion point to the right of the indent after the bullet, waiting for you to type the text.

▶ **2.** Type **Own a refrigerator: top 3%** and then press the **Enter** key.

▶ **3.** Type **Own a car, computer, microwave, or VCR: top 1%**.

▶ **4.** Click in a blank area of the slide pane to deselect the bulleted list text box. The completed Slide 2 should look like Figure 1-8.

Figure 1-8	**Slide 2 after adding text**

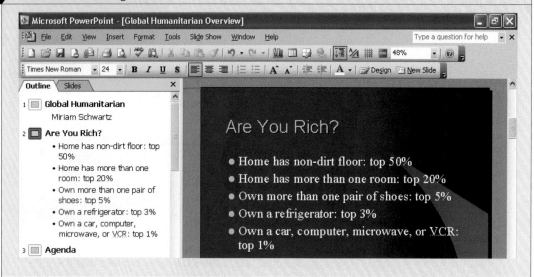

You're now ready to edit the text on another slide and create sub-bullets.

To create sub-bullets:

▶ **1.** Click the **Next Slide** button ▼ at the bottom of the vertical scroll bar four times to move to Slide 6. Slide 6 appears in the slide pane and on the Outline tab.

▶ **2.** Select the title text **Topic One**, and then type **How You Can Help**.

▶ **3.** Select all the text in the body text placeholder, not just the text of the first bulleted item.

▶ **4.** Type **Become a member of Global Humanitarian**, press the **Enter** key, and then type **Contribute to humanitarian projects**. You've added two bulleted items to the body text.

Now you'll add some sub-bullets beneath the first-level bulleted item.

▶ **5.** Press the **Enter** key to insert a new bullet, and then press the **Tab** key. The new bullet changes to a sub-bullet. In this design template, sub-bullets have a dash in front of them, which you won't be able to see until you start typing the text.

▶ **6.** Type **Health and Education**, and then press the **Enter** key. The new bullet is a second-level bullet, the same level as the previous bullet.

▶ **7.** Type **Water and Environment**, press the **Enter** key, type **Income Generation and Agriculture**, press the **Enter** key, and then type **Leadership and Cultural Enhancement**.

Now you want the next bullet to return to the first level.

▶ **8.** Press the **Enter** key to create a new, second-level bullet, and then click the **Decrease Indent** button 🔃 on the Formatting toolbar. The bullet is converted to a first-level bullet. You can also press the Shift+Tab key combination to move a bullet up a level.

▶ **9.** Type the remaining two first-level bulleted items: **Join a humanitarian expedition** and **Become a student intern**, and then click in a blank area of the slide to deselect the text box. See Figure 1-9.

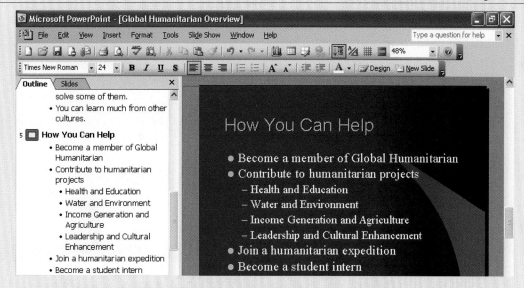

You have completed editing Slide 6. Miriam suggests that you delete the previous three slides, which are unnecessary for your presentation, before you edit the other slides.

Deleting Slides

When creating a presentation, you'll often delete slides. The AutoContent Wizard may create slides that you don't think are necessary, or you may create slides that you no longer want. You can delete slides in several ways: in Normal view, by clicking the slide thumbnail in the Slides tab or by clicking the slide icon in the Outline tab to select the slide, and then pressing the Delete key or using the Delete command on the shortcut or Edit menu; or in Slide Sorter view, by selecting the slide and then pressing the Delete key. Keep in mind that once you delete a slide, you can recover it by immediately clicking the Undo button on the Standard toolbar.

You need to delete Slide 3 ("Agenda"), Slide 4 ("Overview"), and Slide 5 ("Vocabulary").

To delete Slides 3 through 5:

1. With Slide 6 in the slide pane, click the **slide icon** next to Slide 3 ("Agenda") on the Outline tab. You might need to drag the Outline pane scroll box up to view Slide 3. This causes Slide 3 to appear in the slide pane. Now you're ready to delete the slide.

2. Right-click the Slide 3 ("Agenda") **slide icon** on the Outline tab, and then click **Delete Slide** on the shortcut menu. The entire slide is deleted from the presentation, and the rest of the slides are renumbered so that the slide that was Slide 4 becomes Slide 3, and so on. The renumbered Slide 3 ("Overview") appears in the slide pane.

3. Click the **Slides** tab. The Outline tab disappears and the Slides tab appears with thumbnails of all of the slides. With the Slides tab on top, notice that the labels identifying the Slides and Outline tabs change to icons.

4. With **Slide 3** ("Overview") selected in the Slides tab, press and hold the **Shift** key, and then click **Slide 4** on the Slides tab. Slides 3 and 4 are both selected on the Slides tab.

5. Click **Edit** on the menu bar, and then click **Delete Slide**. Both slides are deleted from the presentation. The new Slide 3, entitled "How You Can Help," now appears in the slide pane.

   Trouble? If the Delete Slide command is not on the Edit menu, click the double arrow at the bottom of the menu to display all of the commands on the menu.

Now you'll finish editing the presentation and save your work.

To edit and save the presentation:

▶ **1.** Go to **Slide 4** ("Topic Two"), and then edit the title text to read **Benefits of Joining Global Humanitarian**. Notice that as you type the last word, PowerPoint automatically adjusts the size of the text to fit in the title text box.

   Trouble? If the font size of the text doesn't automatically adjust so that the text fits within the body text placeholder, click the AutoFit Options button ⊞ that appears in the slide pane, and then click the AutoFit Text to Placeholder option.

▶ **2.** Select all the body text, not just the text of the first bulleted item, in the body text place-holder, and then type the bulleted items shown in Figure 1-10.

Figure 1-10	Completed Slide 4

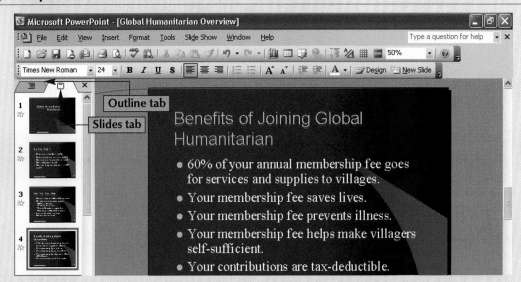

▶ **3.** Go to **Slide 5**, and then modify the title and body text so that the slide looks like Figure 1-11.

Figure 1-11	Completed Slide 5

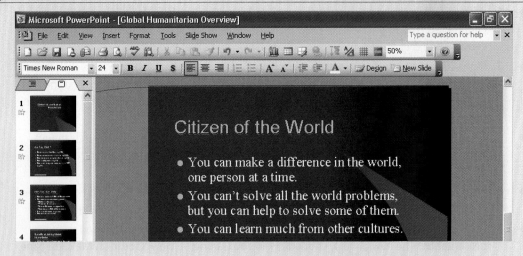

> **4.** Delete **Slide 6** ("Where to Get More Information").
>
> **5.** Click the **Save** button  on the Standard toolbar to save the presentation.

Miriam reviews your presentation and wants you to add a slide at the end of the presentation stating what action you want your readers to take as a result of your presentation.

Adding a New Slide and Choosing a Layout

Miriam suggests that you add a new slide at the end of the presentation explaining how individuals and families can join Global Humanitarian. When you add a new slide, PowerPoint formats the slide using a slide layout. PowerPoint supports four **text layouts**: Title Slide (placeholders for a title and a subtitle, usually used as the first slide in a presentation); Title Only (a title placeholder but not a body text placeholder); Title and Text (the default slide layout, with a title and a body text placeholder); and Title and 2-Column Text (same as Title and Text, but with two columns for text). PowerPoint also supports several **content layouts**—slide layouts that contain from zero to four charts, diagrams, images, tables, or movie clips. In addition, PowerPoint supports combination layouts, called **text and content layouts**, and several other types of layouts.

When you insert a new slide, it appears after the current one, and the Slide Layout task pane appears with a default layout already selected. This default layout is applied to the new slide. To use a different layout, you click it in the Slide Layout task pane.

To insert the new slide at the end of the presentation:

> **1.** Because you want to add a slide after Slide 5, make sure Slide 5 is still in the slide pane.
>
> **2.** Click the **New Slide** button on the Formatting toolbar. The Slide Layout task pane opens with the first layout in the second row under Text Layouts selected as the default, and a new Slide 6 appears in the slide pane with the default layout applied. See Figure 1-12.

New slide added | **Figure 1-12**

You'll accept the default layout for this slide. If you wanted a different layout, you would click the desired layout in the Slide Layout task pane.

Trouble? If the Slide Layout task pane does not appear, click View on the menu bar, click Task Pane, click the Other Task Panes list arrow at the top of the task pane, and then click Slide Layout. To make the Slide Layout task pane open automatically when you insert a new slide, click the Show when inserting new slides check box at the bottom of the task pane.

▶ **3.** Position the pointer over the selected layout in the task pane. A ScreenTip appears, identifying this layout as the Title and Text layout.

Next you'll close the Slide Layout task pane to provide a larger view of the slide pane.

▶ **4.** Click the **Close** button ☒ in the Slide Layout task pane title bar to close the task pane.

Trouble? If you accidentally click the Close button of the PowerPoint window or Presentation window, PowerPoint will ask you if you want to save the changes to your presentation. Click the Cancel button so that the presentation doesn't close, and then click the correct Close button on the task pane title bar.

The new slide contains text placeholders. On a new slide, you don't need to select the text on the slide to replace it with your text. You only need to click in the placeholder text box; the placeholder text will disappear and the insertion point will be placed in the text box, ready for you to type your text. Once you type your text, the dotted line outlining the edge of the text box will disappear. You'll add text to the new slide.

To add text to the new slide:

▶ **1.** Click anywhere in the title text placeholder in the slide pane, where it says "Click to add title." The title placeholder text disappears and the insertion point blinks at the left of the title text box.

▶ **2.** Type **Global Humanitarian Memmbership**. Make sure you type "Memmbership" with two *ms* in the middle. You'll correct this misspelling later. Again, the font size decreases to fit the text within the title placeholder.

▶ **3.** Click anywhere in the body text placeholder. The placeholder text disappears and the insertion point appears just to the right of the first bullet.

▶ **4.** Type **Individual membership: $75 per year**, press the **Enter** key, type **Family membership: $150 per year**, press the **Enter** key, type **Visit our Web site at www.globalhumanitarian.org**, and then press the **Enter** key.

When you press the Enter key after typing the Web site address, PowerPoint automatically changes the Web site address (the URL) to a link. It formats the link by changing its color and underlining it. When you run the slide show, you can click this link to jump to that Web site if you are connected to the Internet.

▶ **5.** Type **Call Sam Matagi, Volunteer Coordinator, at 523–555–SERV**.

You have inserted a new slide at the end of the presentation and added text to the slide. Next you'll create a new slide by promoting text in the Outline tab.

Promoting, Demoting, and Moving Outline Text

You can modify the text of a slide in the Outline tab as well as in the slide pane. Working in the Outline tab gives you more flexibility because you can see the outline of the entire presentation, not only the single slide currently in the slide pane. Working in the Outline tab allows you to easily move text from one slide to another or to create a new slide by promoting bulleted items from a slide so that they become the title and body text on a new slide.

To **promote** an item means to increase the outline level of that item—for example, to change a bulleted item into a slide title or to change a second-level bullet into a first-level bullet. To **demote** an item means to decrease the outline level—for example, to change a slide title into a bulleted item on the previous slide or to change a first-level bullet into a second-level bullet. You'll begin by promoting a bulleted item to a slide title, thus creating a new slide.

To create a new slide by promoting outline text:

1. Click the **Outline** tab. The outline of the presentation appears.

2. Drag the scroll box in the slide pane up until the ScreenTip displays "Slide: 3 of 6" and the title "How You Can Help." Slide 3 appears in the slide pane and the text of that slide appears at the top of the Outline tab.

3. In the Outline tab, move the pointer over the bullet to the left of "Contribute to humanitarian projects" so that the pointer becomes ⊹, and then click the bullet. The text for that bullet and all its sub-bullets are selected.

   Now you'll promote the selected text so that it becomes the title text and first-level bullets on a new slide.

4. Click the **Decrease Indent** button ▤ on the Formatting toolbar. PowerPoint promotes the selected text one level. Because the bullet you selected was a first-level bullet, the first-level bullet is promoted to a slide title on a new Slide 4, and the second-level bullets become first-level bullets on the new slide. See Figure 1-13.

Promoting a bulleted item to become a new slide   **Figure 1-13**

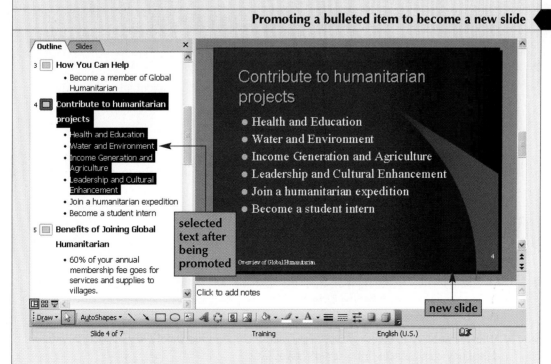

Now you'll edit this text, and then move some of the bulleted items to another slide.

5. Click anywhere to deselect the text, select the Slide 4 title text in the Outline tab, and then type **Types of Humanitarian Projects in Third-World Villages**. Notice that the title changes in the slide pane as well.

   Trouble? If all of the text on the slide becomes selected when you try to select the title text, make sure you position the pointer just to the left of the title text, and not over the slide icon, before you drag to select the text.

6. Click the bullet to the left of "Join a humanitarian expedition" (the fifth bullet in Slide 4) in the Outline tab, and then, while holding down the left mouse button, drag the bullet and its text up until the horizontal line position marker is just under the bulleted item "Become a member of Global Humanitarian" in Slide 3, as shown in Figure 1-14.

Figure 1-14 ▶ **Moving text in the Outline tab**

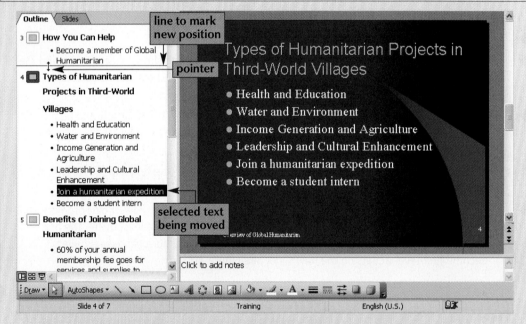

7. Release the mouse button. The bulleted item moves to the new position.

8. Using the same procedure, move the bulleted item "Become a student intern" from the end of Slide 4 to the end of Slide 3 in the Outline tab.

As you review your slides, you notice that in Slide 5, the phrase "Your membership fee" is repeated three times. You'll fix the problem by demoting some of the text.

To demote text on Slide 5:

1. Click the **slide icon** 🔲 next to Slide 5 ("Benefits of Joining Global Humanitarian") in the Outline tab.

2. Click immediately to the right of "Your membership fee" in the second bulleted item in the Outline tab, and then press the **Enter** key. The item "saves lives" becomes a new bulleted item, but you want that item to appear indented at a lower outline level.

3. Press the **Tab** key to indent "saves lives," and then press the **Delete** key, if necessary, to delete any blank spaces to the left of "saves lives."

▶ **4.** Click the bullet to the left of "Your membership fee prevents illness" in the Outline tab, press and hold down the **Shift** key, and then click the bullet to the left of "Your membership fee helps make villagers self-sufficient." This selects both bulleted items at the same time.

▶ **5.** Click the **Increase Indent** button 🔲 on the Formatting toolbar to demote the two bulleted items. Note this has the same effect as pressing the Tab key.

▶ **6.** Delete the phrase "Your membership fee" and the space after it from the two items that you just demoted. Your slide should now look like Figure 1-15.

Slide 5 after demoting text to sub-bullets ◀ **Figure 1-15**

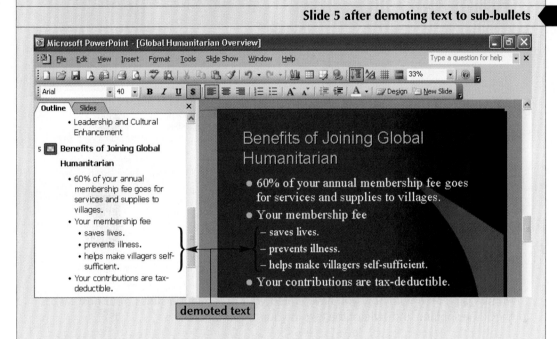

demoted text

Miriam looks at your presentation and suggests that you move the current Slide 4 ahead of Slide 3. You could make this change by clicking the slide icon and dragging it above the slide icon for Slide 3 in the Outline tab. Instead, you'll move the slide in Slide Sorter view.

Moving Slides in Slide Sorter View

In Slide Sorter view, PowerPoint displays all the slides as thumbnails, so that several slides can appear on the screen at once. This view not only provides you with a good overview of your presentation, but also allows you to easily change the order of the slides and modify the slides in other ways.

To move Slide 4:

▶ **1.** Click the **Slide Sorter View** button 🔲 at the bottom of the Outline tab. You now see your presentation in Slide Sorter view.

▶ **2.** Click **Slide 4**. A thick colored frame appears around the slide, indicating that the slide is selected.

▶ **3.** Press and hold down the left mouse button, drag the slide to the left so that the vertical line position marker appears on the left side of Slide 3, as shown in Figure 1-16.

Figure 1-16 ▶ Moving a slide in Slide Sorter view

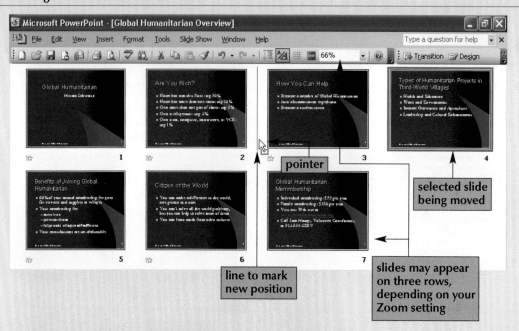

4. Release the mouse button. Slides 3 and 4 have switched places.
5. Click the **Normal View** button ▣ to return to Normal view.

Miriam is pleased with how you have edited your presentation slides. Your next task is to check the spelling and style of the text in your presentation.

Checking the Spelling and Style in a Presentation

Before you print or present a slide show, you should always perform a final check of the spelling and style of all the slides in your presentation. This will help to ensure that your presentation is accurate and professional looking.

Checking the Spelling

If PowerPoint finds a word that's not in its dictionary, the word is underlined with a red wavy line in the slide pane. When you right-click the word, suggestions for alternate spellings appear on the shortcut menu, as well as commands for ignoring the misspelled word or opening the Spelling dialog box. You can also click the Spelling button on the Standard toolbar to check the spelling in the entire presentation.

You need to check the spelling in the Global Humanitarian presentation.

To check the spelling in the presentation:

1. Go to **Slide 7**. The spelling check always starts from the current slide.
2. Click the **Spelling** button 🗹 on the Standard toolbar. The Spelling dialog box opens. The word you purposely mistyped earlier, "Memmbership," is highlighted in the Outline tab and listed in the Not in Dictionary text box in the Spelling dialog box. Two suggested spellings appear in the Suggestions list box, and the selected word in the Suggestions list box appears in the Change to text box.

▶ **3.** With "Membership" selected in the Suggestions list box and in the Change to text box, click the **Change** button. If you knew that you misspelled that word throughout your presentation, you could click the Change All button to change all of the instances of the misspelling in the presentation to the corrected spelling.

The word is corrected, and the next word in the presentation that is not in the PowerPoint dictionary, Matagi, is flagged. This word is not misspelled; it is a surname.

▶ **4.** Click the **Ignore** button. The word is not changed on the slide. If you wanted to ignore all the instances of that word in the presentation, you could click the Ignore All button. A dialog box opens telling you that the spelling check is complete.

Trouble? If another word in the presentation is flagged as misspelled, select the correct spelling in the Suggestions list, and then click the Change button. If your name on Slide 1 is flagged, click the Ignore button.

▶ **5.** Click the **OK** button. The dialog box closes.

Next, you need to check the style in the presentation.

Using the Style Checker

The **Style Checker** checks your presentation for consistency in punctuation, capitalization, and visual elements and marks problems on a slide with a light bulb. For this feature to be active, you need to turn on the Style Checker.

To turn on the Style Checker:

▶ **1.** Click **Tools** on the menu bar, click **Options** to open the Options dialog box, and then click the **Spelling and Style** tab.

▶ **2.** Click the **Check style** check box to select it, if necessary. Now you'll check to make sure the necessary Style Checker options are selected.

Trouble? If a message appears telling you that the Style Checker needs to use the Office Assistant, click the Enable Assistant button. If another message appears telling you that PowerPoint can't display the Office Assistant because the feature is not installed, click the Yes button only if you are working on your own computer. If you are in a lab, ask your instructor or technical support person for assistance.

▶ **3.** Click the **Style Options** button in the Options dialog box, click the **Slide title style** check box to select it, if necessary, click the list arrow to the right of this option, and then click **UPPERCASE**. When you run the Style Checker, it will suggest changing all of the titles to all uppercase.

▶ **4.** Click the **Body text style** check box to select it, if necessary, click the list arrow to the right of this option, and then click **Sentence case**, if necessary. When you run the Style Checker, it will check to make sure that the text in each bullet in the body text has an uppercase letter as the first letter, and that the rest of the words in the body text start with a lowercase letter.

▶ **5.** Click the bottom two check boxes under End punctuation to clear them, if necessary. Some of the bulleted lists in this presentation are complete sentences and some are not, so you want PowerPoint to allow variation in the end punctuation. See Figure 1-17.

Figure 1-17   **Style Options dialog box**

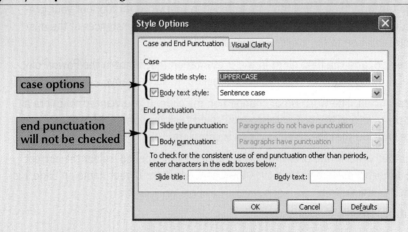

6. Click the **OK** button to close the Style Options dialog box, and then click the **OK** button to close the Options dialog box.

From now on, PowerPoint will check the style in your presentation as you display each slide in the slide pane. Now you'll go through your presentation and check for style problems.

To fix problems marked by the Style Checker:

1. Go to **Slide 1**. A light bulb appears next to the title. This indicates that the Style Checker found a problem with the slide title. Since you did not type any of the titles in all uppercase letters, a light bulb will appear on every slide marking the titles as not matching the style.

2. Click the **light bulb**. The Office Assistant appears and displays a dialog box with a description of the problem and three options from which you can choose. See Figure 1-18.

Figure 1-18   **Using the Style Checker**

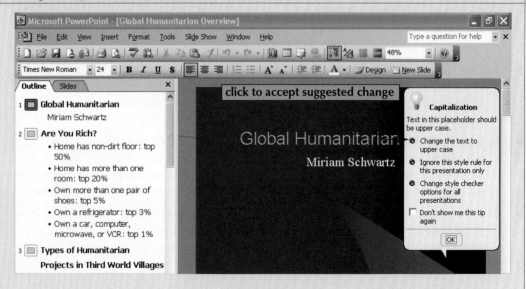

Trouble? If a message appears telling you that PowerPoint can't display the Office Assistant because the feature is not installed, click the Yes button only if you are working on your own computer. If you are in a lab, ask your instructor or technical support person for assistance.

3. Click the **Change the text to upper case** option button in the Office Assistant dialog box. All of the title text is now changed to uppercase.

4. Go to **Slide 2**.

5. Use the Style Checker to change the title text to uppercase.

6. Go to **Slide 3**, and then change the title text to uppercase. Another light bulb appears on Slide 3 next to the body text.

   Trouble? If, in this or subsequent steps, the light bulb doesn't appear by the body text, go to the next or the previous slide, and then return to the current slide as a way of telling the Style Checker to recheck the slide.

7. Click the **light bulb** to see that the error in the body text is another capitalization error, and then click the **Change the text to sentence case** option button in the Office Assistant dialog box. All the words in the bulleted items are converted to lowercase (except the first word in each bulleted item); that is, all the bulleted items are converted to sentence case.

8. Go to **Slide 4**, change the title text to uppercase, and then click the **light bulb** next to the body text. The Style Checker detects that the first bulleted item is in mixed case (the words "Global Humanitarian" are capitalized), but the organization's name should remain capitalized, so you don't need to make any changes here.

9. Click the **OK** button in the Office Assistant dialog box. PowerPoint ignores the style for that slide, and the light bulb no longer appears.

10. Correct the title and body text on Slide 5, and the title text on Slide 6, and then go to Slide 7.

11. Correct the title text on Slide 7, but do not correct the capitalization in the body text on Slide 7. The words that start with an uppercase letter in the body text on this slide are proper nouns or are part of the phone number. Now you need to turn off the Style Checker.

12. Click **Tools** on the menu bar, click **Options**, click the **Check style** check box on the Spelling and Style tab to clear it, and then click the **OK** button. The Style Checker is turned off.

As you create your own presentations, watch for the problems marked by the Style Checker. Of course, in some cases, you might want a certain capitalization that the Style Checker detects as an error. In these cases, just ignore the light bulb, or click it, and then click the OK button. The light bulb never appears on the screen during a slide show or when you print a presentation.

Using the Research Task Pane

PowerPoint enables you to use the Research task pane to search online services or Internet sites for additional help in creating a presentation. Using these resources helps you make your presentations more professional. For example, you could look up specific words in a thesaurus. A **thesaurus** contains a list of words and their synonyms, antonyms, and other related words. Using a thesaurus is a good way to add variety to the words you use or to choose more precise words. You could also look up information in online encyclopedias, news services, libraries, and business sites.

Miriam thinks the word "rich" in Slide 2 may be too informal. She asks you to find an appropriate replacement word. You'll now look for synonyms in the Office thesaurus.

To do research using the thesaurus:

▶ 1. Go to **Slide 2**, and then highlight the word **RICH** in either the Outline tab or the slide pane. Be careful not to highlight the question mark at the end of the phrase.

▶ 2. Click the **Research** button on the Standard toolbar. The Research task pane opens with the word "RICH" in the Search for text box.

▶ 3. Click the list arrow next to All Reference Books in the task pane, and then click **Thesaurus: English (U.S.)**.

▶ 4. Click the **green arrow** button next to the Search for text box to begin a search for synonyms for the word "rich," if necessary. The thesaurus provides several suggestions in a list organized so that the most relevant words are in bold, and additional synonyms are indented under the bold terms.

▶ 5. Scroll down, if necessary, to see the word "full" in boldface, and then click the **minus sign** button next to "full (adj.)." The minus sign changes to a plus sign, and the list of words under "full" collapses.

After looking over the list, Miriam decides that "full" and "opulent" do not convey the correct meaning. She decides that "wealthy" is the most appropriate synonym.

▶ 6. Position the pointer over the word **wealthy**, indented under the bold term **wealthy (adj.)**. A box appears around the term and a list arrow appears at the right side of the box.

▶ 7. Click the list arrow on the side of the box, as shown in Figure 1-19.

Figure 1-19	Using the Thesaurus in the Research task pane

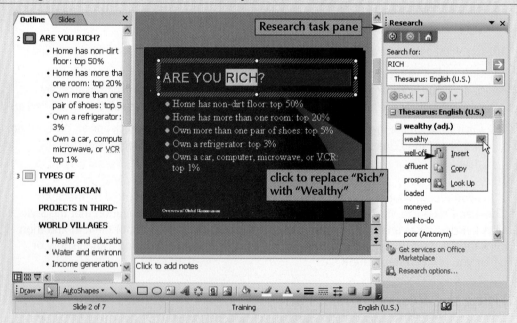

▶ 8. Click **Insert**. "WEALTHY" replaces "RICH" in the slide.

▶ 9. Close the task pane.

Creating Speaker Notes

When you show the presentation to Miriam, she is satisfied. Now you're ready to prepare the other parts of Miriam's presentation: the notes (also called speaker notes) and audience handouts (a printout of the slides). **Notes** are printed pages that contain a picture of and notes about each slide. They help the speaker remember what to say when a particular slide appears during the presentation. **Handouts** are printouts of the slides; these can be arranged with several slides printed on a page.

You'll create notes for only a few of the slides in the presentation. For example, Miriam wants to remember to acknowledge special guests or Global Humanitarian executives at any meeting where she might use this presentation. You'll create a note reminding her to do that.

To create notes:

1. Click the **Slides** tab, and then click **Slide 1** in the Slides tab. Slide 1 appears in the slide pane. The notes pane currently contains placeholder text.

2. Click in the notes pane, and then type **Acknowledge special guests and Global Humanitarian executives.** See Figure 1-20.

Notes on Slide 1 ◀ **Figure 1-20**

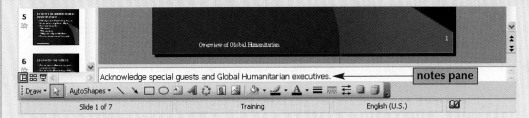

Acknowledge special guests and Global Humanitarian executives. ◀———— notes pane

3. Click **Slide 2** in the Slides tab, click in the notes pane, and then type **Everyone in this room is in the top one percent of wealthy people who have ever lived on earth.**

4. Go to **Slide 3**, click in the notes pane, and then type **Give an example of each of these project types.** These are all the notes that Miriam wants.

5. Click the **Save** button 🖫 on the Standard toolbar to save the changes to the presentation.

Before Miriam gives her presentation, she'll print the notes of the presentation so she'll have them available during her presentations. You can now view the completed presentation to make sure that it is accurate, informative, and visually pleasing.

To view the slide show:

1. Go to **Slide 1**, and then click the **Slide Show from current slide** button 🖵 at the bottom of the Slides tab.

2. Proceed through the slide show as you did earlier, clicking the left mouse button or pressing the spacebar to advance from one slide to the next.

3. If you see a problem on one of your slides, press the **Esc** key to leave the slide show and display the current slide on the screen in Normal view, fix the problem on the slide, save your changes, and then click the **Slide Show from current slide** button 🖵 to resume the slide show from the current slide.

4. When you reach the end of your slide show, press the **spacebar** to move to the blank screen, and then press the **spacebar** again to return to Normal view.

Now you're ready to preview and print your presentation.

Previewing and Printing a Presentation

Before you give your presentation, you may want to print it. PowerPoint provides several printing options. For example, you can print the slides in color using a color printer; print in grayscale or pure black and white using a black-and-white printer; print handouts with 2, 3, 4, 6, or 9 slides per page; or print the notes pages (the speaker notes printed below a picture of the corresponding slide). You can also format and then print the presentation onto overhead transparency film (available in most office supply stores).

Usually you'll want to open the Print dialog box by clicking File on the menu bar, and then clicking Print, rather than clicking the Print button on the Standard toolbar. If you click the Print button, the presentation prints with the options chosen last in the Print dialog box. If you're going to print your presentation on a black-and-white printer, you should first preview the presentation to make sure the text will be legible. You'll use Print Preview to see the slides as they will appear when they are printed.

To preview the presentation:

▶ 1. Go to **Slide 1**, if necessary, and then click the **Print Preview** button 🔍 on the Standard toolbar. The Preview window appears, displaying Slide 1.

▶ 2. Click the **Options** button on the Preview toolbar, point to **Color/Grayscale**, and then click **Grayscale**. The slide is displayed in grayscale.

▶ 3. Click the **Next Page** button 🔽 on the Preview toolbar. As you can see, part of the background graphic covers the text on Slide 2. See Figure 1-21. You'll need to remove the background from the slides so you can read them after you have printed them.

| Figure 1-21 | Slide 2 in Preview window |

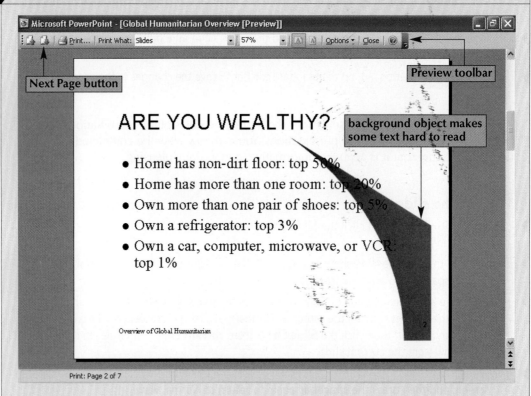

▶ **4.** Click the **Close** button on the Preview toolbar to return to Normal view.

▶ **5.** Click **Format** on the menu bar, click **Background** to display the Background dialog box, click the **Omit background graphics from master** check box, and then click the **Apply to All** button. The slide appears as before, but without the background graphic.

▶ **6.** Click the **Print Preview** button 🔍 on the Standard toolbar, and then click the **Next Page** button 🔽 on the Preview toolbar. You can now easily read the text on Slide 2.

▶ **7.** Click the **Print What** list arrow on the Preview toolbar, and then click **Handouts (4 slides per page)**. The preview changes to display four slides on a page.

▶ **8.** Click the **Print** button on the Preview toolbar. The Print dialog box opens. See Figure 1-22.

Print dialog box ◀ **Figure 1-22**

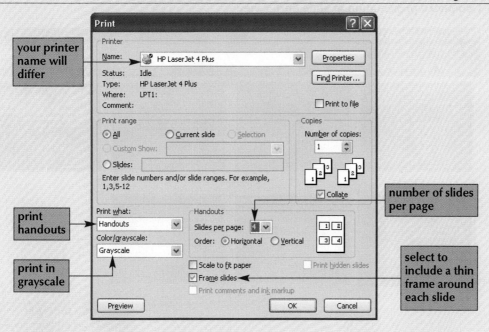

▶ **9.** Compare your dialog box to the one shown in Figure 1-22, make any necessary changes, and then click the **OK** button to print the handouts on two pages. Now you're ready to print the notes.

▶ **10.** Click the **Print What** list arrow on the Preview toolbar, and then click **Notes Pages**. The current slide is displayed as a notes page, with the slide on the top and the notes on the bottom.

▶ **11.** Click the **Print** button on the Print Preview toolbar, click the **Slides** option button in the Print range section of the Print dialog box, and then type **1-3**. These are the only slides with notes on them, so you do not need to print all seven slides as notes pages.

▶ **12.** Click the **OK** button to print the notes. Slides 1-3 print on three pieces of paper as notes pages.

▶ **13.** Click the **Close** button on the Preview toolbar. The view returns to Normal view.

Your last task is to view the completed presentation in Slide Sorter view to see how all the slides look together. First, however, you'll restore the background graphics.

To restore the background graphics and view the completed presentation in Slide Sorter view:

▶ **1.** Click **Format** on the menu bar, click **Background**, click the **Omit background graphics from master** check box to clear it, and then click the **Apply to All** button. The background graphics are restored to the slides.

▶ **2.** Click the **Slide Sorter View** button ⊞ at the bottom of the Slides tab. The slides appear on the screen in several rows, depending on the current zoom percentage shown in the Zoom box on the Standard toolbar and on the size of your monitor. You need to see the content on the slides better.

▶ **3.** Click the **Zoom** list arrow on the Standard toolbar, and then click **75%**. See Figure 1-23.

Figure 1-23	Completed presentation in Slide Sorter view

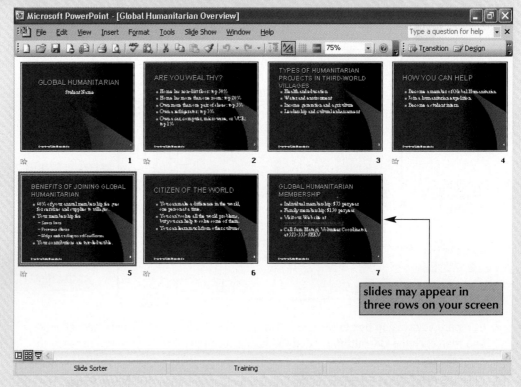

slides may appear in three rows on your screen

▶ **4.** Compare your handouts with the slides shown in Slide Sorter view.

▶ **5.** Click the **Close window** button ✕. A dialog box appears asking if you want to save your changes.

▶ **6.** Click the **Yes** button to save the changes and close the presentation.

You have created a presentation using the AutoContent Wizard, edited it according to Miriam's wishes, and created and printed notes and handouts. Miriam thanks you for your help; she believes that your work will enable her to make an effective presentation.

Review

Session 1.2 Quick Check

1. Explain how to do the following in the Outline tab:
   a. move text up
   b. delete a slide
   c. change a first-level bullet to a second-level bullet
2. What does it mean to promote a bulleted item in the Outline tab? To demote a bulleted item?
3. Explain a benefit of using the Outline tab rather than the slide pane.
4. What is the Style Checker? What is an example of a consistency or style problem that it might mark?
5. What are notes? How do you create them?
6. Why is it beneficial to preview a presentation before printing it?

Review

Tutorial Summary

In this tutorial, you learned how to plan and create a PowerPoint presentation by modifying AutoContent slides. You learned how to edit the text in both the Outline tab and the slide pane; add a new slide and choose a slide layout; delete slides; and promote, demote and move text in your outline. You also learned how to check your presentation for consistency, create speaker notes, and preview and print your presentation.

Key Terms

animation	note	slide pane
body text	notes pane	slide transitions
bulleted item	numbered list	Slides tab
bulleted list	object	Style Checker
content layout	Outline tab	sub-bullet
demote	placeholder	text and content layout
design template	PowerPoint	text box
first-level bullet	progressive disclosure	text layout
footer	promote	thesaurus
handout	second-level bullet	thumbnail
layout	sizing handle	title text
main text		

Practice

Practice the skills you learned in the tutorial using the same case scenario.

Review Assignments

Data File needed for the Review Assignments: VillageOP.ppt

Miriam Schwartz, the managing director of the Austin, Texas headquarters of Global Humanitarian, asks you to prepare a PowerPoint presentation explaining the Village Outreach Program to potential donors and volunteers. She gives you a rough draft of a PowerPoint presentation. Your job is to edit the presentation. Complete the following:

1. Open the presentation **VillageOP** in the Tutorial.01\Review folder included with your Data Files.
2. Save the file as **Village Outreach Program** in the same folder.
3. In Slide 1, change the subtitle placeholder ("Global Humanitarian") to your name.

4. In Slide 2, use the Outline tab to demote the bulleted items "Health," "Education," "Clean water," and "Environment," so that they become second-level bulleted items.
5. Below the sub-bulleted item "Clean water," insert another second-level bulleted item: "Agriculture and Income-producing Projects."
6. In Slide 3, delete all occurrences of the word "the" to reduce the number of words in each bulleted item and thus approach the 6 × 6 rule.
7. Move the last bulleted item in Slide 3 ("Assist villagers in organizing health committees") in the Outline tab so it becomes the second bulleted item in the body text of Slide 3.
8. Go to Slide 5, and then promote the bulleted item "Agriculture and Income-producing Opportunities" in the Outline tab so it becomes the title of a new slide (Slide 6).
9. Return to Slide 5 and promote the last three second-level bulleted items so they become bullets on the same level as "Help villagers build."
10. In Slide 7, move the second bulleted item ("Mobilize resources") so it becomes the fourth bulleted item.
11. Add a new Slide 8 with the default Title and Text layout.
12. In Slide 8, type the slide title "Village Projects."
13. Type the following as first-level bulleted items in Slide 8: "Wells," "Water Pumps," "Greenhouses," "Lorena Stoves," "First aid supplies," and "School supplies."
14. In Slide 2, add the following speaker note: "Relate personal experiences for each topic."
15. In Slide 3, add the following speaker note: "Explain that we need volunteers, especially physicians, dentists, optometrists, and nurses."
16. Switch to Slide Sorter view, and then drag Slide 5 to the left of Slide 4.
17. Use the Research task pane to replace "Agriculture" on Slide 6 with another word, and then make this same change on Slide 2.
18. Check the spelling in the presentation and change or ignore each flagged word as appropriate.
19. Turn on the Style Checker, set the Case options so that the slide title style is uppercase and the body text style is sentence case, and then examine the slides for elements that the Style Checker flags, correcting slides as appropriate. Turn off the Style Checker when you are finished.
20. View the presentation in Slide Show view. Look carefully at each slide and check the content. If you see any errors, press the Esc key to end the slide show, fix the error, and then start the slide show again.
21. Go to Slide 6. When you viewed the presentation, did you notice the typographical error "load" in the final bulleted item? (It should be "loan.") If you did not fix this error already, fix it now.
22. Save the changes to the presentation, preview the presentation in grayscale, and then print the presentation in grayscale as handouts, four slides per page.
23. Print Slides 2 and 3 as notes pages in grayscale, and then close the file.

Case Problem 1

There are no Data Files needed for this Case Problem.

e-Commerce Consultants Kendall Koester founded e-Commerce Consultants, a consulting company that helps local businesses with their e-commerce needs, including Web page design, order fulfillment, and security. Kendall hired you to prepare a presentation to businesses to sell the services of e-Commerce Consultants. Complete the following:

1. Start PowerPoint, and then start the AutoContent Wizard.
2. In the Presentation type window, select the Sales/Marketing category, and then select Selling a Product or Service.
3. In the Presentation style window, select On-screen presentation.

4. In the Presentation options window, type "Developing Strategies for Your Future" as the presentation title, and type "e-Commerce Consultants" as the footer.
5. Omit the date last updated from the presentation, but include the slide number.
6. In Slide 1, change the subtitle placeholder to your name, if necessary.
7. In Slide 2 ("Objective"), replace the slide title with "What We Offer," and replace the body text with the following first-level bulleted items: "Overcoming barriers to e-commerce," "Surviving today's shaky market," "Setting up your Web site," and "Managing your orders."
8. In Slide 3 ("Customer Requirements"), leave the title text as is, and then replace the body text with the following bulleted items: "Web site design and development," "Order taking and fulfillment," "Security," and "Other." Don't modify or delete the radial diagram on the slide.
9. In Slide 4, change the slide title to "Meeting Your Needs," and then replace the body text with the following first-level bulleted items: "Promoting your product," "Securing startup funds," "Arranging for credit card accounts," and "Answering all your questions." Don't modify or delete the three pyramid diagrams.
10. Delete Slides 5 ("Cost Analysis") and 6 ("Our Strengths").
11. In the new Slide 5 ("Key Benefits"), leave the title text as is, and then replace the body text with the following first-level bulleted items: "You can focus on your products, your services, and your bottom line."; and "We'll help you sell your product on the Internet."
12. In Slide 6 ("Next Steps"), leave the title text as is, and then replace the body text with the following first-level bulleted items: "List what you want us to do," "Draw up an agreement," "Determine a timeline," "Establish the order-fulfillment process," and "Launch the Web-based e-commerce system."
13. Save the presentation as **e-Commerce Consultants** in the Tutorial.01\Cases folder included with your Data Files.
14. In Slide 2, indent (demote) "Managing your orders" so it is a sub-bullet under "Setting up your Web site," and then add another sub-bullet, "Handling online credit."
15. In Slide 3, add the following sub-bulleted items under "Web site design and development": "know-how," "graphic design," "software," and "programming."
16. In Slide 4, insert a new first bullet "We can help by," and then make all the other phrases the sub-bullets.
17. Move the last bulleted item "Answering all your questions" up to become the first sub-bullet.
18. In Slide 6 ("Next Steps"), delete excess words like "a," "an," and "the" to achieve the 6 × 6 rule as closely as possible.
19. Add a new slide after Slide 6 with the Title and Text layout, type "Your Account Representative" as the title text, and then type the following information in five bullets: Kendall Koester, e-Commerce Consultants, 1666 Winnebago St., Pecatonica, IL 61063, 555-WEB-PAGE. The city, state, and Zip code should all be part of the same bulleted item. (Note that the first letter of "e-Commerce" changes to an uppercase letter as soon as you press the spacebar. This is PowerPoint's AutoFormat.)
20. Click to the right of the first letter "E" in "E-Commerce," press the Backspace key, and then type "e."
21. Turn on the Style Checker, set the Case options so that the slide title style is title case and the body text style is sentence case, and then go through each slide of the presentation to see if the Style Checker marks any potential problems. (Don't forget to double-check each slide by moving to the next or previous slide and then back to the current slide to recheck it.) When you see the light bulb, click it, and then assess whether you want to accept or reject the suggested change. You'll want to accept

most of the suggested changes, but make sure you leave words like "Web" and "Internet" capitalized, and don't change the capitalization of the address and phone number you typed on Slide 7. Turn off the Style Checker when you are finished.

22. Check the spelling in the presentation. Correct any misspellings, and ignore any words that are spelled correctly.
23. View the presentation in Slide Show view.
24. Save the presentation, preview it in grayscale, print the presentation in grayscale as handouts with four slides per page, and then close the file.

Case Problem 2

Data File needed for this Case Problem: Seafoods.ppt

Northwest Seafoods   Paul Neibaur is president of Northwest Seafoods, a seafood distribution company with headquarters in Vancouver, British Columbia. He buys fish and other seafood from suppliers and sells to restaurant and grocery store chains. Although his company has been in business and profitable for 27 years, Paul wants to sell the company and retire. He wants you to help him create a PowerPoint presentation to prospective buyers. Complete the following:

1. Open the file **Seafoods** located in the Tutorial.01\Cases folder included with your Data Files, and then save it as **Northwest Seafoods** in the same folder.
2. In Slide 1, replace the subtitle placeholder ("Paul Neibaur") with your name.
3. In Slide 2, add the speaker's note "Mention that regular customers are large grocery stores and fast-food franchises."
4. Add a sixth bulleted item to Slide 2: "Contracts with 13 distributors."
5. Move the second bulleted item ("Low debt") so that it becomes the last bulleted item.
6. In Slide 3, edit the third bulleted item so that "walk-in freezers," "cutting devices," and "other equipment" are second-level bulleted items below the main bullet.
7. Promote the bulleted item "Experienced employees" and its sub-bullets so that they become a new, separate slide.
8. Use the Slides tab to move Slide 5 ("Profitability") to become Slide 4.
9. Add a new slide after Slide 7 with the Title and Text layout, and then replace the title placeholder text with "British Columbia Business Brokers."
10. Create three new bulleted items with the address on the first line ("107-5901 Granville Street"), the city, province, and postal code on the second line ("Coquitlam, BC V6M 4J7"), and the phone number on the third line ("604.555.SELL").
11. Check the spelling in the presentation. Correct any spelling errors and ignore any words that are spelled correctly.
12. Turn on the Style Checker, change the options so that the slide title style is uppercase and the body text style is sentence case, and then go through all the slides correcting any flagged style problems. Be sure not to let the Style Checker change the case for "Small Business Administration" or modify the address you typed on Slide 8; otherwise, accept the Style Checker's suggested case changes. Turn off the Style Checker when you are finished.
13. View the presentation in Slide Show view.
14. Go to Slide 4. When you viewed the presentation, did you notice the two typographical errors on this page? If you did not fix these errors, fix them now.
15. Save the presentation, preview the presentation in grayscale, print the presentation in grayscale as handouts with four slides per page, and then print Slide 2 as a notes page, and then close the file.

Challenge

Explore more advanced features of PowerPoint by formatting text, paragraphs, and lists, and by changing slide layouts and adding a design template.

Case Problem 3

Data File needed for this Case Problem: LASIK.ppt

Camellia Gardens Eye Center   Dr. Carol Wang, head ophthalmologist at the Camellia Gardens Eye Center in Charleston, South Carolina, performs over 20 surgeries per week using laser-assisted in situ keratomileusis (LASIK) to correct vision problems of myopia (nearsightedness), hyperopia (farsightedness), and astigmatism. She asks you to help prepare a PowerPoint presentation to those interested in learning more about LASIK. Complete the following:

1. Open the file **LASIK** located in the Tutorial.01\Cases folder included with your Data Files, and then save it as **Camellia LASIK** in the same folder.
2. In Slide 1, replace the subtitle placeholder ("Camellia Gardens Eye Center") with your name.
3. In Slide 2, move the first bulleted item down to become the third bulleted item.
4. Edit the sub-bullets "Myopia," "Hyperopia," and "Astigmatism" in the first item so they're part of the first-level bullet and there are no sub-bullets. Be sure to add commas after the first two words, and add the word "and" before the last word.
5. Add a fourth bulleted item with the text "Patients no longer need corrective lenses."
6. Still in Slide 2, center the text in the title text box. (*Hint*: Click anywhere in the title text, and then position the pointer over the buttons on the Formatting toolbar to see the ScreenTips to find a button that will center the text.)
7. In Slide 3, change the bulleted list to a numbered list. (*Hint*: Select all of the body text, and then look for a button on the Formatting toolbar that will number the list.)
8. Have PowerPoint automatically split Slide 3 into two slides. (*Hint*: First, click the AutoFit Options button in the slide pane and click the Stop Fitting Text to This Placeholder option button. Then, with the insertion point in the body text box, click the AutoFit Options button again, and then click the appropriate option.)
9. On the new Slide 4, change the numbering so it continues the numbering from Slide 3 rather than starting over at number 1. (*Hint*: Right-click anywhere in the first item in the numbered list, click Bullets and Numbering on the shortcut menu, click the Numbered tab, and then change the Start at value.)
10. At the end of the title in Slide 4, add a space and "(cont.)," the abbreviation for continued.
11. In Slide 5, demote the two bullets under "With low to moderate myopia," so they become sub-bullets.
12. Still in Slide 5, tell the PowerPoint Spell Checker to ignore all occurrences of the word "hyperopia," which is not found in PowerPoint's dictionary. (*Hint*: Right-click the word to see a shortcut menu with spelling commands.)
13. If any of the bulleted text doesn't fit on the slide, but drops below the body text box, set the text box to AutoFit. (*Hint*: Click anywhere in the text box, click the AutoFit Options button that appears, and then click the desired option.)
14. In Slide 6, join the final two bullets to become one bullet. Be sure to add a semicolon between the two bullets and change the word "Other" to lowercase.
15. In Slide 8, move the second bullet "Schedule eye exam to determine" (along with its sub-bullets) up to become the first bullet.
16. In Slide 8, edit the bulleted item ("Analysis of . . .") so that "eye pressure," "shape of cornea," and "thickness of cornea" are sub-bullets below "Analysis of."
17. Change the layout of Slide 8 so that the body text appears in two columns. (*Hint*: Click the AutoFit Options button in the slide pane, and then click Change to Two-Column Layout.) Drag the last two bullets over to the second column in the body text. (*Hint*: After you select the bulleted item, position the pointer over the selected

text instead of over the bullet, and then drag the pointer to immediately after the new bullet in the second column, using the vertical line indicator that appears to help guide you.)

18. Add a new Slide 9, and then apply the Title Only layout in the Text Layout section of the Slide Layout task pane.

Explore

19. In Slide 9, add the title "Camellia Gardens Eye Center," create a new text box near the center of the slide, and then add the address "8184 Camellia Drive" on the first line, "Charleston, SC 29406" on the second line, and the phone number "(843) 555-EYES" on the third line. (*Hint*: Click the Text Box button on the Drawing toolbar, and then click on the slide at the desired location.)

Explore

20. Change the size of the text in the new text box on Slide 9 so that it's 32 points. (*Hint*: Click the edge of the text box to select the entire text box and all of its contents, and then click the Font Size list arrow on the Formatting toolbar.)

Explore

21. Turn on the Style Checker, and then set the style options for end punctuation so that the Style Checker checks to make sure that slide titles do not have end punctuation, and that paragraphs in the body text have punctuation. Set the slide title style to title case and the body text style to sentence case. Also, set the Visual Clarity options so that the maximum number of bullets should not exceed six, the number of lines per title should not exceed two, and the number of lines per bulleted item should not exceed two. (*Hint*: Use the End punctuation section of the Case and End Punctuation tab and the Legibility section of the Visual Clarity tab in the Style Options dialog box.)

Explore

22. Go through all the slides, correcting problems of case (capitalization) and punctuation. Be sure not to let the Style Checker change the case for proper nouns. Let the Style Checker correct end punctuation for complete sentences, but you shouldn't allow (or you should remove) punctuation for words or phrases that don't form complete sentences. Do not accept the Style Checker's suggestions to remove question marks in the slide titles.

Explore

23. Change the Style Options back so that the next time the Style Checker is run, only the Slide title style and Body text style options on the Case and End Punctuation tab and the Fonts options on the Visual Clarity tab are selected, and then turn off the Style Checker.

24. Check the spelling in the presentation.

Explore

25. Apply the design template called "Watermark," which has a white background with violet circles. (*Hint*: Click the Design button on the Formatting toolbar, and then use the ScreenTips in the Slide Design task pane to find the Watermark design template.) If you can't find the Watermark design template, choose a different design template.

26. View the presentation in Slide Show view.

27. Save the presentation, preview it in grayscale, print the presentation in grayscale as handouts with four slides per page, and then close the file.

Research

Use the Internet to research bestsellers and use PowerPoint's Help system to find out how to format text.

Case Problem 4

There are no Data Files needed for this Case Problem.

Book Review Your English teacher asks you to prepare a book review for presentation to the class. The teacher asks you to review any book from a bestseller list, past or present, such as the Barnes & Noble Top 100 Books or Amazon's Top 100 Bestsellers. To help you give your class presentation, you want to use PowerPoint slides. Your task is to prepare a presentation of at least six PowerPoint slides. Complete the following:

1. Go to **www.bn.com**, **www.amazon.com**, or any other bestseller list, and find the title of a book you have read. If you can't find a book from among these lists, get approval from your instructor to report on another book.

2. Use the AutoContent Wizard to begin developing slides based on "Generic" from the General category of presentation types.
   a. Title the presentation "Review of" followed by your book title, and then add "Review of" followed by the book subject as the footer. For example, the title might be "Review of Harry Potter and the Order of the Phoenix," along with the footer "Review of a Recent Bestseller."
   b. Include both the date and the slide number.

Explore

3. Use PowerPoint's Help system to find out how to italicize text. Close the Help window and the task pane, and then edit Slide 1 so that the book title is italicized.
4. In Slide 1, change the subtitle to your name, if necessary.
5. In Slide 2 ("Introduction"), include the following information in the bulleted list: title, author(s), publisher, publication year, and the number of pages in the book.
6. In Slide 3 ("Topics of Discussion"), include the categories used in reviewing the book, for example, "Plot," "Action," "Characterization," "Description," "Humor," and "Comparison with Other Books in the Series."
7. Delete Slides 4 through 9.
8. Create at least one slide for each of the topics you listed on Slide 3, and then include bulleted lists explaining that topic.

Explore

9. Connect to the Internet, and then use the Research task pane to find additional information about the topic of the book you've chosen or about the author. (*Hint*: In the Research task pane, type the topic or author name into the Search for text box, make sure your computer is connected to the Internet, select a research site such as Encarta Encyclopedia, and then click the green arrow button, if necessary, to start searching.) You might want to create one or more new slides, cut and paste information into the new slides, and then edit the information into one or more appropriate bulleted lists.
10. Create a slide titled "Summary and Recommendations" as the last slide in your presentation, giving your overall impression of the book and your recommendation for whether the book is worth reading.
11. View the presentation on the Outline tab. If necessary, change the order of the bulleted items on the slides, or change the order of the slides.

Explore

12. If you see any slides with more than six bulleted items, split the slide in two. (*Hint*: With the insertion point in the body text box, click the AutoFit Options button that appears near the lower-left corner of the text box, and then click the appropriate option.)
13. Turn on the Style Checker, and then go through all the slides, correcting problems of case (capitalization), punctuation, number of bulleted items per slide, and number of lines per bulleted item. Be sure not to let the Style Checker change the case for proper nouns. Let the Style Checker correct end punctuation for complete sentences, but you shouldn't allow (or you should remove) punctuation for words or phrases that don't form complete sentences.
14. Check the spelling of your presentation.
15. View the presentation in Slide Show view. If you see any typographical errors or other problems, stop the slide show, correct the problems, and then continue the slide show. If you find slides that aren't necessary, delete them.
16. Save the presentation as **Book Review** in the Tutorial.01\Cases folder included with your Data Files.
17. Preview the presentation in grayscale, and then print the presentation in grayscale as handouts with four slides per page. Print speaker notes if you created any, and then close the file.

Research

Go to the Web to find information you can use to create presentations.

Internet Assignments

The purpose of the Internet Assignments is to challenge you to find information on the Internet that you can use to work effectively with this software. The actual assignments are updated and maintained on the Course Technology Web site. Log on to the Internet and use your Web browser to go to the Student Online Companion for New Perspectives Office 2003 at **www.course.com/np/office2003**. Click the Internet Assignments link, and then navigate to the assignments for this tutorial.

Assess

SAM Assessment and Training

If you have a SAM user profile, you may have access to hands-on instruction, practice, and assessment of the skills covered in this tutorial. Log in to your SAM account and go to your assignments page to see what your instructor has assigned.

Review

Quick Check Answers

Session 1.1

1. A presentation's components can consist of individual slides, speaker notes, an outline, and audience handouts.
2. The slide pane shows the slide as it will look during your slide show. The notes pane contains speaker notes. The Outline tab shows an outline of your presentation. The Slides tab displays thumbnails of each slide.
3. a. a feature that causes each element on a slide to appear one at a time
   b. the manner in which a new slide appears on the screen during a slide show
   c. a file that contains the colors and format of the background and the font style of the titles, accents, and other text
   d. a predetermined way of organizing the objects on a slide
4. What is my purpose or objective? What type of presentation is needed? What is the physical location of my presentation? What is the best format my presentation?
5. The AutoContent Wizard lets you choose a presentation category and then creates a general outline of the presentation.
6. The view you use to present an on-screen presentation to an audience.

Session 1.2

1. a. Click a slide or bullet icon, and then drag the selected item up.
   b. Right-click the slide icon of the slide to be deleted in the Outline tab, and then click Delete Slide on the shortcut menu; or, move to the slide you want to delete in the slide pane, click Edit on the menu bar, and then click Delete Slide.
   c. Click the slide or bullet icon in the Outline tab, and then click the Decrease Indent button on the Formatting toolbar.
2. Promote means to decrease the level (for example, from level two to level one) of an outline item; demote means to increase the level of an outline item.
3. In the Outline tab, you can see the text of several slides at once, which makes it easier to work with text. In the slide pane, you can see the design and layout of the slide.
4. The Style Checker automatically checks your presentation for consistency and style. For example, it will check for consistency in punctuation.
5. Notes are notes for the presenter. They appear in the notes pane in Normal view or you can print notes pages, which contain a picture of and notes about each slide.
6. By previewing your presentation, you make sure that the slides are satisfactory, and that the presentation is legible in grayscale if you use a monochrome printer.

Applying and Modifying Text and Graphic Objects

Presenting and Preparing for an Expedition to Peru

Case

Global Humanitarian, Lima Office

The objectives of Global Humanitarian's expeditions are to help villagers build homes, schools, greenhouses, wells, culinary water systems, and Lorena adobe stoves; to provide medical and dental services; and to teach basic hygiene, literacy, and gardening skills. The village council of Paqarimuy, a small village in the puna (also called the altiplano, or high-altitude plains of the Andes Mountains), requested help in accomplishing some of these objectives. Therefore, Pablo Fuentes, the managing director of Global Humanitarian in Lima, Peru, is organizing a service expedition to that village. He plans the expedition as a two-week trip. To complete everything he hopes to accomplish, he needs approximately 25 volunteers. He thinks that the best way to recruit volunteers is to present a PowerPoint slide show to interested students at local colleges and universities. During the presentation, he can give an overview to the audience members so that they will have enough information to consider the trip. He can answer questions that the audience might have during and after the presentation. He asks you to help prepare a PowerPoint presentation to prospective expedition participants.

In this tutorial, you'll create a new presentation based on a design template, modify the design template, apply a design template to an existing presentation, and then enhance the presentation by adding graphics to the slides. You will also add a slide summarizing the content of the presentation.

Student Data Files

▼ **Tutorial.02**

▽ **Tutorial folder**

GHLogo.jpg
MntTop.jpg
PeruExp2.ppt

▽ **Review folder**

Boots.jpg
Camera.jpg
Food.jpg
GHLogo.jpg
PackList.ppt
Personal.jpg
PrMeds.jpg
SlpBag.jpg
Vitamins.jpg

▽ **Cases folder**

Excycle.jpg	SBpaper.jpg
MyBody.ppt	SBpens.jpg
Payroll.ppt	SBphoto.jpg
PESLogo.jpg	SBsciss.jpg
PKPBadg.jpg	StrMach.jpg
PKPKey.jpg	Treadmil.jpg
SBcam.jpg	Vitamins.jpg
SBfile.jpg	Weights.jpg
SBpages.jpg	

Session 2.1

Planning a Presentation

Before creating his text presentation, Pablo and his staff planned the presentation as follows:

- **Purpose of the presentation**: to convince potential volunteers to apply for a position in the Peru expedition
- **Type of presentation**: an onscreen (electronic) information presentation
- **Audience**: students, health professionals, and other people interested in serving villages in a third-world country
- **Location of the presentation**: a conference room at the offices of Global Humanitarian, as well as classrooms and business offices
- **Audience needs**: to recognize the services they can provide and the adventure they can enjoy as expedition volunteers
- **Format**: one speaker presenting an onscreen slide show consisting of seven to 10 slides

After planning the presentation, Pablo and his staff discuss how they want the slides to look.

Creating a New Presentation from a Design Template

Plain white slides with normal text (such as black Times New Roman or Arial) often fail to hold an audience's attention. In today's information age, audiences expect more interesting color schemes, fonts, graphics, and other effects.

To make it easy to add color and style to your presentations, PowerPoint comes with design templates. A **design template** is a file that contains the color scheme, text formats, background colors and objects, and graphics in the presentation. The **color scheme** is the eight colors used in a design template. A **graphic** is a picture, clip art, photograph, shape, design, graph, chart, or diagram that you can add to a slide. A graphic, like a text box, is an object. Pablo asks you to create a new presentation with the Teamwork design template so that he can see what it looks like.

Reference Window | **Creating a New Presentation from a Design Template**

- Click File on the menu bar, and then click New.
- Click the From design template link in the New Presentation task pane.
- Click the design template you want to use.

You'll begin enhancing Pablo's presentation by changing the design template.

To create a new presentation from a design template:

1. Start PowerPoint, and then click the **Create a new presentation** link at the bottom of the Getting Started task pane. The New Presentation task pane opens.

   Trouble? If you don't see the Create a new presentation link in the Getting Started task pane, point to the small, downward-pointing triangle at the bottom of the task pane to scroll the task pane automatically so that you can see the commands at the bottom of the task pane.

Trouble? If PowerPoint is already running and the task pane is not open, click File on the menu bar, and then click New to open the New Presentation task pane.

2. Click the **From design template** link in the New Presentation task pane. Slide 1 (the title slide) of a new blank presentation opens in Normal view and the Slide Design task pane opens. Notice that Default Design appears in the status bar below the slide pane to indicate that this is the current design template. A thumbnail showing the Default Design template also appears in the Slide Design task pane under Used in This Presentation. In the Default Design template, the slides have black text on a plain white background.

3. Move the pointer over the **Default Design template** thumbnail under Used in This Presentation in the task pane. A ScreenTip appears, identifying the template. See Figure 2-1.

Blank presentation with Default Design template applied | **Figure 2-1**

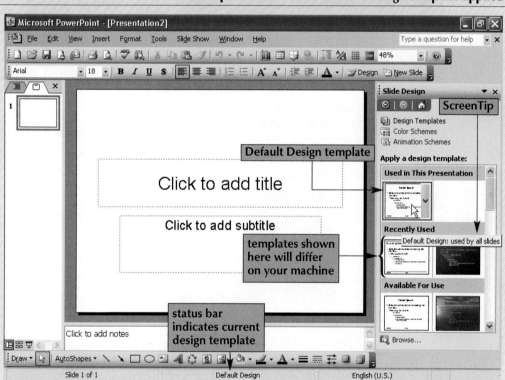

4. Scroll down through the thumbnail views of the design templates, and move the pointer over the thumbnails under **Available For Use** until you find **Teamwork**, a dark green thumbnail.

Trouble? If the Teamwork template is not in the task pane, you must install it. If you are working in a lab, ask your instructor or technical support person for help. If you are working on your own computer, click the Additional Design Templates thumbnail to install additional templates.

5. Click the **Teamwork** design template. The design template of the new presentation changes from Default Design to Teamwork. See Figure 2-2.

Figure 2-2 ▶ Teamwork design template applied

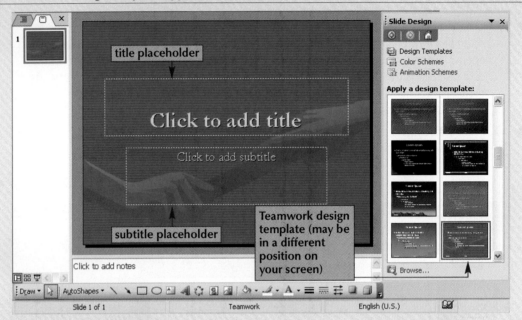

▶ **6.** Click in the **title** placeholder in the slide pane, and then type **Peru Expedition 2006**.

▶ **7.** Click in the **subtitle** placeholder and then type your own name.

▶ **8.** Click the **Close** button ✕ in the Slide Design task pane.

▶ **9.** Save the presentation as **PeruExp** in the Tutorial.02\Tutorial folder included with your Data Files.

▶ **10.** Click **File** on the menu bar, and then click **Print** to open the Print dialog box.

▶ **11.** Click the **Color/grayscale** list arrow, click **Grayscale**, click the **Print what** list arrow, and then click **Slides**, if necessary.

▶ **12.** Click the **OK** button. The one-page presentation prints in full slide format (one slide fits the entire page).

▶ **13.** Close the presentation (but leave PowerPoint running).

Pablo takes the new presentation you created, adds more slides to the presentation, and saves the file as PeruExp2. After considering the Teamwork design template, he decides that he doesn't like it because the hands in the background are hard to see. You'll change the design template now.

Applying a Design Template

The design template you choose for your presentation should reflect the content and the intended audience. For example, if you are presenting a new curriculum to a group of elementary school teachers, you might choose a template that uses bright, primary colors. Likewise, if you are presenting a new marketing plan to a mutual fund company, you might choose a plain-looking template that uses dark colors formatted in a way that appears sophisticated.

Although Pablo's presentation is serious, he wants to make the trip seem attractive to prospective participants. He decides that he wants to use a color scheme that includes a dark blue background with a color gradient and some graphics representing the Peruvian Andes Mountains. He thinks such a design would give his presentation more interest.

Applying a Different Design Template

- Display the Slide Design templates in the task pane by clicking the Design button on the Formatting toolbar.
- Scroll through the design template thumbnails until you see one you'd like to apply, and then click the design template thumbnail.

To change the design template:

1. Open the presentation file **PeruExp2** located in the Tutorial.02\Tutorial folder included with your Data Files.

2. Save the file in the same folder using the filename **Peru Expedition**. The presentation title slide appears in the slide pane.

3. Click the **Design** button on the Formatting toolbar to open the Slide Design task pane.

4. Scroll down through the thumbnail views of the design templates in the task pane under Available For Use, and then click the **Mountain Top** template. Don't forget to move the pointer over the templates to see their names. The design template of Peru Expedition changes from Teamwork to Mountain Top. See Figure 2-3.

Presentation with Mountain Top design template applied   **Figure 2-3**

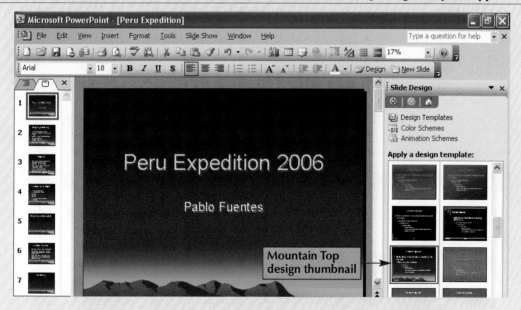

As you can see, the title slide has a dark blue background with varying color, and a background graphic of a mountain top along the bottom of the slide. Next, you'll modify this template to make it more appropriate for this presentation.

Understanding Graphics

Graphics add information, clarification, emphasis, variety, and even pizzazz to a PowerPoint presentation. PowerPoint enables you to include many types of graphics in your presentation: graphics created using another Windows program; scanned photographs, drawings, or cartoons; and other picture files or clip art located on a CD or other disk. You can also create graphics using the drawing tools in PowerPoint. In addition, you can add graphical bullets to a bulleted list.

Inserting Clip Art

Slide 6, "Expedition Information," has six bulleted items of text. Pablo wants to include some clip art to add interest to this slide. In PowerPoint, **clip art** refers specifically to images in the Media Gallery that accompanies Office 2003, or images that are available from the Clip Art and Media section of Microsoft Office Online. Pablo decides that an image of a globe would help emphasize the global aspects of the expedition.

To add clip art to a slide, you can use a slide layout that has a place for clip art, or you can insert the clip art as you would a picture. If you insert clip art using the Insert Clip Art button on the Drawing toolbar, the Clip Art task pane opens and you can search for clips that match keywords you type, and then browse the results. If you insert clip art by clicking a button on a layout that includes a placeholder for clip art, you can browse through all of the clips stored on your machine as well as search for clips that match keywords you type. You'll change the existing slide layout before adding clip art.

To change the layout of a slide and add clip art:

1. Go to **Slide 6** ("Expedition Information").

2. Click **Format** on the menu bar, and then click **Slide Layout** to display the Slide Layout task pane.

3. Scroll down the task pane until you see Text and Content Layouts, and then click the **Title, Text, and Content** layout (the first layout under Text and Content Layouts). The bulleted list moves to the left side of the slide and the content placeholder appears on the right of the slide. See Figure 2-4. Notice that PowerPoint automatically reduces the size of the text in the bulleted list so that it will fit properly within the reduced text box.

Figure 2-4 ▷ **Slide 6 after changing slide layout to Title, Text, and Content**

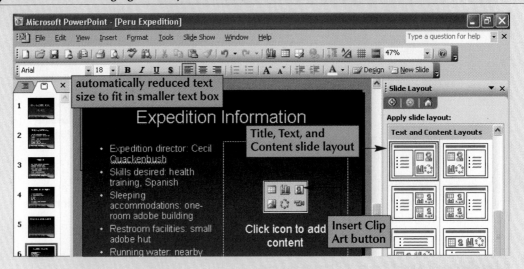

Trouble? If the text size doesn't automatically change or if it doesn't change to a small enough size, click anywhere in the body text, click the AutoFit Options button that appears near the lower-left corner of the body text, and then click the AutoFit Text to Placeholder option button.

4. Click the **Close** button ✕ in the task pane title bar to close the task pane.

5. Click the **Insert Clip Art** button in the content placeholder. The Select Picture dialog box opens. If necessary, drag the box by its title bar so you can see all of it. Now you'll search for a piece of clip art that relates to a globe.

6. Type **globe** in the Search text box at the top of the dialog box, and then click the **Go** button. Depending upon how Office was installed on your computer, PowerPoint displays from just a few to over 250 pieces of clip art that contain a representation of a globe.

7. If necessary, drag the scroll button up to the top of the scroll bar in the Select Picture dialog box, and then double-click the image of a globe in the center of a red circular background. The Select Picture dialog box closes, the content placeholder disappears from the slide, and the clip art you selected appears in its place. See Figure 2-5.

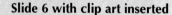 Slide 6 with clip art inserted | Figure 2-5

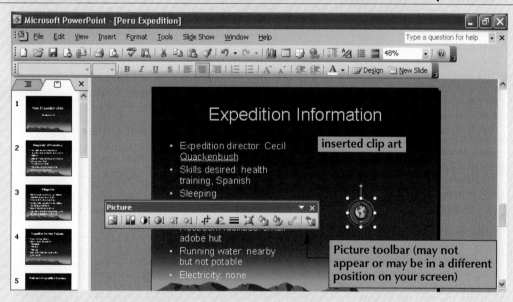

Now you'll modify this clip art image by changing its size and some of its colors.

Resizing Clip Art

The clip art is too small, and so is the body text box, making the autofit text in the bulleted list too small. You will increase the size of the clip art and the text box.

To resize the clip art image:

1. Drag the upper-right corner sizing handle of the globe clip art toward the upper-right corner of the slide until the image is approximately tripled in size.

2. Position the pointer over the selected clip art image so that it changes to ⁺↕↔, and then drag the entire clip art image so that it's centered between the top and bottom of the slide, and near the right edge of the slide. Compare your screen to Figure 2-6 and adjust the size or position of the graphic as necessary.

Figure 2-6 ▶ **Slide 6 with repositioned clip art**

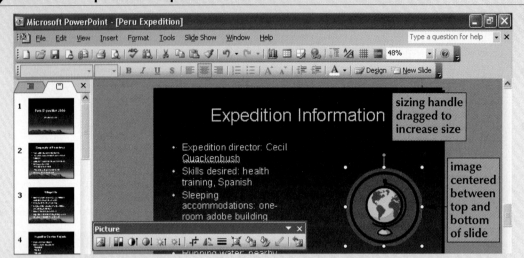

▶ **3.** Click anywhere in the body text to display the text box and its sizing handles, and then drag the right-center sizing handle to the right until it just touches the left edge of the clip art.

With the clip art inserted and resized, you're ready to change some of the colors.

Recoloring Clip Art

Pablo thinks the red colors on the clip art don't match the blue hues of the design template, so he asks you to change the red to dark blue. You can recolor clip art, but you may not always be able to change the color on other types of pictures.

To recolor a clip art image:

▶ **1.** Click the **clip art** in Slide 6 to select it. The sizing handles appear around the image, and the Picture toolbar appears.

Trouble? If the Picture toolbar doesn't appear automatically, click View on the menu bar, point to Toolbars, and then click Picture.

▶ **2.** Click the **Recolor Picture** button [icon] on the Picture toolbar to display the Recolor Picture dialog box. The colored rectangular tiles under Original are all of the colors used in this piece of clip art.

▶ **3.** Drag the scroll box down to the bottom of the scroll bar in the dialog box so you can see the red and off-red tiles. See Figure 2-7.

Recolor Picture dialog box ◀ **Figure 2-7**

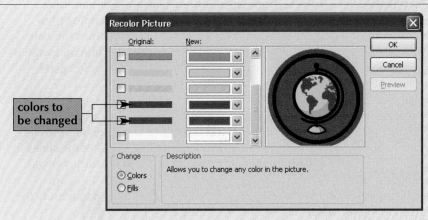

colors to
be changed

4. Click the **off-red color tile** list arrow in the New column, and then click the **light violet tile** on the palette of default colors. The **default colors** are those colors associated with the overall color scheme of the design template. The globe's shadow in the Preview box changes from off-red to light violet.

5. Change the **red tile** in the New column to the **royal blue tile** (not the dark blue tile) on the palette of default colors.

6. Click the **Preview** button in the Recolor Picture dialog box, and then drag the dialog box by its title bar so that you can see the colors applied to the clip art on the slide. The recolored clip art looks much better than the red colors did.

7. Click the **OK** button, and then click outside the selected object to deselect it. See Figure 2-8.

Recolored clip art and resized body text box ◀ **Figure 2-8**

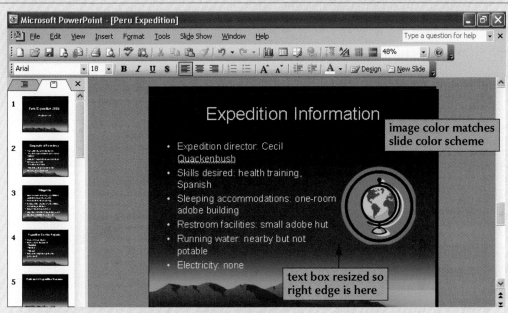

image color matches
slide color scheme

text box resized so
right edge is here

8. Click the **Save** button 🖫 on the Standard toolbar to save your changes.

You'll now add a picture to one of the slides. To add a picture to a slide, the picture must be a computer file located on an electronic medium, such as a CD or hard disk. Picture files are generated by taking photographs with a digital camera, scanning photographs taken with a conventional camera, or drawing pictures using graphics software (such as Microsoft Paint). These types of picture files are bitmap images. A **bitmap image** is a grid (or "map") of colored dots that form a picture. The colored dots are called **pixels**, which stands for picture elements.

Instead of using the current background graphic of the Mountain Top design template, Pablo prefers an actual photograph of the Andes Mountains, in the form of a bitmap image. To get a bitmap file of the Andes Mountains, Pablo scanned a picture he took with a 35mm camera. Pablo also wants to add Global Humanitarian's logo to all of the slides in the presentation. To get a bitmap file of the logo, Pablo hired a graphic artist to create the file using graphics software.

To make these changes to all of the slides in the presentation, you'll need to modify the design template in Slide Master view.

Modifying the Design Template in the Slide Master

A **master** is a slide that contains the elements and styles of the design template, including the text and other objects that appear on all the slides of the same type. Masters never appear when you show or print a presentation. PowerPoint presentations have four types of masters: the **title master**, which contains the objects that appear on the title slide (most presentations have only one title slide, but some have more than one); the **slide master**, which contains the objects that appear on all the slides except the title slide; the **handout master**, which contains the objects that appear on all the printed handouts; and the **notes master**, which contains the objects that appear on the notes pages.

You use slide and title masters so that all the slides in the presentation have a similar design and appearance. This ensures that your presentation is consistent. To make changes to the masters, you need to switch to Slide Master view. You'll do this now.

To switch to Slide Master view:

1. Click **View** on the menu bar, point to **Master**, and then click **Slide Master**. The view changes to Slide Master view, and the Slide Master View toolbar appears. See Figure 2-9.

| Figure 2-9 | Slide Master view |

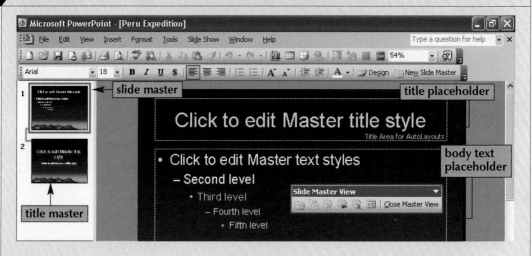

As you can see from the thumbnail slides in the Slides tab, Slide Master view includes two slides: the slide master (as Slide 1) and the title master (as Slide 2). The slide master is currently selected and appears in the slide pane. In Slide Master view, you always see both the slide master and the title master. They appear in Slide Master view as a set, and this is referred to as a **slide-title master pair**.

▶ **2.** Click the **title master** (Slide 2) in the Slides tab. The slide pane now displays the master for the title slide.

▶ **3.** Click **View** on the menu bar, point to **Master**, and then click **Handout Master**. The layout of handouts appears in the slide pane, and the Handout Master View toolbar appears. You can click the buttons on this toolbar to change the layout of the handout master.

▶ **4.** Click **View** on the menu bar, point to **Master**, and then click **Notes Master**. The layout of the notes pages appears in the slide pane, and the Notes Master View toolbar opens.

▶ **5.** Click the **Close Master View** button on the Notes Master View floating toolbar. PowerPoint returns to Normal view.

You can modify the slide and title master in Slide Master view by changing the size and design of the title and body text, adding or deleting graphics, and changing the background. You cannot delete or add objects to the background unless you are in Slide Master view.

Modifying Slide and Title Masters

Reference Window

- Click View on the menu bar, point to Master, and then click Slide Master; *or* press and hold the Shift key and then click the Normal View button at the bottom of the Slides or Outline tab to switch to Slide Master view.
- Click the thumbnail of the master slide type that you'd like to modify, either the slide master (Slide 1) or the title master (Slide 2).
- Make any changes to the slide or title master such as changing the background color; modifying the text size, color, font, or alignment; inserting clip art, bitmap images, or other graphics; and changing the size or location of text placeholders.
- Click the Normal View button or click the Close Master View button on the Slide Master View toolbar to return to Normal view.

Before you can insert Pablo's photograph of the Andes Mountains, you must delete the graphic of the mountains currently in the design template.

To modify the slide master:

▶ **1.** Switch again to Slide Master view. The slide master appears.

You're going to delete the background image containing the mountain tops. The image is made up of three bitmaps that need to be deleted individually: the sky, the brown mountains, and the dark shading on the mountains.

▶ **2.** Position the pointer over the bitmap image so that it changes to ⁺↖, and then click the teal-green area at the lower-right side of the slide as shown in Figure 2-10. Be careful not to click inside the placeholder titled Object Area for AutoLayouts or inside the placeholder for the Number Area. Sizing handles appear around the selected bitmap.

Figure 2-10 ▷ **First bitmap in background image selected**

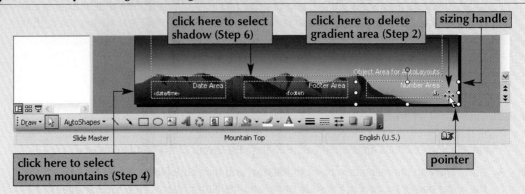

3. Press the **Delete** key. The selected bitmap is deleted.

   Trouble? If you accidentally deleted the Number Area placeholder, click the Undo button 🔄 on the Standard toolbar, and then repeat Steps 2 and 3.

4. Click the brown mountain at the lower-left side of the slide as indicated in Figure 2-10. Be careful not to click inside the Date Area placeholder.

5. Press the **Delete** key. The bitmap of the mountains is deleted.

   Trouble? If you accidentally deleted the Date Area placeholder, click the Undo button 🔄 on the Standard toolbar, and then repeat Steps 4 and 5.

6. Click the dark brown shadow in the area just above and to the left of the Footer Area place-holder, as indicated in Figure 2-10. Be careful not to click inside the Footer Area placeholder.

7. Press the **Delete** key. The last bitmap is deleted. The bottom of the slide no longer contains any graphics.

   Trouble? If you have difficulty selecting the shadow, click the Footer Area placeholder, press the ↓ key three times, and then repeat Steps 6 and 7. After you delete the shadow, click the Footer Area placeholder again, and then press the ↑ key three times to return the Footer Area placeholder to its original position.

8. Click the **Save** button 💾 on the Standard toolbar to save your changes.

Because you deleted the mountain graphic in Slide Master view, it will be deleted from every slide in the presentation, except the title slide. Now you'll insert the new photo of the Andes Mountains on all of the slides.

Inserting and Modifying a Bitmap Image on a Slide

To add the new bitmap image to all of the slides, you will insert it on the slide master in Slide Master view. To insert a bitmap image on just one slide, you use the same procedure in Normal view.

Inserting a Graphic on a Slide

- If necessary, switch to Normal view, and then open the Slide Layout task pane by clicking Format on the menu bar and clicking Slide Layout.
- Click one of the Content layouts or one of the Text and Content layouts to change the layout of the current slide.
- Click the Insert Clip Art or Insert Picture button in the content placeholder, and then find the desired clip art or navigate to the folder containing the desired picture file.
- Double-click the graphic that you want to insert into the slide.
   or
- Click the Insert Picture button on the Drawing toolbar, navigate to and click the picture file you want to insert, and then click the Insert button.

To insert a graphic into a slide:

▶ **1.** Click the **Insert Picture** button 🖼 on the Drawing toolbar. The Insert Picture dialog box opens.

▶ **2.** Navigate to the Tutorial.02\Tutorial folder included with your Data Files.

▶ **3.** Click **MntTop**, the bitmap image file of the photograph, and click the **Insert** button. The picture is inserted into your slide master in the middle of the slide, and the Picture toolbar appears.

   Trouble? If the Picture toolbar doesn't appear, click View on the menu bar, point to Toolbars, and then click Picture.

You need to move and resize the image to fit along the bottom of the slide master.

To reposition and resize a picture on a slide:

▶ **1.** Position the pointer over the bitmap image so that it changes to ⁺ℝ, and then drag the photo to the lower-left corner of the slide. See Figure 2-11.

Slide master with bitmap image ◀ **Figure 2-11**

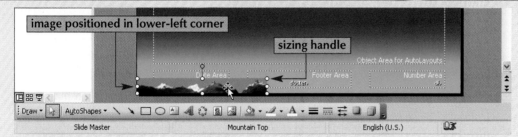

   Trouble? If the Picture or Slide Master View toolbar covers the lower-left corner, drag the toolbar by its title bar to another location on the screen.

   As you can see, the selected bitmap image has sizing handles in each corner and on each side of the picture. You'll drag a sizing handle to resize the image to the width of the slide.

▶ **2.** Drag the upper-right sizing handle up and to the right until the width of the bitmap image is the same as the width of the slide, and approximately double its original height. See Figure 2-12. Because you are dragging a corner sizing handle, the height and width of the image resizes proportionally.

Figure 2-12 ▶ **Resized picture of Andes Mountains**

You have two tasks left to perform on the bitmap image. First, the blue sky in the background of the photo interrupts the gradient colors in the background. You'll set a transparent color, which is a color on the bitmap image that becomes transparent (invisible). Second, you'll change the order of objects so that the bitmap image is behind the placeholders at the foot of the slide.

To set a color to transparent in a bitmap image:

1. Make sure the image is still selected, and then click the **Set Transparent Color** button ✎ on the Picture toolbar. The pointer changes to ✎.

2. Click anywhere in the blue sky above the mountain tops in the bitmap image. The sky color becomes transparent so that the slide background color appears.

Now you want to make sure the mountain top picture is behind the three text placeholders at the bottom of the slide. To do this, you will change the order of the objects on the slide. Imagine each object is on a piece of paper and you lay each piece of paper down on the slide as you add objects. Objects you add last will be on top of the other objects on the slide.

To change the order of objects on a slide:

1. Make sure the image is still selected, click the **Draw** button on the Drawing toolbar, point to **Order**, and then click **Send to Back**. The bitmap image is sent to the back of all the objects on the slide master, including the slide background, so you can no longer see the mountains. Therefore, you need to move the mountains one object forward.

2. Make sure you can still see the sizing handles of the selected image, click the **Draw** button on the Drawing toolbar, point to **Order**, and then click **Bring Forward**. The mountains now properly appear in the slide master, in front of the background but behind the text placeholders.

   Trouble? If you accidentally deselected the mountain image before you brought it forward again, click the Undo button ↺ on the Standard toolbar to bring the image to the front again, and then repeat Steps 1 and 2.

As you can see, changing the drawing of mountaintops to a digital photograph of Andean mountaintops makes the background graphic more realistic. Now you'll make the same changes on the title master that you just made on the slide master.

To change the background graphic on the title master:

▶ 1. Make sure the resized bitmap image that you just added to the slide master is still selected, and then click the **Copy** button on the Standard toolbar. The image is copied to the Clipboard.

▶ 2. Click the **title master** thumbnail (Slide 2) in the Slides tab. The title master appears in the slide pane. The original drawing of the mountain top appears at the bottom of the slide.

▶ 3. Delete all three components of the original mountain top drawing, as you did before.

▶ 4. Click the **Paste** button on the Formatting toolbar to paste the bitmap image on the slide.

▶ 5. Send the image to the back, so that it's behind all the other objects on the title master, and then bring it forward one object to place it in front of the background. Now both the title master and the slide master have the bitmap image of Andean mountaintops as a background picture in the design template.

▶ 6. Click the **Save** button on the Standard toolbar to save your changes.

Next, Pablo wants you to change the font of the body text on the slide master, and to modify the color of the title text on the slide master.

Modifying Text on a Slide

In PowerPoint, text is described in terms of the font, font size, and font style. A **font** is the design of a set of characters. Some names of fonts include Arial, Times New Roman, Helvetica, and Garamond. Font size is measured in **points**. Text in a book is typically printed in 10- or 12-point type. **Font style** refers to special attributes applied to the characters; for example, bold and italics are font styles.

Pablo wants you to replace the current subtitle and body text font (Arial) with a different font (Times New Roman), and to change the color of the title text from light violet to light blue. He also wants you to add the Global Humanitarian logo on the slides by placing it next to the title text on each slide.

Modifying the Format of Text on a Slide

To change the format of all the text in a text box, you first need to select the text box. To do this, you click the edge of it. This changes the text box border to a thick line composed of little dots. On the other hand, when you click *inside* a text box, you make the box active—that is, ready to accept text that you type or paste—but this doesn't select the text box, as indicated by the borders composed of slanted lines. When you select a text box (with a border of a thick line composed of little dots), any formatting changes you make are global formatting changes and are applied to all of the text in the text box. (This is different than if you select specific text within the text box and make a local formatting change to the selected text.)

You'll now select text boxes in the slide and title to change the font on all the slides.

To modify the fonts in text boxes on a slide:

▶ **1.** Click the **slide master** thumbnail (Slide 1) in the Slides tab.

▶ **2.** Click the dotted-line edge of the body text placeholder on the slide master in the slide pane. The entire placeholder text box is selected, as indicated by the border, which is now a thick line composed of little dots and sizing handles.

   Trouble? If the box surrounding the placeholder is composed of slanted lines, the text box is active, not selected. Click the edge of the text box to change it to a thick line composed of dots.

▶ **3.** Click the **Font** list arrow Arial on the Formatting toolbar, scroll down, if necessary, and then click **Times New Roman** to change the body text font from Arial to Times New Roman.

▶ **4.** Click the dotted-line edge of the title placeholder to select the entire text box, click the **Font Color** list arrow **A ·** on the Drawing or Formatting toolbar, click **More Colors** to open the Colors dialog box, and then click the **Standard** tab. You can now see a honey-comb of color cells from which to select a new font color. See Figure 2-13.

| Figure 2-13 | Standard tab in the Colors dialog box |

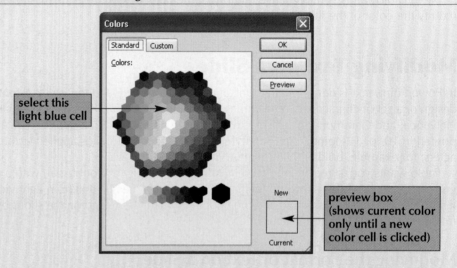

select this
light blue cell

preview box
(shows current color
only until a new
color cell is clicked)

▶ **5.** Click the light blue cell, as indicated in Figure 2-13. The light blue color appears under New in the preview box in the lower-right corner of the dialog box.

▶ **6.** Click the **OK** button. The font color of the title on the slide master changes from light violet to light blue. Now you'll change the text alignment so that the title text on the slide master is left-aligned rather than centered.

▶ **7.** With the title text box still selected, click the **Align Left** button 🔲 on the Formatting tool-bar. The title text is now left-aligned.

▶ **8.** Click the **title master** thumbnail (Slide 2) in the Slides tab. Note that the changes you made to the text boxes on the slide master have also been applied to the text boxes on the title master. Any changes you make to the format of the text on the slide master are also applied to the text on the title master. This does not, however, work in reverse; in other words, text-formatting changes that you make to the title master do not affect the text on the slide master.

You don't want the title text on the title master left-aligned.

► **9.** Select the **title** text box on the title master, and then click the **Center** button on the Formatting toolbar. The text is center-aligned, while the title text on the slide master stays left-aligned.

Next, you need to resize the title text box on the slide so you can insert the Global Humanitarian logo next to the title.

Resizing a Text Box on a Slide

To resize a text box, you need to select it, and then drag a sizing handle. You'll resize the title text box on the slide master by dragging the left-center sizing handle. As with the formatting changes you made to the text, you would follow this same procedure to resize text boxes in Normal view.

To resize a text box:

► **1.** Click the **slide master** thumbnail in the Slides tab, and then select the title text box. The sizing handles appear.

► **2.** Drag the left-center sizing handle to the right approximately one inch, as shown in Figure 2-14, and then release the mouse button. This leaves room for the logo, which will go in the upper-left corner of the slide master, to the left of the title text box.

Resizing the title text placeholder ◄ **Figure 2-14**

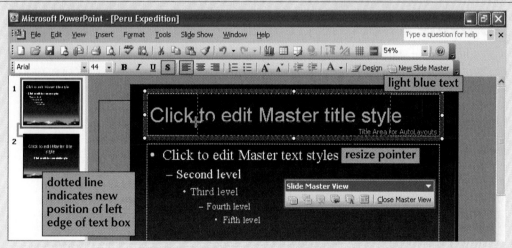

► **3.** Insert the picture file **GHLogo**, located in the Tutorial.02\Tutorial folder included with your Data Files, into the slide master.

► **4.** Drag the logo up near the upper-left corner of the slide, so that the top of the logo is aligned with the top of the title text box.

► **5.** Drag the lower-right sizing handle up and to the left until the logo just fits in the space to the left of the title placeholder.

► **6.** Set the black area surrounding the globe to transparent, and then click a blank area of the slide to deselect the logo. See Figure 2-15.

Figure 2-15 | Slide master after adding and reformatting logo

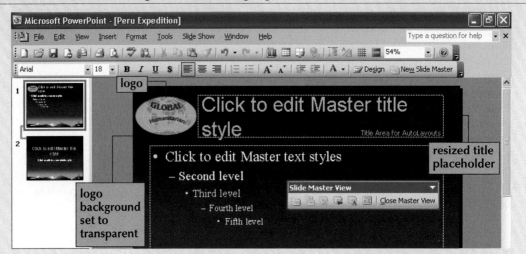

Trouble? If your slide master does not look like the one shown in Figure 2-15, make any necessary adjustments now.

▶ 7. Click the **Close Master View** button on the Slide Master View toolbar. The presentation returns to Normal view.

▶ 8. Save the presentation.

Applying a Second Design Template

Normally all your slides in one presentation will have the same design template. On occasion, however, you might want to apply a second design template to only one, or a few, of the slides in your presentation. Pablo wants you to change the design template for Slide 8, "Expedition Costs (Per Person)" from the modified Mountain Top design template to the Globe design template. All of the other slides present points about the expedition itself. He wants this slide to stand out from the others because it lists the costs of the trip for each participant.

To apply a second design template to a presentation:

▶ 1. Go to **Slide 8** ("Expedition Costs (Per Person)"). When you want to apply a design template to only one slide, you'll usually want that slide to appear in the slide pane.

▶ 2. Click the **Design** button on the Formatting toolbar to open the Slide Design task pane.

▶ 3. Scroll the task pane until you locate the Globe design template, but do not click it. If you just click the Globe design template, it will appear on all the slides rather than just the selected slide.

▶ 4. Position the pointer over the **Globe** design template, and then click the **Design Template** list arrow. See Figure 2-16.

Applying a new design template to this slide only ◄ **Figure 2-16**

Trouble? If you clicked the design thumbnail instead of the Design Template list arrow, click the Undo button ⟳ on the Standard toolbar, and then repeat Step 4.

► **5.** Click **Apply to Selected Slides**. Because Slide 8 is the only selected slide in the Slides tab, it's the only one to which the design template is applied.

► **6.** Click the **Close** button ✕ in the Slide Design task pane, select the title text box in the slide pane, and then adjust the size and alignment of the title text box so that it's similar to the title text box on the other slides and so that the text doesn't overlap the Global Humanitarian logo. You need to change the body text font to match the other slide.

► **7.** Select the body text box, change the font to Times New Roman, change the font size to 36, and then click a blank area of the slide. See Figure 2-17.

Slide 8 with Globe design template ◄ **Figure 2-17**

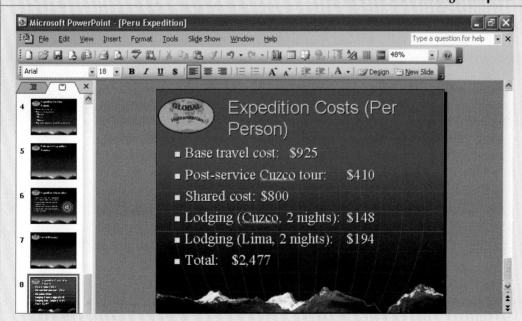

► **8.** Save your changes.

You applied the Globe design template to only one slide in the presentation. The modified Mountain Top design remains on the other slides. The next time you switch to Slide Master view, you will see a second slide-title master pair for the Globe design template below the customized Mountain Top slide-title master pair. Now you need to modify the tab stops on Slide 8 to align the dollar amounts.

Adding and Modifying Tab Stops

A **tab** adds space between the left margin and the beginning of the text on a particular line, or between the text in one column and the text in another column. (When you create several long columns of data, however, you probably want to use a table instead of tabs.) For example, in Slide 8 ("Expedition Costs"), Pablo typed the cost description and a colon, pressed the Tab key to add space, and then typed the dollar amounts for each expense. A **tab stop** is the location where the insertion point moves (including any text to the right of it) when you press the Tab key. The default tab stops on a slide are set at one-inch intervals. You can add your own tab stops to override the default tab stops to align text on a slide. You can set tab stops so that the text left-aligns, right-aligns, center-aligns, or aligns on a decimal point.

The default tab stops on the ruler are left tabs, which position the left edge of text at the tab stop and extend the text to the right. However, you want to align the right sides of the dollar amounts in Slide 8, so you want to use a right tab stop, which positions the right edge of text at the tab stop and extends the text to the left. You'll change the tab stops on Slide 8 now.

To change the tab stops:

► **1.** Click **View** on the menu bar, and then click **Ruler**. Horizontal and vertical rulers appear on the screen.

Trouble? If rulers were already visible on your screen, then clicking Ruler on the View menu hid them. Click View on the menu bar, and then click Ruler again to redisplay the rulers.

► **2.** Click anywhere in the body text box. The default tab stops for the body text appear as light gray rectangles, or hash marks, under the ruler, and the Left Tab button appears to the left of the horizontal ruler. When Pablo typed the text on this slide, he pressed the Tab key after typing the colon in each line, so the dollar amounts on each line are aligned at the next available tab stop. See Figure 2-18.

Tabs for body text box on ruler | **Figure 2-18**

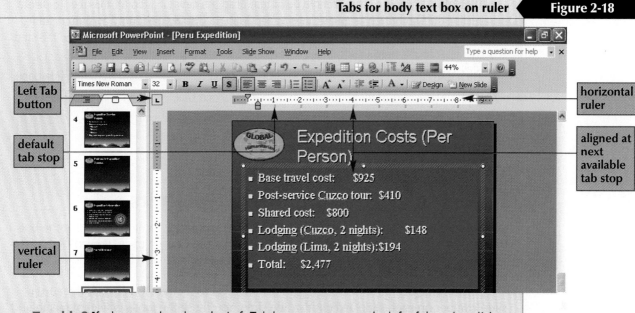

Trouble? If a button other than the Left Tab button appears to the left of the ruler, click the Tab button as many times as necessary until the Left Tab button appears.

3. Click the **Left Tab** button L to the left of the horizontal ruler so that the button changes to the Center Tab button ⊥, and then click the **Center Tab** button ⊥ to change it to the Right Tab button ⌐. If you were to click the Tab button again, the Decimal Tab button ⊥ would appear, and if you were to click once more, the Left Tab button would appear again.

4. Position the pointer immediately before the word "Base" in the first bulleted item, and then click and drag to the bottom of the body text to select all of the bulleted items. The selected text is highlighted.

5. Click just below the 8-inch mark in the white area of the horizontal ruler, and then click anywhere within the selected text. A new, right tab stop appears at the location you clicked, the default tab stops to the left of the new tab stop disappear, and the dollar amounts in the body text box become right-aligned at the new tab stop. See Figure 2-19.

Slide 8 after inserting new tab stop in body text paragraphs | **Figure 2-19**

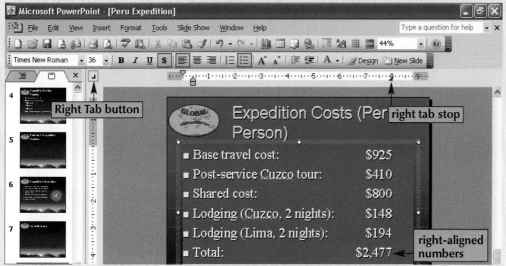

Trouble? If you used the wrong type of tab, drag the new tab stop off the ruler to delete it, click the Tab button as many times as necessary to display the Right Tab button, and then repeat Steps 4 and 5. If you clicked in the wrong place on the ruler, drag the tab stop character to the right or left until it's positioned where you want it.

6. Click **View** on the menu bar, and then click **Ruler**. The rulers disappear from the slide pane.

7. Click a blank area of the slide pane to deselect the text box, and then save your changes.

Next, you'll insert footers and slide numbers.

Inserting Footers and Slide Numbers

When you used the AutoContent wizard, you typed footer text to be displayed at the bottom of each slide. A **header** is text that appears at the top of each page. PowerPoint already provides a footer placeholder on the slide master, and both header and footer placeholders on the notes and handout masters.

As part of the overall slide design, Pablo wants you to include footers and the current slide number on each slide, except the title slide. You'll use the footer placeholders to add the footer and the slide number to each of the slides (except the title slide).

To insert a footer into your presentation:

1. Click **View** on the menu bar, click **Header and Footer** to open the Header and Footer dialog box, and then click the **Slide** tab, if necessary, to display the slide footer information. In the Preview box in the lower-right corner of the dialog box, two of the rectangles at the bottom of the preview slide are black. These black rectangles correspond to the selected check boxes on the Slides tab, in this case, the Date and time and the Footer check boxes.

2. Click the **Date and time** check box to clear it. The left rectangle in the Preview box turns white.

3. Click the **Slide number** check box to select it. The right rectangle in the Preview box turns black. Now the slide number will appear on each slide.

4. Make sure the Footer check box is selected, and then click in the **Footer** text box.

5. Type **Peru Expedition 2006**, and then click the **Don't show on title slide** check box to select it. See Figure 2-20. The slide number and the text you typed in the Footer text box will appear on every slide except the title slide.

Header and Footer dialog box ◄ **Figure 2-20**

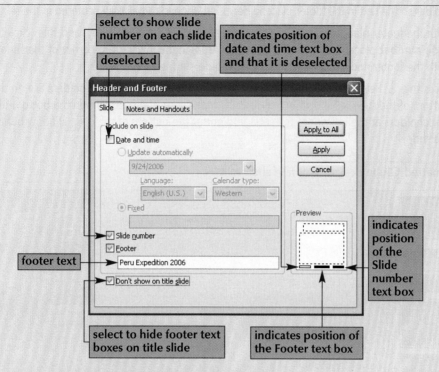

select to show slide
number on each slide

deselected

indicates position of
date and time text box
and that it is deselected

footer text

indicates
position
of the
Slide
number
text box

select to hide footer text
boxes on title slide

indicates position of
the Footer text box

▶ **6.** Click the **Apply to All** button in the Header and Footer dialog box. All the slides (except the title slide) now contain a footer.

The footer has several problems. First, after you applied the new design template to Slide 8, the mountains at the bottom of the slide appear in front of the footer. Second, the footer text isn't legible because the font is too small and its white color makes it unreadable against the white peak of an Andean mountaintop. You can solve these problems by modifying the slide master of the Globe design template, moving the footer on the slide master so that it appears on the left side of the slide, and increasing the font size of the text in the footer. Before you can reposition the footer placeholder text box, you need to delete the date and time placeholder text box.

To delete and reposition text boxes:

▶ **1.** Display the slide master, make sure the slide master of the Globe design (Slide 3 in the Slides tab) is selected, and send the mountain bitmap image to the back and bring it forward in front of the background, as before.

▶ **2.** On the same slide master, click the edge of the **date and time** placeholder (labeled Date Area) in the lower-left corner of the slide, and press the **Delete** key. The placeholder text box is deleted.

▶ **3.** Select the **footer** placeholder (labeled Footer Area), currently located in the bottom middle of the slide, and then press the ← key until the placeholder is aligned on the left with the body text placeholder. By using the ← key rather than dragging and dropping, you ensure that you move the placeholder horizontally but not vertically.

4. With the footer placeholder still selected, click the **Align Left** button ▤ on the Formatting toolbar so the text in the footer placeholder is left-aligned rather than centered in the text box.

5. With the footer placeholder still selected, press and hold the **Shift** key, and then click the **slide number** placeholder (labeled Number Area) in the lower-right corner of the slide. Both the footer and the slide number placeholders are selected.

6. Press the ↓ key two or three times until the bottoms of the two placeholders are on the bottom of the slide, as shown in Figure 2-21. Make sure that you position the bottom of the placeholders at the bottom of the slide and not at the bottom of the drop shadow behind the slide.

Figure 2-21	Reformatted Globe design template slide master

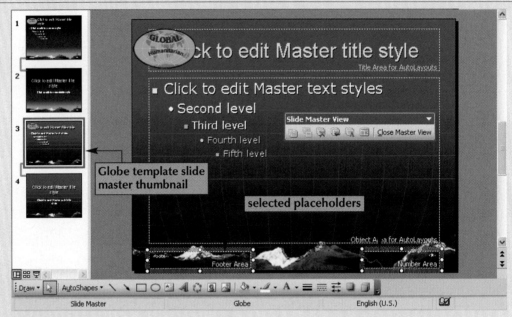

Trouble? If you can't position the text boxes where you want to, press and hold the Ctrl key while you press the ↓ key to nudge the placeholders in smaller increments than pressing the ↓ key alone.

7. With the footer and slide number placeholders still selected, click the **Font Size** list arrow `10 ▾` on the Formatting toolbar, and then click **24** to change the font size to 24 points.

8. Click the **Mountain Top slide master** (Slide 1) in the Slides tab and then repeat Steps 2 through 7 to make the same changes on the slide master of the Mountain Top design template.

9. Click the **Close Master View** button on the Slide Master View toolbar. Now you can read the footer text and the slide number, but the footer text wraps to a second line because the footer placeholder is too small to contain all the footer text on one line.

10. Switch back to Slide Master view, select the footer placeholder, and then drag the right-center sizing handle of the footer placeholder to the right until the right edge of the text box is near the center of the slide.

11. Repeat Step 10 on the Mountain Top slide master, and then click the **Normal View** button ▤ at the bottom of the Slides tab.

▶ **12.** Go to **Slide 4** to make sure that you can read the footer and the slide number on a slide with the Mountain Top design template. See Figure 2-22.

Slide 4 with adjusted footer and slide number ◀ **Figure 2-22**

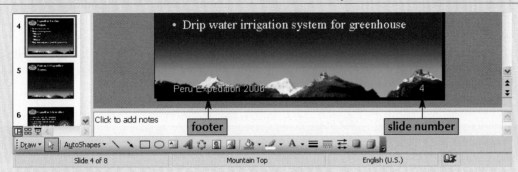

Trouble? If your footer and slide number aren't the same font size and color and in the same position as shown in Figure 2-22, return to Slide Master view and make any necessary adjustments.

▶ **13.** Save the presentation.

Pablo is pleased with how the footer and page number appear at the bottom of each slide. You've completed most of Pablo's presentation. In Session 2.2, you'll finalize the slides by creating a table, diagram, and simple drawing.

Session 2.1 Quick Check

Review

1. List at least three reasons to add graphics to your presentation.
2. Explain the meaning of the following terms:
   a. design template
   b. bitmap image
   c. graphic
   d. Default Design template
3. Describe how to do the following:
   a. make a text box active
   b. select a text box
   c. scale a graphic to change its size
   d. move an object on a slide
   e. apply a second design template to selected slides
   f. recolor clip art
4. What is the difference between the title master and the slide master?
5. What are tabs? What are tab stops? Describe how to insert a right tab stop on the ruler.
6. What are the three objects included in a footer on a slide as part of the master?

Creating a Table in a Slide

Pablo wants you to create a table listing the travel itinerary for the Peru expedition in Slide 7. A **table** is information arranged in horizontal rows and vertical columns. The area where a row and column intersect is called a **cell**. Each cell contains one piece of information and is identified by a column and row label; for example, the cell in the upper-left corner of a table is cell A1 (column A, row 1), the cell to the right of that is B1, the cell below A1 is A2, and so forth. A table's structure is indicated by borders, which are lines that outline the rows and columns.

Reference Window | Inserting a Table on a Slide

- Click Format on the menu bar, and then click Slide Layout to open the Slide Layout task pane.
- Change the slide layout of the desired slide to one of the Content layouts.
- Click the Insert Table button.
- Specify the desired table size—the numbers of columns and rows—and then click the OK button.
- Add information to the cells. Use the Tab key to move from one cell to the next, and the Shift+Tab keys to move to previous cells.
- Modify the borders as desired.
- Click in a blank area of the slide to deselect the table.

The itinerary table you'll create needs to have four columns: one for the date of travel, one for the departure or arrival city, one for the time of departure or arrival, and one for the flight number. The table needs to have nine rows: one row for column labels, and eight rows for the data. Now you'll create the travel itinerary table.

To create a table:

1. If you took a break after the previous session, make sure PowerPoint is running, and then open the presentation **Peru Expedition** located in the Tutorial.02\Tutorial folder included with your Data Files.

2. Go to **Slide 7** ("Travel Itinerary"), click **Format** on the menu bar, and then click **Slide Layout** to open the Slide Layout task pane.

3. Click the **Title and Content** layout. The layout of the current slide changes.

4. Click the **Insert Table** button ▦ in the content placeholder in the slide pane. The Insert Table dialog box opens.

5. Type **4** in the Number of columns text box, press the **Tab** key to move the insertion point to the Number of rows text box, type **9**, and then click the **OK** button. A table made up of four columns and nine rows is inserted in the slide with the insertion point blinking in the first cell (cell A1), and the Tables and Borders toolbar opens.

    Trouble? If the table doesn't have four columns and nine rows, click the Undo button ⟲ on the Standard toolbar to undo your creation of the table, and then repeat Steps 4 and 5.

Trouble? If the Tables and Borders toolbar doesn't appear, click View on the main menu bar, point to Toolbars, and then click Tables and Borders.

▶ 6. Close the task pane.

Now you're ready to fill the blank cells with information. To enter data in a table, you click in the cell in which you want to enter data. Once you start typing in a cell, you can use the Tab and arrow keys to move from one cell to another. If you want to add a new row at the bottom of the table, move the insertion point to the last cell in the table, and then press the Tab key. A new row will be inserted automatically.

To add information to the table:

▶ 1. With the insertion point blinking in the first cell, type **Date**, press the **Tab** key to move to cell B1, type **City**, press the **Tab** key to move to cell C1, type **Time**, press the **Tab** key to move to cell D1 (the last cell in the first row), and then type **Flight**. This completes the column labels.

Trouble? You might have to drag the Tables and Borders toolbar by its title bar to see the table cells.

▶ 2. Press the **Tab** key. The insertion point moves to cell A2.

▶ 3. Type **Dec. 25**, and then press the **Tab** key to move to cell B2.

▶ 4. Type **Lv Dallas** (short for "Leave Dallas") in cell B2, type **4:22 PM** in cell C2, and then type **AA 982** (short for American Airlines flight 982) in cell D2. This completes the first row of data.

▶ 5. Complete the information in the rest of the cells, as shown in Figure 2-23, and then click a blank area of the slide to deselect the table.

Slide 7 with completed table ◀ **Figure 2-23**

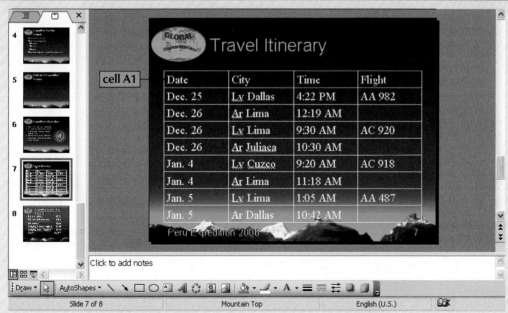

Trouble? If you pressed the Tab key after typing the last enty, you added a new row to the table. Click the Undo button on the Standard toolbar to remove the extra row.

To make the column labels appear visually separated from the data, you'll change the border below the top row so that it is more visible.

To draw a border:

▶ 1. Click anywhere in the table to make it active and display the Tables and Borders toolbar.

▶ 2. Click the **Draw Table** button ⬚ on the Tables and Borders toolbar, and then move the pointer off of the toolbar. The pointer changes to ✎.

▶ 3. Click the **Border Width** list arrow ⬚1 pt ▾⬚ on the Tables and Borders toolbar, and then click **3 pt** to change the border line width to three points.

▶ 4. Click the **Border Color** button ✎ on the Tables and Borders toolbar, and then click the light blue tile (the custom color *below* the main row of tiles). Now when you draw a border, it will be a 3-point, light blue line.

▶ 5. Drag ✎ along the border between the first and second rows in the table. As you draw the border, a dotted line appears to indicate the border as it is drawn. When you release the mouse button, the light blue line appears.

▶ 6. Click the **Draw Table** button ⬚ on the Table and Borders toolbar to deselect it.

In addition to changing the border lines in a table, you can add and change diagonal lines within cells of a table. First, click the Table button on the Tables and Borders toolbar, click Borders and Fill, click the Borders tab, and then click one or both of the Diagonal Line buttons.

Although the colored border visually separates the column labels from the data in the table, the labels would stand out more if they were formatted differently from the data. You will format the text in the top row to be a light blue, bold, Arial font.

To modify the font in a table:

▶ 1. Drag I across all the text in the top row to select it.

▶ 2. Change the font to **Arial**, as you would any other type of text.

▶ 3. Click the **Bold** button ⬚B⬚ on the Formatting toolbar to make the selected text bold.

▶ 4. Click the **Font Color** list arrow ⬚A ▾⬚ on the Drawing or Formatting toolbar, and then click the light blue tile (the custom color *below* the main row of tiles).

▶ 5. Click a blank area of the slide pane to deselect the table. See Figure 2-24.

Table after modifying border and column headings   **Figure 2-24**

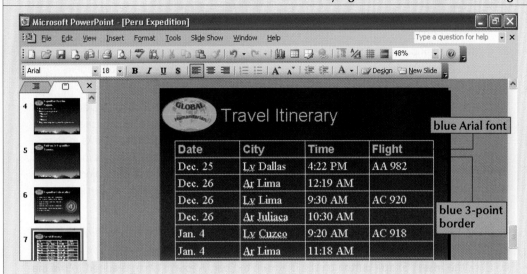

▶ **6.** Save your changes.

You have completed the table that shows the flight itinerary for the Peru expedition. The Tables and Borders toolbar also lets you remove rows, add and remove columns, combine cells, split cells, and perform other modifications to the table. If you want to do any of these tasks, use PowerPoint's Help system. In addition, try right-clicking anywhere on the table to see a shortcut menu containing commands specific to working with tables.

Your next task is to create a diagram on Slide 5 to show the relationship between the four major parties involved in a humanitarian service project.

Creating a Diagram on a Slide

PowerPoint allows you to create the following types of diagrams on slides:

- **Cycle diagrams**—show a process that has a continuous cycle
- **Organizational charts**—show the relationship between individuals or units within an organization
- **Radial diagrams**—show the relationships of a core element
- **Pyramid diagrams**—show foundation-based relationships
- **Venn diagrams**—show areas of overlap between elements
- **Target diagrams**—show steps toward a goal

In the Peru Expedition presentation, Pablo wants you to add a Venn diagram on Slide 5 ("Partners in Expedition Success") to show the relationship between the four major parties involved in a humanitarian service project: the village for which the service is being performed, the volunteers who perform the service, the humanitarian organization that sponsors the service, and the donors who contribute money to support the service. You'll create the Venn diagram now.

To create a Venn diagram:

▶ **1.** Go to **Slide 5**, and then change the layout to the **Title and Content** layout in the Content Layouts section.

▶ **2.** Close the task pane, and then click the **Insert Diagram or Organization Chart** button 🔆 in the content placeholder in the slide pane. The Diagram Gallery dialog box opens.

▶ **3.** Click the **Venn Diagram** icon (the middle icon in the second row), and then click the **OK** button. A diagram with three intersecting circles and text box placeholders is added to the slide, and the Diagram toolbar opens. The text box placeholders are hard to see on the dark blue part of the background. Selection handles—gray circles with small *X*s in them—appear around the top circle in the diagram. When you see selection handles instead of sizing handles on a slide, it means that the selected object is part of a larger object, and although you can modify the selected object by changing its color or other attributes, you can't resize the individual object.

   Next, you'll edit the diagram by adding another circle, adding text, and modifying the circle colors.

▶ **4.** Click the **Insert Shape** button on the Diagram toolbar. A fourth circle is added to the diagram. The new circle is the same color as the bottom circle. You'll change the color of the bottom circle.

▶ **5.** Right-click the bottom circle, click **Format AutoShape** on the shortcut menu to open the Format AutoShape dialog box, and then click the **Colors and Lines** tab, if necessary.

▶ **6.** Click the **Color** list arrow in the Fill section at the top of the dialog box, and then click the light blue tile (the custom color) located on its own row just above the More Colors command.

▶ **7.** Click the **OK** button. The bottom circle is recolored light blue. See Figure 2-25.

Figure 2-25 ▶ **Venn diagram with new shape added**

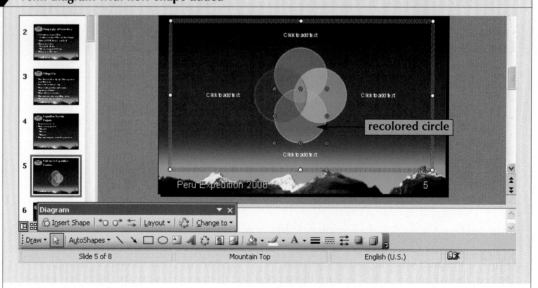

Now you'll label each circle in the Venn diagram.

To add and modify text in the Venn diagram:

▶ **1.** Click in the text box placeholder (labeled "Click to add text") above the top circle, and then type **Village**.

▶ **2.** Type **Volunteers** in the text box placeholder to the right of the right circle.

▶ **3.** Click in the text box placeholder to the left of the left circle, type **Global**, press the **Enter** key, and then type **Humanitarian**.

▶ **4.** Type **Donors** in the text box placeholder below the bottom circle.

Because the font of the text around the Venn diagram is small, the text is hard to read. You'll increase the font size now.

▶ **5.** Shift-click the four text boxes (press and hold the Shift key, and then click each of the text boxes) to select them all, and then change the font size to **24** points.

▶ **6.** Click a blank area of the slide pane to deselect everything in the slide. See Figure 2-26.

Slide 5 with completed Venn diagram ◀ **Figure 2-26**

▶ **7.** Save your changes.

This completes the diagram on Slide 5. When Pablo uses this slide show to give a presentation, he'll discuss how the roles of the village, volunteers, donors, and Global Humanitarian overlap to make a successful project.

Pablo now asks you to insert a new Slide 6, and create a shape in the slide.

Creating and Manipulating a Shape

For the last graphic to be included in his presentation, Pablo asks you to add an inverted triangle with labels along each side to a new Slide 6. The labels on each side of the triangle will list the three components of the Global Humanitarian strategy—village outreach projects, expeditions, and internships. Pablo wants you to use an equilateral triangle to point out that each of the three strategies is equally important. This graphic will be a strong visual reminder to potential Global Humanitarian contributors and volunteers of this threefold strategy.

To create the triangle, you'll use the triangle AutoShape. When you click the AutoShapes button on the Drawing toolbar, you are presented with the following categories of shapes from which to choose: lines, connectors, basic shapes (for example, rectangles and triangles), block arrows, flowchart shapes, stars and banners, callouts, and action buttons.

To insert a shape in a slide using AutoShapes:

1. Insert a new Slide 6, change the slide layout to **Title Only** (under Text Layouts), and then close the Slide Layout task pane.

2. Type **Global Humanitarian Strategy** in the title placeholder.

3. Click the **AutoShapes** button on the Drawing toolbar, and then point to **Basic Shapes**. The Basic Shapes palette opens.

4. Click the **Isosceles Triangle** button on the Basic Shapes palette, as indicated in Figure 2-27, and then position the pointer over the slide in the slide pane. The pointer changes to ⊹.

| Figure 2-27 | Selecting an AutoShape |

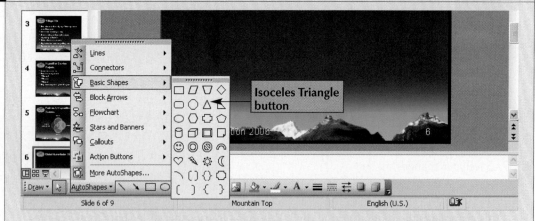

5. Position ⊹ approximately one inch below the "o" in "Global" (in the title of the slide), press and hold down the **Shift** key, and then click and and drag the pointer down and to the right. The outline of a triangle appears as you drag. Pressing the Shift key while you drag makes the triangle equilateral—the three sides are of equal length. (Similarly, if you click the Oval button, you can press and hold the Shift key while you drag to draw a circle, and if you click the Rectangle button, you can press and hold the Shift key while you drag to draw a square.)

6. Release the mouse button and the Shift key when your triangle is approximately the same size and shape as the one shown in Figure 2-28.

Slide 6 with isosceles triangle shape | Figure 2-28

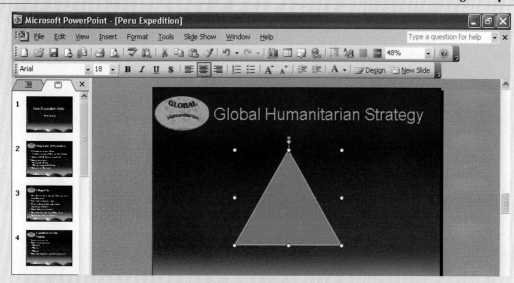

Trouble? If your triangle doesn't look like the one in Figure 2-28, you can move it by dragging it to a new location, resize or change its shape by dragging one or more of the sizing handles, or delete it by pressing the Delete key, and then repeating Steps 3 through 6 to redraw it.

In addition to the sizing handles, the selected triangle has a yellow diamond and a green circle at its top. The yellow diamond is an **adjustment handle**; if you drag it, the shape of the tip of the triangle changes without changing the overall size of the object. The green circle is the **rotate handle**, which you can drag to rotate the shape.

The default color of the drawn object is the blue color from the set of default colors, but Pablo prefers the same color of blue as the title text.

To change the fill color of an AutoShape:

1. With the triangle still selected, click the **Fill Color** list arrow ⬛ ▾ on the Drawing toolbar. The color palette appears on the screen.

2. Click the light blue tile (the custom color located below the row of default tiles). The color of the triangle changes to light blue.

The triangle is the desired size and color, but Pablo wants you to flip (invert) the triangle so that it points down instead of up. You can use commands on the Draw menu on the Drawing toolbar to rotate and flip objects.

To flip an object:

▶ **1.** With the triangle still selected, click the **Draw** button on the Drawing toolbar, point to **Rotate or Flip**, and then click **Flip Vertical**.

▶ **2.** Click a blank region in the slide pane to deselect the triangle. Your triangle should be sized, positioned, colored, and oriented like the one shown in Figure 2-29.

Figure 2-29 ▶ **Slide 6 after recoloring and flipping triangle**

▶ **3.** Save the presentation.

Now you'll add the text labels along the sides of the triangle.

Inserting Text Boxes

Sometimes you need to add a text box in a different location than any of the text box placeholders on the layouts. You need to add text boxes on each of the three sides of the triangle in Slide 6.

Adding Text to the Diagram

You're ready to add the text naming the three strategies of Global Humanitarian on each side of the triangle. You'll now add three text boxes around the AutoShape triangle you just created.

To add a text box to the slide:

▶ **1.** Click the **Text Box** button 🔲 on the Drawing toolbar, and then position the pointer over the slide. The pointer changes to ↓.

▶ **2.** Position ↓ so it is just above and centered on the top side of the triangle, and then click. A small text box appears above the triangle with the insertion point blinking in it. The position doesn't have to be exact.

Trouble? If the insertion point is blinking in the middle of the triangle instead of in a new text box above the triangle, you clicked the edge of the triangle. Click the Undo button ↺ on the Standard toolbar, and then repeat Steps 1 and 2.

3. Click the **Center** button ≣ on the Formatting toolbar, and then type **Village Outreach Projects**.

4. Click the **Text Box** button 🔲 on the Drawing toolbar, click ↓ to the right of the triangle, and then type **Expeditions**.

5. Create a third text box to the left of the triangle, click the **Align Right** button ≣ on the Formatting toolbar, and then type **Internships**.

6. Click the **Text Box** button 🔲 again, and then drag to draw a text box *inside* the triangle.

7. Type **Global Humanitarian**.

   Trouble? If the text you type appears upside down, you did not drag to create the text box inside the triangle, you simply clicked. Click the Undo button on the Standard toolbar twice, and then repeat Steps 6 and 7.

8. If the text inside the triangle does not fit on one line, drag a sizing handle on the text box to increase the size of the text box.

9. Select the three text boxes that you created outside the triangle by Shift-clicking them, and then change the font size to **24** points.

10. Click in a blank area of the slide to deselect the text boxes. Your slide should now look similar to Figure 2-30.

Text boxes added in and around triangle | **Figure 2-30**

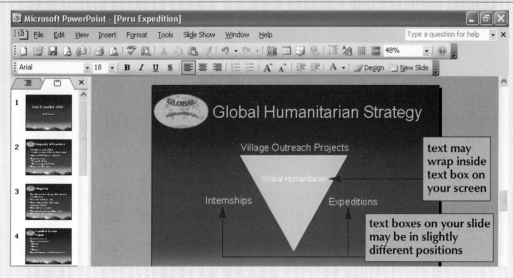

Next you'll rotate the text boxes to make them parallel to the sides of the triangle.

Rotating and Moving Text Boxes

The method for rotating text is similar to the one for rotating graphics (or rotating any other object). You use the Rotate or Flip commands on the Draw menu on the Drawing toolbar, or you drag the rotate handle on the object. You will rotate the text boxes on the left and right sides of the triangle.

To rotate and move the text boxes:

1. Click anywhere within the "Expeditions" text box. The sizing handles and the rotate handle appear around the text box.

2. Position the pointer over the rotate handle. The pointer becomes ↻.

3. Press and hold the **Shift** key, and then drag the rotate handle counterclockwise until the top edge of the box is parallel to the lower-right edge of the triangle. Holding down the Shift key causes the rotation to occur in 15-degree increments.

4. Drag the "Expeditions" text box to position it against and centered on the lower-right edge of the triangle. See Figure 2-31.

| Figure 2-31 | Slide 6 with rotated and repositioned text box |

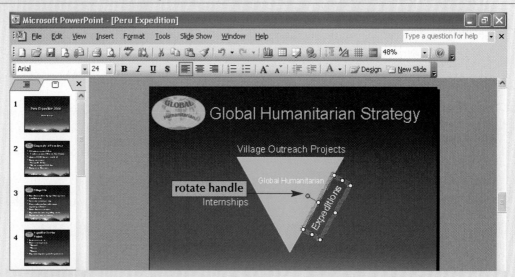

Trouble? If the edge of the text box isn't parallel to the edge of the triangle, you can repeat Steps 2 and 3 to fix the rotation. If necessary, try it without pressing the Shift key.

Trouble? If the text box jumps from one location to another as you drag it, and you can't position it exactly where you want it, hold down the Alt key as you drag the box. (The Alt key temporarily disables a feature that forces objects to snap to invisible gridlines on the slide.)

5. Rotate the "Internships" text box clockwise so that the top edge of the text is parallel to the lower-left edge of the triangle, and then position the text box so it's against and centered on the left edge of the triangle.

6. Adjust the position of (but don't rotate) the "Village Outreach Projects" text box so it's centered over the triangle.

7. Reposition the text box inside the triangle so that it is centered in the triangle.

8. Click a blank area of the slide pane to deselect the text box. Your slide should look like Figure 2-32.

Slide 6 with completed diagram | **Figure 2-32**

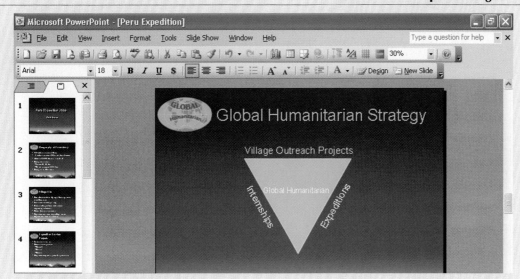

▶ **9.** Save the presentation.

Pablo asks you to perform one final task before the presentation is finished. He wants you to add a summary at the end of the presentation.

Adding a Summary Slide

A **summary slide** is a slide containing the slide titles of selected slides in the presentation. PowerPoint helps you create a summary slide automatically. You'll do this now.

To create a summary slide:

▶ **1.** Click the **Slide Sorter View** button ▦ at the bottom of the Slides tab. The presentation appears in Slide Sorter view.

▶ **2.** Click **Slide 2**, press and hold down the **Shift** key, and then click **Slide 9**. All of the slides except Slide 1 are selected. (If you wanted to select nonsequential slides, you would press and hold the Ctrl key while you clicked the desired slides.)

▶ **3.** Click the **Summary Slide** button 🖾 on the Slide Sorter toolbar. PowerPoint creates a new slide in front of the first selected slide with the title "Summary Slide" and body text consisting of a list of the titles of the selected slides.

Trouble? If you don't see the Summary Slide button on the Slide Sorter toolbar, click the Toolbar Options button ⁞ on the Slide Sorter toolbar.

▶ **4.** Drag **Slide 2** (the new summary slide) to the right of Slide 10. Slide 2 becomes Slide 10, and the other slides are renumbered automatically.

▶ **5.** Double-click **Slide 10** to return to Normal view with Slide 10 in the slide pane.

▶ **6.** Double-click **Slide** in the title text to select the entire word, press the **Delete** key, and then deselect the text box. The selected text is deleted and the title becomes "Summary." See Figure 2-33.

Figure 2-33 | New summary slide

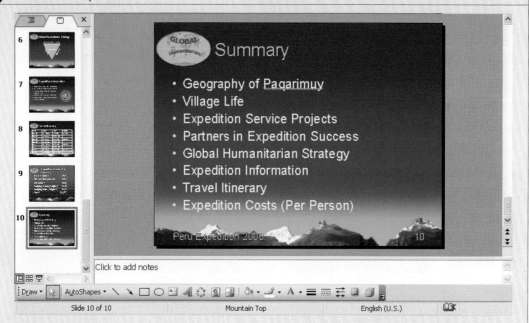

You have completed the entire presentation, so you should save the final version to the disk.

▶ **7.** Save the file.

As usual, you should finish up your presentation by checking the spelling, viewing it in Slide Show view, and printing it.

To check, view, and print the presentation:

▶ **1.** Click the **Spelling** button on the Standard toolbar to start checking the spelling of your presentation. Decide how to handle each word that is flagged because it was not found in the PowerPoint dictionary. (In most cases, you should click the Ignore All button because the words are proper nouns, such as "Paqarimuy" and "Cuzco.")

▶ **2.** Go to **Slide 1**, and then click the **Slide Show from current slide** button at the bottom of the Slides tab. The slide show starts.

▶ **3.** Press the **spacebar** or click the mouse button to advance through the slide show.

▶ **4.** If you see any problems while you are watching the slide show, press the **Esc** key to exit the slide show and return to Normal view, make the necessary corrections, and then return to Slide Show view.

▶ **5.** Go to **Slide 1**, and then replace Pablo's name with your own name.

▶ **6.** Print the presentation in grayscale as handouts, with six slides per page. Don't worry that the footers and one of the graphics are illegible in grayscale.

▶ **7.** Save the presentation, and then close the presentation.

Pablo is pleased with the additions and modifications you made to the presentation. He is anxious to use it to recruit volunteers for the next Peru expedition.

Review

Session 2.2 Quick Check

1. How do you add a table to a slide?
2. Where is cell A1 in a table?
3. What is a Venn diagram?
4. How do you add a text box to a slide?
5. How do you draw a shape, such as a rectangle or a circle, on a slide?
6. How do you rotate or flip an object using menu commands?
7. How do you rotate an object without using menu commands?
8. Describe the Summary Slide command in PowerPoint.

Review

Tutorial Summary

In this tutorial, you learned how to create a new presentation using a design template, and how to apply a new design template to selected (or all) the slides in the presentation. You learned how to insert, format, and resize graphics, including clip art and photographs. You also learned how to modify the design template in the slide master and the title master. You learned how to add tab stops to align text on a slide. You learned how to insert footer information on slides. You also learned how to insert a table, a diagram, a shape, and a text box on slides. And finally, you learned how to add a summary slide to a presentation.

Key Terms

adjustment handle	font style	rotate handle
bitmap image	graphic	slide master
cell	handout master	slide-title master pair
clip art	header	summary slide
color scheme	master	tab
default colors	notes master	tab stop
design template	pixel	table
font	point	title master

Practice

Practice the skills you learned in the tutorial using the same case scenario.

Review Assignments

Data Files needed for the Review Assignments: PackList.jpg, GHLogo.jpg, SlpBag.jpg, Boots.ppt, Camera.jpg, Food.jpg, Personal.jpg, PrMeds.jpg, Vitamins.jpg

One of the common questions from volunteers who sign up for a service expedition is, "What items will I need for the trip?" In other words, they want to see a packing list to give them an idea of what they'll have to purchase and pack if they decide to go on the trip. Pablo decides to give a presentation to all volunteers to explain what they must take on the service expedition. He asks you to create a PowerPoint presentation on the Peru expedition packing list. Complete the following:

1. Open the file **PackList** located in the Tutorial.02\Review folder included with your Data Files, and then save it as **Peru Packing List** in the same folder.
2. Apply the design template titled "Teamwork," and then replace the subtitle in Slide 1 with your name.

3. Add the footer "Packing List" and slide numbers to all the slides except Slide 1.

4. In the title master, insert the logo file **GHLogo**, also located in the Tutorial.02\Review folder, position the graphic near the lower-right corner of the slide, just above the Number Area (the slide number placeholder text box), and then make the background of the logo transparent.

5. On both the title master and the slide master, change the title font color from light blue to the light yellow-green color found among the scheme colors. Switch back to Normal view when you are finished.

6. On Slide 2, change the slide layout so you can place clip art to the right of the bulleted list, search for clip art that deals with money, and then insert the piece of clip art that shows a dollar sign in an orange circle.

7. Recolor the clip art so that it is green (the third color from the right in the color palette).

8. Resize the clip art so it fits properly on the slide, and then resize the bulleted-list text box as needed so the text is as large as possible without overlapping the clip art. If the font size does not increase automatically when you increase the size of the text box, then use the Font Size button on the Formatting toolbar.

9. In Slide 3, insert the bitmap image file **SlpBag** ("sleeping bag") located in the Tutorial.02\Review folder.

10. Resize the sleeping bag image to increase its size so it fills more of the space on the right side of the slide, and then make the background of the image transparent.

11. In Slides 4 through 9, insert appropriate bitmap images located in the Tutorial.02\Review folder, resize the images as large as possible, and make the backgrounds transparent. Modify the layouts or resize the body text boxes as needed.

12. Add a new Slide 10 using the Title Only layout (under Text Layouts), type "Areas of Personal Preparation" as the title, draw a square in the middle of the blank area of the slide below the title, and change the fill color to the light blue color in the default color palette.

13. Add text just outside of the square on each of its four sides, using the words "Physical," "Mental," "Social," and "Spiritual." It doesn't matter which word you place on which side.

14. Rotate the text on the sides of the box so the bottom edges of the text boxes face toward the square. Adjust the text boxes so that each word is centered along the edge of the square and almost resting on the box. Resize the font to a readable size.

15. Add a new Slide 11 with the Title and Content layout, type "Discount Items" as the title, insert a table with three columns and five rows, and then add the text as follows:

Item	Regular Price	Discount Price
Boots	$198	$118
Sleeping bag	$162	$98
Water filter	$51	$32
Flashlight	$26	$16

16. Select the text and numbers in columns 2 and 3, and then right-align it.

17. Draw a light yellow-green, 4½ point border below the top row, and then modify the format of the text in the top row so it is 32 points and light yellow-green.

18. Drag the bottom-center sizing handle of the table up so that the table stays the same width but decreases in height so the text fits better in the cells of the table.

19. To Slide 11 only, apply the design template titled "Glass Layers," and then change the font and alignment of the title text on the slide master for this slide so that it matches the rest of the slides.
20. Add a new Slide 12 with the Title and Content layout, type "Thank You" as the title, and then insert a Pyramid diagram. Apply the teamwork design template to this slide.
21. Click the bottom placeholder in the diagram, type "You," click the middle placeholder, type "Global Humanitarian," click the top placeholder, type "The World," and then reformat all three labels to 28-point bold Arial.
22. Create a summary slide that includes titles from all the slides except Slides 1 and 12, and change the title to "Summary." Notice that PowerPoint creates two summary slides, because all of the slide titles will not fit on a single slide.
23. Check the spelling in the presentation, view the slide show, fix any problems you see, save the presentation, print it in grayscale as handouts with six slides per page, and then close the file.

Case Problem 1

Data Files needed for this Case Problem: MyBody.ppt, Weights.jpg, StrMach.jpg, Excycle.jpg, Treadmil.jpg, Vitamins.jpg

MyBodyTrainer.com   Several years ago, Jerry Wursten received an M.S. degree in exercise physiology and became a board-certified strength and conditioning specialist (CSCS). Recently, he started a new e-commerce company called MyBodyTrainer.com, which provides services and products for health, fitness, weight loss, and sports conditioning. The services include personalized training and weight-loss programs, and the products include fitness equipment and dietary supplements. Jerry's business is expanding rapidly, and he needs additional capital. He needs to hire three more CSCS employees and several other employees to process orders, and he needs to purchase additional inventory and rent additional warehouse and office space. He asks you to help him prepare a PowerPoint presentation giving an overview of his business. He will give the presentation to bankers and investors to help him raise money for his company. Complete the following:

1. Open the file **MyBody** located in the Tutorial.02\Cases folder included with your Data Files, and then save it as **MyBodyTrainer** in the same folder.
2. Apply the design template titled "Shimmer," and then replace the subtitle in Slide 1 with your name.
3. In the slide master, change the title text box so it is center-aligned, rather than left-aligned.
4. Using the AutoShapes, draw a heart in the upper-left corner of the slide master, to the left of the title text box.
5. Change the fill color of the heart to red.
6. In Slides 7 and 8, change the slide layout to Title, Text, and 2 Content, and then add two bitmap images to each slide. In Slide 7, use the **Weights** and **StrMach** (strength machines) files, and in Slide 8 use the **Excycle** (exercise cycle) and **Treadmil** (treadmill) files; these bitmap images are located in the Tutorial.02\Cases folder.
7. In Slide 8, adjust the two images so they are side-by-side and fill the area to the right of the text. Similarly, in Slide 7, adjust the size and position of the images so they are visible and attractive.

8. In Slide 9, change the layout to Title, Text, and Content, and then add the bitmap image **Vitamins**, located in the Tutorial.02\Cases folder.

9. In Slide 3, change the layout to Title, Text, and Content, insert appropriate clip art, and then, if necessary, recolor the clip art so it matches the design template color scheme. (Note that if the image you choose is a bitmap image, you will not be able to recolor it.)

10. In Slide 4, draw a large equilateral Regular Pentagon in the middle of the blank area of the slide below the title.

11. Invert the pentagon so it's pointed down.

12. Add white, 18-point Arial text just outside the pentagon on each of its five sides, using the phrases (starting at the top of the pentagon and going clockwise): "Motivation," "Strength Training," "Cardio Exercise," "Nutrition," and "Flexibility."

13. Rotate the text boxes so they are parallel to their respective sides of the pentagon. Adjust the size of the pentagon and the position of the text so that each phrase is centered along an edge, and almost resting on the shape.

14. In Slide 11, insert a table with two columns and five rows, and then add the text as follows:

Expense Item	Amount Needed
CSCS Employees	$230,000
Other Employees	$312,000
Inventory	$186,000
Rent	$21,000

Explore ▶ 15. Add a new row with "Total" in the left column and "$749,000" in the right column. (*Hint*: To add a row to an existing table, click in the last cell, in this case cell B5, and then press the Tab key.)

16. Drag the bottom-center sizing handle of the table up so that the table stays the same width but decreases in height so the text fits better in the cells of the table.

17. Right-align the text and numbers in column 2.

Explore ▶ 18. Change the fill color of the top row of the table to dark amber. (*Hint*: Use the Fill Color button on the Tables and Borders toolbar.)

19. Create a summary slide that includes titles from Slides 5 through 10, and change the slide title to "Products and Services." Leave the slide as the new Slide 5 in the presentation.

20. Check the spelling, view the slide show, fix any problems you see, and then save the presentation.

21. Print the presentation in grayscale as handouts with six slides per page, and then close the file.

Challenge

Apply the skills you learned in this tutorial, and explore some new ones, to modify a presentation for an accountancy firm.

Case Problem 2

Data File needed for this Case Problem: Payroll.ppt

Payroll Partners   Payroll Partners, founded by Sara Ostergaard, is a Wichita, Kansas-based accountancy office that helps small businesses process payroll and perform other financial tasks. Recently, Sara was approached by lawyers of a national chain of payroll-processing offices who expressed interest in buying her business. Sara is interested in exploring the idea, and asks you to prepare a presentation that she can use to present to the board of directors of the national chain in hopes of getting the best deal possible. Complete the following:

1. Open the file **Payroll** located in the Tutorial.02\Cases folder included with your Data Files, and then save it as **Payroll Partners** in the same folder.
2. Apply the design template titled "Textured," and then replace the subtitle in Slide 1 with your name.
3. In the title master and slide master, change the title text so it's the same color (sky blue) as the square bullets in the main text of the slide master.

Explore

4. In the slide master, add a yellow-gold, 3-point border around the title text box. (*Hint*: Use the Line Color and Line Style buttons on the Drawing toolbar. Note that yellow-gold is one of the default colors.)
5. Add the footer "Payroll Partners" and slide numbers to all the slides except Slide 1.
6. Change the layout of Slide 3 to Title and Content, and then insert a Venn diagram consisting of three circles.
7. Add text labels next to each of the circles (in the designated placeholders): "Software Development," "Accounting," and "Small Business Payroll."
8. Near the bottom of the slide and centered below the Venn diagram, insert a text box with the phrase "Niche Region." Change the text to 32-point, yellow-gold text.

Explore

9. Add a yellow-gold line border around the "Niche Region" text box. (*Hint*: Select the box and then click the Line Color button on the Drawing toolbar.)

Explore

10. Draw a black, 3-point arrow from this text box to the center of the Venn diagram where the three circles overlap. (*Hint*: Use the Arrow and Line Style buttons on the Drawing toolbar.)
11. In Slide 5, change the layout to Title, Text, and Content, and then insert clip art that deals with money. If necessary, recolor the clip art to match the slide color scheme. If necessary, use the AutoFit option to fit the text in the placeholder.
12. In Slide 6, change the font color of the asking price to yellow-gold.
13. In Slide 7, insert a table with three columns and five rows, and then add the text as follows:

Year	Gross Revenues	Earnings
2002	$180,000	$70,000
2003	$270,000	$122,000
2004	$350,000	$188,000
2005	$510,000	$238,000

14. Drag the bottom-center sizing handle of the table up so that the table stays the same width but decreases in height so the text fits better in the cells of the table.

Explore

15. Select the top row of text, and change the vertical alignment so the text appears at the bottom of each cell in the row. (*Hint*: Use the Align Bottom button on the Tables and Borders toolbar.)

16. Right-align the text and numbers in columns 2 and 3.
17. Create a summary slide that includes titles from Slides 3 through 8, move the slide to the end of the presentation so it becomes Slide 9, and then change the title to "Summary."
18. Check the spelling, view the slide show, fix any problems you see, and then save the presentation.
19. Print the presentation in grayscale as handouts with six slides per page, and then close the file.

Create

Create a new presentation about scrapbooking by using and expanding on the skills you learned in this tutorial.

Case Problem 3

Data Files needed for this Case Problem: SBcam.jpg, SBfile.jpg, SBpages.jpg, SBpaper.jpg, SBpens.jpg, SBphoto.jpg, SBsciss.jpg

Sally's Scrapbooking Four years ago, Brian and Sally DiQuattro started a business called Sally's Scrapbooking Supplies, which distributes wholesale scrapbooking supplies to retail stores in the Atlanta area. More recently, Brian and Sally opened their own specialty retail store (called Sally's Scrapbooking) and stocked it with scrapbooking supplies, which include binders, paper and plastic sheets and protectors, colored pens and markers, stickers and die cuts, stencils, scissors and cutting boards, glues and adhesives, and other miscellaneous items. As part of their marketing, Brian and Sally give presentations to scrapbooking clubs, women's clubs, crafts clubs, church groups, genealogical societies, and others interested in preserving their family histories through picture scrapbooks. The DiQuattros asked you to prepare a presentation for members of these organizations. The seven slides in your completed presentation should look like the slides shown in Figure 2-34.

Figure 2-34

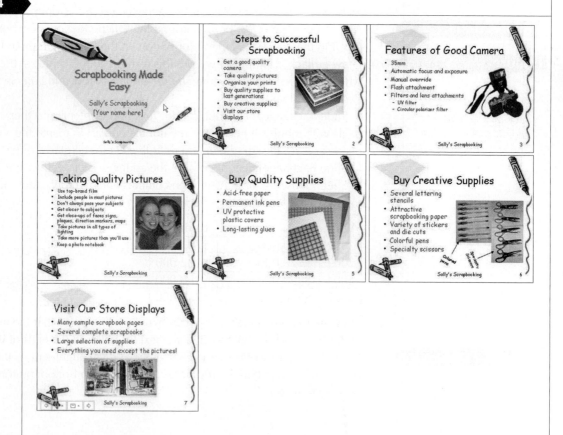

The following information will help you in creating the slide show. Read all the steps before you start creating your presentation.

1. The design template is called "Crayons."
2. The font is Comic Sans MS, the default font for the Crayons design template, but if your system doesn't support Comic Sans MS, you could use Eras Medium BT, Futura Bk BT, Kids, Microsoft Sans Serif, Technical, or some other font of your choosing.
3. In Slide 1, add your name in the subtitle placeholder.
4. Slides 2 through 7 contain one or more bitmap images. You'll find all these images in the Tutorial.02\Cases folder. You should use each image once.
5. The text at the bottom of the slides is a footer and an automatic slide number.
6. Modify the slide master so that the footer on your slides is in the same place as shown in the figure.
7. The content on Slides 2 through 7 reviews the following points:
   a. Quality supplies are critical in scrapbooking.
   b. Scrapbookers need acid-free and lignin-free paper to protect their photos from damage. (Lignin is a substance in paper that yellows over time.)
   c. Scrapbookers need archival-quality pens with ink that won't bleed through the paper.
   d. Page layout is easy with the right die cuts and stickers.
   e. Buy quality cutting tools and keep them sharpened.
   f. File photos in groups to prepare to lay out pages.
8. Remember to check the spelling in the final presentation, and to view the slide show.
9. Print the final presentation in grayscale as handouts with four slides per page.
10. Save the file as **Sally's Scrapbooking** to the Tutorial.02\Cases folder.

Case Problem 4

Data Files you might use in this Case Problem: PESLogo.jpg, PKPBadge.jpg, PKPKey.jpg,

College Honor Society Honor societies recognize students who distinguish themselves in academics and leadership. Your assignment is to prepare a PowerPoint presentation on an honor society at your college or university. Complete the following:

1. Gather information on an honor society from honor society advisors, college advisement centers, or the office of the Dean of Students. For the names, locations, and phone numbers, call information at your college, or consult your student directory or catalog. You can also gather information from the Internet. For general information about members of the Association of College Honor Societies, including a list of most honor societies in the United States and Canada, consult **www.achsnatl.org**. For information on a specific national, nondiscipline-specific honor society, Phi Kappa Phi, consult **www.phikappaphi.org**. For a national freshman honor society, Phi Eta Sigma, consult **www.phietasigma.org**.
2. Create a new PowerPoint presentation based on an appropriate design template. Type the name of the society on the title slide, and type your name as the subtitle.
3. Create at least eight slides with information about the society. Information on your slides might include local and national names and addresses of advisors and officers, purposes, eligibility, activities, scholarships, recognition programs, famous members, history, meetings, local and national conventions, merchandise, and publications.
4. Modify the slide master by adding a text box or graphics object, changing the font attributes, or making some other desired change that will appear on all the slides.

Research

Use the Internet to collect information about a collegiate honor society and create a new presentation based on this information.

5. Include the slide number and an appropriate footer on each slide, except the title slide. In the slide master, change the font style, size, and color, and change the position of the footer and slide number text.

6. Include in your presentation at least one piece of clip art.

Explore

7. Click Insert on the menu bar, point to Picture, and then click Clip Art to open the Clip Art task pane. Click the Clip Art on Office Online link in the task pane to go to Microsoft's Design Gallery Live, where you can search through hundreds of pieces of clip art. Find and insert at least one image connected specifically to the honor society you are describing. If you can't find the image on the Design Gallery Live site, look elsewhere on the Web, or request an image from the local chapter of the honor society. If you choose to describe Phi Kappa Phi or Phi Eta Sigma, bitmap images of their logos are located in the Tutorial.02\Cases folder.

8. Recolor the clip art you inserted to match the presentation color scheme or the colors of the other graphics in your presentation.

9. Include a table or an organizational chart in your presentation. (For information on organizational charts, use the PowerPoint Help system.) You might include a table with the name, description, location, and dates of chapter activities; a table listing the chapter merchandise and prices; or a table with names, addresses, phone numbers, and e-mail addresses of chapter officers. You might include an organizational chart showing the structure of officers in the honor society.

10. Include a drawing that you create from lines, arrows, AutoShapes, or text boxes. For example, you might create a diagram showing the procedure for becoming a member of the honor society, using text boxes and arrows.

11. Apply a second design template to one of the slides.

12. Create a summary slide, and change its title to "Summary of Phi Kappa Phi" (but use the name of your selected honor society).

13. Check the spelling in your presentation, view the slide show, and then save the presentation to the Tutorial.02\Cases folder using the filename **Honor Society**.

14. Print the presentation in grayscale as handouts with four slides per page, and then close the file.

Research

Go to the Web to find information you can use to create presentations.

Internet Assignments

The purpose of the Internet Assignments is to challenge you to find information on the Internet that you can use to work effectively with this software. The actual assignments are updated and maintained on the Course Technology Web site. Log on to the Internet and use your Web browser to go to the Student Online Companion for New Perspectives Office 2003 at **www.course.com/np/office2003**. Click the Internet Assignments link, and then navigate to the assignments for this tutorial.

Assess

SAM Assessment and Training

If you have a SAM user profile, you may have access to hands-on instruction, practice, and assessment of the skills covered in this tutorial. Log in to your SAM account and go to your assignments page to see what your instructor has assigned.

Quick Check Answers

Session 2.1

1. Graphics add information, clarification, emphasis, variety, and pizzazz.
2. a. a file that contains the color scheme, graphics, text formats, and background colors and objects in the presentation
   b. a grid (or "map") of colored dots that form a picture
   c. a picture, clip art, photograph, shape, design, graph, chart, or diagram
   d. the design template applied to a presentation if no other template is chosen (black text on a white background)
3. a. Click anywhere in the text box.
   b. Click the edge of the text box.
   c. Drag a sizing handle.
   d. Drag the object (or in the case of a text box, the edge of the box).
   e. Display the slide in the slide pane, click the list arrow of the desired design template in the Design Template task pane, and then click Apply to Selected Slides.
   f. Select the clip-art image, click the Recolor Picture button on the Picture toolbar, and modify the original colors to new colors.
4. The title master is a slide that contains the objects that appear on the title slide of the presentation. The slide master is a slide that contains the objects that appear on all the slides except the title slide.
5. Tabs add space between the left margin and the beginning of the text on a particular line, or between the text in one column and the text in another column. Tab stops are the locations where text moves when you press the Tab key. Click the Tab button until the Right Tab button appears, and then click the desired location on the ruler.
6. date and time, footer, and slide number

Session 2.2

1. Change the slide layout to a Content layout, click the Insert Table button, set the desired number of columns and rows, insert information into the cells, and modify the table format as desired.
2. upper-left corner
3. a diagram used to show overlap between different elements
4. Click the Text Box button on the Drawing toolbar, and click or drag at the desired location in the slide.
5. Click the AutoShapes list arrow on the Drawing toolbar, point to the appropriate category (such as Basic Shapes), click the desired shape button, move the pointer into the slide pane, and then drag the pointer to draw the figure.
6. Select the triangle, click the Draw button on the Drawing toolbar, point to Rotate or Flip, and then click the appropriate command.
7. Drag the rotate handle of the object in the slide pane.
8. a method for automatically creating a slide with the titles of the slides selected in Slide Sorter view

New Perspectives on
Microsoft® Office PowerPoint® 2003

Read This Before You Begin: Tutorials 3–4

To the Student

Data Files

To complete the Level II PowerPoint Tutorials (Tutorials 3 and 4), you need the starting student Data Files. Your instructor will either provide you with these Data Files or ask you to obtain them yourself.

The Level II PowerPoint tutorials require the folders indicated to complete the Tutorials, Review Assignments, and Case Problems. You will need to copy these folders from a file server, a standalone computer, or the Web to the drive and folder where you will be storing your Data Files. Your instructor will tell you which computer, drive letter, and folder(s) contain the files you need. You can also download the files by going to www.course.com; see the inside back or front cover for more information on downloading the files, or ask your instructor or technical support person for assistance.

If you are storing your Data Files on floppy disks, you will need **five** blank, formatted, high-density disks for these tutorials. Label your disks as shown, and place on them the folder(s) indicated.

▼ **PowerPoint 2003 Level II: Data Disk 1**
Tutorial.03\Tutorial folder

▼ **PowerPoint 2003 Level II: Data Disk 2**
Tutorial.03\Review folder

▼ **PowerPoint 2003 Level II: Data Disk 3**
Tutorial.03\Cases folder

▼ **PowerPoint 2003 Level II: Data Disk 4**
Tutorial.04\Tutorial folder
Tutorial.04\Review folder

▼ **PowerPoint 2003 Level II: Data Disk 5**
Tutorial.04\Cases folder

When you begin a tutorial, refer to the Student Data Files section at the bottom of the tutorial opener page, which indicates which folders and files you need for the tutorial. Each end-of-tutorial exercise also indicates the files you need to complete that exercise. For Tutorials 3 and 4, you should save all your work to a high-capacity disk, such as a Zip disk or the hard disk on your computer. Because of the file sizes generated, you will not be able to save all the files back to your Data Disks if you are working from floppy disks. If you don't have access to a hard disk or some other high-capacity disk, in Tutorial 3, skip those steps in which you're asked to insert a digital image or movie into the presentation; and in Tutorial 4, skip those steps in which you're asked to create a Web page. If you have any questions about the Data Files, see your instructor or technical support person for assistance.

To the Instructor

The Data Files are available on the Instructor Resources CD for this title. Follow the instructions in the Help file on the CD to install the programs to your network or standalone computer. See the "To the Student" section above for information on how to set up the Data Files that accompany this text.

You are granted a license to copy the Data Files to any computer or computer network used by students who have purchased this book.

System Requirements

If you are going to work through this book using your own computer, you need:

- **Computer System** Microsoft Windows 2000, Windows XP, or higher must be installed on your computer. These tutorials assume a complete installation of Microsoft PowerPoint 2003.

- **Data Files** You will not be able to complete the tutorials or exercises in this book using your own computer until you have the necessary starting Data Files.

www.course.com/NewPerspectives

Objectives

Session 3.1
- Insert slides from another presentation
- Create and apply a custom design template
- Apply graphics and sounds
- Add a textured background

Session 3.2
- Create a chart (graph)
- Create an organization chart
- Apply slide transitions and animations
- Use the pointer pen during a slide show
- Hide slides in a presentation
- Prepare a presentation to run on another computer

Labs

Student Data Files

Presenting a Slide Show

Customizing and Preparing a Presentation

Case

Global Humanitarian, Peru Expedition

Pablo Fuentes, the managing director of Global Humanitarian in Lima, Peru, recently led a humanitarian expedition to Paqarimuy, a village in the Peruvian altiplano. The board of directors of Global Humanitarian asked Pablo to give a report on the expedition. He decided that he wants to present the report using a PowerPoint presentation, and he now asks you to help him prepare the presentation. He emphasizes the importance of preparing a high-quality presentation that includes a custom design template, graphics, sound effects, animations, charts, graphs, and other elements to maximize the visual effects of the presentation.

To help you get started, Pablo prepared a presentation with most of the text and some of the graphics of the expedition report. He also gave you access to other PowerPoint presentations from which you can extract slides.

In this tutorial, you'll insert slides from one presentation into another presentation; create a custom design template; add a digital image, movie, and sound clips to a presentation; create a graph and organization chart; apply special visual effects to your slides; and save the presentation ro a CD so it can be run on another computer.

▼ **Tutorial.03**

▽ **Tutorial folder**
MPLogo.jpg
Paq.wav
PaqaPic.jpg
PaqMovie.avi
PeruPlan.ppt
PeruRep.ppt
Taq.wav

▽ **Review folder**
Cuzco.wav
CuzcTour.ppt
HuaynaP.wav
MachPicc.wav
PeruExp.ppt
PeruLogo.jpg
SacsMov.avi
SacsSnd.wav

▽ **Cases folder**
ACWBus.ppt GeNetics.ppt
Alaskan.ppt kitchen.jpg
Applause.wav livingrm.jpg
Atorv.jpg Totem.jpg
bedrm1.jpg
bedrm2.jpg
Bonnie.jpg
Bowls.jpg.
cabinfnt.jpg
Drugs.jpg
fireplac.jpg
fitness.jpg

Planning the Presentation

Before you begin to create Pablo's slide show, he discusses with you the purpose of, and the audience for, his presentation:

- **Purpose of the presentation**: to present details of the recent humanitarian expedition to Paqarimuy
- **Type of presentation**: report
- **Audience**: Global Humanitarian's board of directors
- **Audience needs**: an overview of the expedition with pictures and data
- **Location of the presentation**: small boardroom for the Board of Directors; office or classroom for other interested parties
- **Format**: on-screen slide show

   With this general plan for the presentation, Pablo prepares the text and some of the pictures for the report.

Inserting Slides from Another Presentation

After Pablo discusses his presentation plan with you, he gives you two presentation files: PeruRep, which contains the text and some pictures to include with his report; and PeruPlan, a presentation used to show expedition plans to prospective volunteers. First, you'll open PeruRep and look through it to see what information Pablo has already included. Then, you'll add slides to it from the PeruPlan presentation.

   To insert slides from another presentation, you first need to open the presentation to which you want to add the slides. Then you use the Slides from File command on the Insert menu to insert specific slides from any other presentation. If the inserted slides have a different design than the current presentation, the design of the current presentation will override the design of the inserted slides.

Reference Window | **Inserting Slides from Another Presentation**

- Go to the slide after which you want to insert slides from another presentation.
- Click Insert on the menu bar, and then click Slides from File to open the Slide Finder dialog box.
- Click the Browse button, and then open the presentation file in the Slide Finder dialog box from which you want to get the slides.
- Click the slides that you want inserted into your presentation to select them.
- Click the Insert button, and then click the Close button in the Slide Finder dialog box.

To open the PeruRep presentation and save it with a new name:

1. Open the file **PeruRep**, located in the Tutorial.03\Tutorial folder included with your Data Files.

2. Maximize the PowerPoint window, if necessary.

3. Save the presentation file as **Peru Expedition Report**. See Figure 3-1.

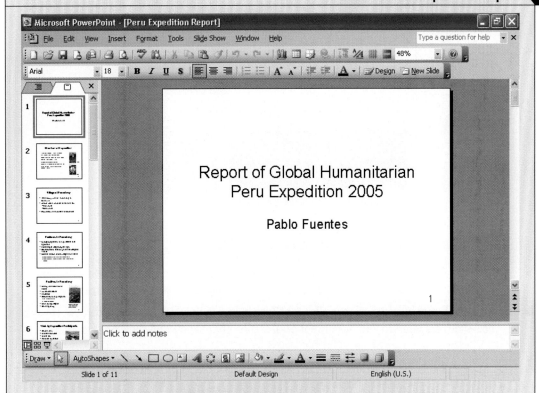

Trouble? If you're using a floppy disk for your Data Files, you won't have enough space to save the file you create in this tutorial. If you don't have access to a hard disk or some other high-capacity disk, skip those steps in which you're asked to insert a digital image or a movie into the presentation. Then you'll have enough room to save the results to a floppy disk.

4. Scroll through all 11 slides of the presentation so you have an idea of its current content. Notice that there is no design template applied to this presentation because you are going to create your own design template later in this tutorial.

Your first task is to insert slides from the presentation file PeruPlan. Pablo told you that he wants you to insert Slides 2 and 3 from PeruPlan.

To insert slides from one presentation into another:

1. Go to **Slide 2** of Peru Expedition Report. When you insert slides from another presentation, they are inserted after the current slide.

2. Click **Insert** on the menu bar, and then click **Slides from Files**. The Slide Finder dialog box opens.

3. Click the **Browse** button, navigate to the **Tutorial.03\Tutorial** folder included with your Data Files, and then double-click **PeruPlan**. The slides in PeruPlan are listed horizontally in the Slide Finder dialog box. Notice that the slides have a shaded red background and that the slide titles are yellow. See Figure 3-2.

Figure 3-2 | **Slide Finder dialog box**

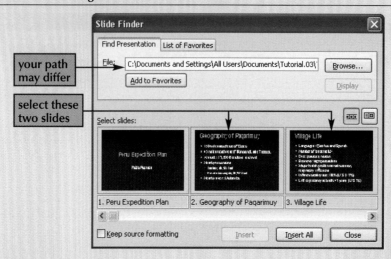

4. Click the **Slide 2** thumbnail ("Geography of Paqarimuy"), and then click the **Slide 3** thumbnail ("Village Life") to select them. The two selected slides have a dark-blue frame around them.

5. Click the **Insert** button, and then click the **Close** button in the Slide Finder dialog box. The two new slides are inserted into the current presentation after the current slide. See Figure 3-3.

Figure 3-3 | **New Slide 4 after inserting two slides from other presentation**

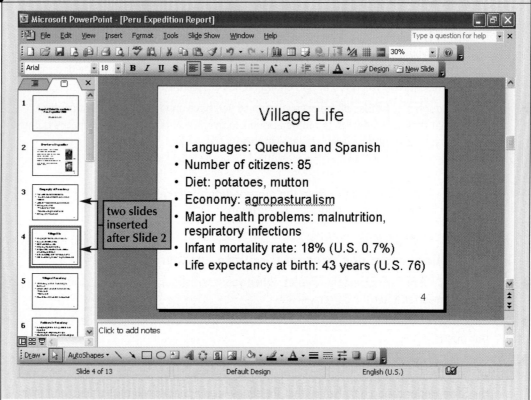

Slides 2 and 3 from PeruPlan are now Slides 3 and 4 in Peru Expedition Report. The two new slides contain detailed information about the village that was helped during the Peru expedition. The Peru Expedition Report presentation now has 13 slides.

With most of the slides now created for the presentation, you're ready to create a custom design template.

Creating a Custom Design Template

As you recall, a design template is a file that contains the color scheme, attributes, and format for the titles, main text, other text, and background for the presentation. You have used several of the design templates that come with PowerPoint. Sometimes, however, you'll want to design your own, custom template. When you create a design template, you need to make sure that the colors go well together, that the text remains clear and legible, and that the color scheme meets the needs of your presentation.

Reference Window

Creating a Custom Design Template

- Using an existing or new presentation, create the desired color scheme, bullets, fonts, background color, and background graphics.
- If you don't want any existing slides, text, or other objects in your custom design template, delete all but the first slide, and delete any text or foreground objects from the slide.
- Click File, click Save As, click the Save as type list arrow, and then click Design Template.
- Navigate to the desired location in the Save in list box, type a filename, and then click the Save button.

For the report on the Peru expedition, Pablo doesn't want you to use any of the built-in design templates; instead, he wants you to create a completely original design that better matches the subject and the colors of the pictures.

Creating a Custom Color Scheme

A **color scheme** is a set of matching colors that makes up the background, fonts, and other elements of a presentation. Each of the design templates included with PowerPoint, including the Default Design template, has several color schemes associated with it. It is easy to select colors that don't match or make text illegible; for example, red text on a blue background might seem like a good combination, but it's actually difficult to read at a distance from the screen. It's usually safer, therefore, to select one of the built-in color schemes and stick to it, or make only minor modifications.

A PowerPoint color scheme includes eight items to which you can assign a color:

- **Background**—the default color of the area on which you add text and other objects.
- **Text and lines**—the default color of the body text and of lines drawn on the slide.
- **Shadows**—the default color of the shadow applied to an object (e.g., a shape or a text box). This does not, however, specify the color of the text shadow that you apply using the Font dialog box.
- **Title text**—the default color of the title (but not the subtitle) text on the title slide and of the title text on other slide layouts.
- **Fills**—the default color that fills shapes (e.g., the color of a square or circle).
- **Accent**—a color that might appear automatically in a PowerPoint chart or graph or one that you can use, if you choose, for bullets, fills, and accented text. Accent colors appear by default only in multicolored charts, but not automatically in text, AutoShapes, lines, and other objects.

- **Accent and hyperlink**—the default color for hyperlink text and another color that might appear by default in multicolored charts.
- **Accent and followed hyperlink**—the default color for hyperlinks that have been followed; in other words, if you click a hyperlink and thereby jump to another location, when you return to the original slide, the color of the hyperlink text will be changed to indicate that you have followed that hyperlink. This color also appears by default in some multicolored charts.

Once you have specified a coordinated set of eight colors, they will appear by default in text and objects, but you can use any of the eight to change the default color of text, fills, shadows, and so forth.

As you look at the pictures of Paqarimuy, you can see that the colors are mostly earth tones—browns and yellows—so you'll create a color scheme now using those colors.

To create a custom color scheme:

1. Click the **Design** button on the Formatting toolbar to display the Slide Design task pane, and then click the **Color Schemes** link in the task pane. The task pane changes to show the color schemes associated with the current design. You can create the color scheme with any slide in the slide pane.

2. If necessary, scroll down so you can see the last color scheme in the task pane, the one with the dark-brown background. See Figure 3-4.

Figure 3-4 | Slide Design task pane open

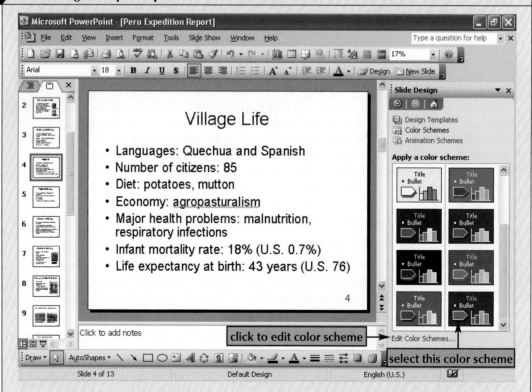

3. Click the color scheme thumbnail with the dark-brown background and tan title text, located in the bottom-right corner of the task pane. PowerPoint applies the color scheme to all the slides in your presentation.

You think the title text could stand out a little more, so next, you'll modify the color of the title text.

4. Click the **Edit Color Schemes** link at the bottom of the task pane. The Edit Color Scheme dialog box opens with the Custom tab on top. Here you can see color tiles of each of the major elements of the slide—the background, the text and lines, the shadows, and so forth.

5. Click the **Title text** tile, click the **Change Color** button to open the Title Text Color dialog box, and then click the **Standard** tab. See Figure 3-5.

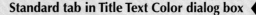 **Standard tab in Title Text Color dialog box** **Figure 3-5**

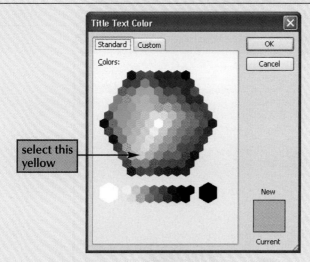

6. Click the bright-yellow tile indicated in Figure 3-5, and then click the **OK** button. The Title Text Color dialog box closes. The Title text color tile changes from tan to yellow, and the title text in the preview pane on the right side of the dialog box changes to yellow also.

7. Click the **Apply** button. The Edit Color Scheme dialog box closes and the new color scheme is applied to your presentation. As you can see in the slide pane, the title is now bright yellow. If you look at the other slides on the Slides tab on the left, you see that the titles on those slides are also bright yellow.

8. Click the **Close** button ✕ on the task pane title bar.

You'll now change the background of the slides. You could have used the Edit Color Scheme dialog box to change to a solid color for the background (by clicking the Background tile), but if you want special effects, such as shading, you must use the Background dialog box.

Creating a Custom Background

The color scheme of your presentation has a brown background, but Pablo asks you to add shading to the background to add interest and a professional touch to the presentation. You decide to use a **gradient fill**, which is a type of shading in which one color blends into another or varies from one shade to another.

When you use a gradient fill, you also choose a shading style and a variant. The **shading style** identifies the direction in which the shading will be applied—horizontally, vertically, diagonally up, diagonally down, from a corner, or from the title. A **variant** is a variation of a particular shading style; there are four variants of each shading style.

You'll change the background of your presentation to a two-color gradient fill.

To create a custom background with a two-color gradient fill:

1. Click **Format** on the menu bar, and then click **Background**. The Background dialog box opens.

2. Click the **Background fill** list arrow (underneath the preview box), and then click **Fill Effects**. The Fill Effects dialog box opens.

3. Click the **Gradient** tab, if necessary, and then click the **Two colors** option button in the Colors section. Two shades of the background color appear on the right side of the Colors section. See Figure 3-6.

| Figure 3-6 | Gradient tab in Fill Effects dialog box |

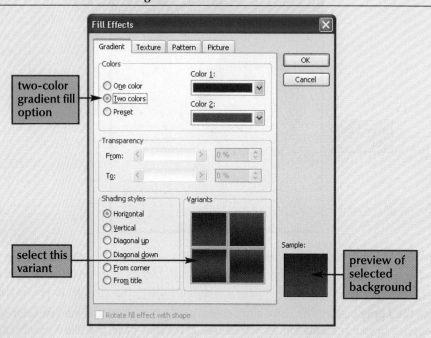

PowerPoint automatically sets the two colors to dark brown and medium brown. You can change one or both of these colors by clicking the Color 1 or Color 2 list arrows and then selecting the desired color, but a dark gradient fill works well with light text colors, so you choose to keep the two colors as they are. The horizontal shading style is selected by default, and this style works well for most presentations. The default variant is the variant in the upper-left corner of the Variants section of the dialog box in which the color varies from dark to light. You'll use the default shading style, but you'll select a different variant.

4. Click the variant in the lower-left corner of the Variants section, as indicated in Figure 3-6. This variant places the dark brown at the top and bottom of the slide, and the lighter brown in the middle.

5. Click the **OK** button. The Fill Effects dialog box closes.

6. Click the **Apply to All** button in the Background dialog box. The Background dialog box closes, and the background gradient fill and variant you selected are applied to all the slides.

7. Save the presentation.

As you can see from the slide pane and the Slides tab, all of the slides now have a background with a gradient fill. You'll now modify the fonts used on the slides.

Modifying Fonts and Bullets

All the current text in your presentation is in a sans serif font called Arial. This is a good general-purpose font, but Pablo wants something with a bit more pizzazz. In this case, he wants you to change the title font from Arial to Impact, a thicker sans serif font, and change the body text font from Arial to Book Antiqua, an attractive serif font. Rather than change the fonts on each of the individual slides, you can make these changes for all the slides at once by changing the fonts on the slide master and title master. As you might recall, the title master contains the objects that appear on the title slide, and the slide master contains the objects that appear on all the slides except the title slide. Now you'll modify the fonts on these two masters.

To modify the fonts on the slide master:

▶ 1. Shift-click the **Normal View** button 🖽. (If you position the mouse pointer over the Normal button while you hold down the Shift key, you'll see that the ScreenTip becomes Slide Master View.)

▶ 2. Click the border of the title placeholder text box to select the entire box, click the **Font** list arrow `Arial` ▾ on the Formatting toolbar, scroll down until you see **Impact**, and then click that font name. The title font changes from Arial to Impact.

Trouble? If your computer doesn't have the Impact font installed, keep Arial as the font, but make it bold by clicking the Bold button **B** on the Formatting toolbar.

▶ 3. Select the placeholder text box for the bulleted list text (the body text), and change the font to **Book Antiqua**. See Figure 3-7.

Trouble? If your computer doesn't have the Book Antiqua font installed, select Times New Roman instead.

Slide master with new fonts ◀ **Figure 3-7**

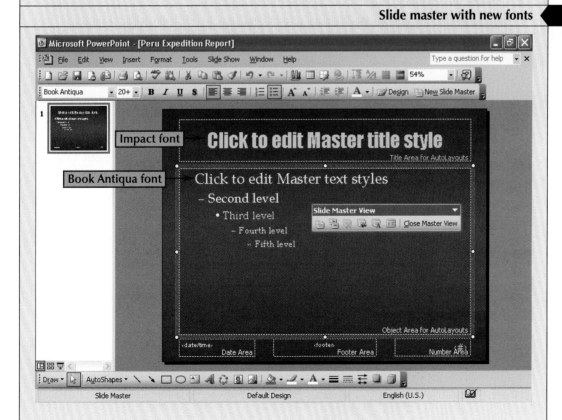

You have made the fonts more interesting. Now you're ready to change the bullets.

To change the bullets style on the slide master:

▶ 1. Right-click the line that reads "Click to edit Master text styles," and then click **Bullets and Numbering** on the shortcut menu. The Bullets and Numbering dialog box opens with the Bulleted tab on top. See Figure 3-8.

| **Figure 3-8** | **Bullet tab in Bullets and Numbering dialog box** |

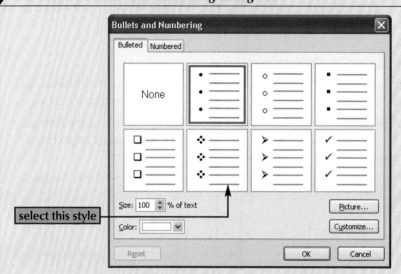

select this style

▶ 2. Click the four-diamond bullet style, as indicated in Figure 3-8.

Trouble? If you don't see the four-diamond bullet style in your dialog box, choose another style.

▶ 3. Click the **Color** list arrow, and then click the bright-yellow tile. The new bullets will be bright yellow.

▶ 4. Click the **OK** button to accept the changes to the top-level bullets. You now see a yellow four-diamond bullet on the first-level bulleted item.

▶ 5. Using the same procedure, change the bullet in the second line ("Second level") to a solid, blue-gray, small square. (The blue-gray color is the right-most tile on the color palette.)

▶ 6. Click the **Normal View** button ▣ to return to Normal view, and then click the **Slide 3** thumbnail in the Slides tab to see the effect of the changes you made. See Figure 3-9.

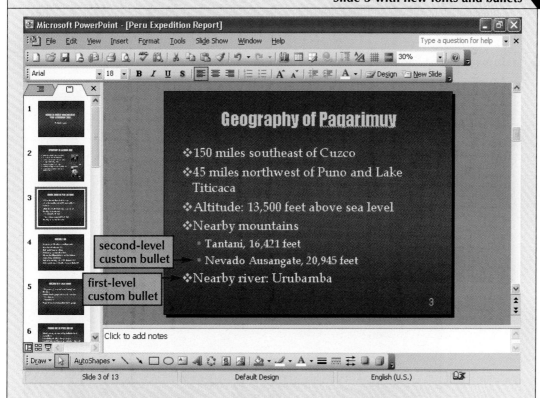

Trouble? If your bullet characters or colors are different from those shown in Figure 3-9, return to the slide master and make any necessary changes.

7. Save the presentation.

You've almost completed the custom design template. Your final task is to add a digital image to the title and slide masters.

Adding a Background Image

Pablo realizes that the best-known image of Peru is Machu Picchu, the ancient Incan ruins located on the edge of the Peruvian jungle. He wants you to add a photo of Machu Picchu to the background of all the slides in the presentation.

Because Pablo wants this image to be on all the slides in the presentation, you'll add it to the title and slide masters. (You'll recall that you added an image to the background when you worked with the title and slide masters in Tutorial 2.)

To add a background image to the slide master:

1. Shift-click the **Normal View** button ▣ to return to Slide Master view.

2. Click the **Insert Picture** button ▣ on the Drawing toolbar. The Insert Picture dialog box opens.

3. Click the **Look in** list arrow and navigate to the **Tutorial.03\Tutorial** folder included with your Data Files, click **MPLogo**, if necessary, and then click the **Insert** button. A small picture of Machu Picchu appears in the middle of the slide master.

4. Drag the picture so it's positioned with its left edge flush with the left edge of the title placeholder text box, and then adjust the size of the title text box so its left edge is to the right of the picture. See Figure 3-10.

Figure 3-10 | **Slide master after adding logo and adjusting title placeholder**

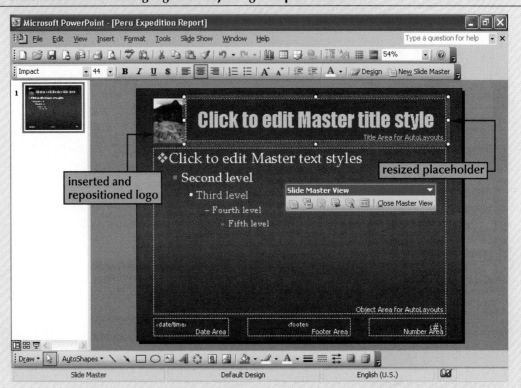

Trouble? If the Slide Master View toolbar is in the way, drag it out of the way by its title bar.

Recall that the title text on the title slide is in a different position than the title text on the rest of the slides. But notice that PowerPoint doesn't automatically include a title master with the Default Design template. You'll need to add a title master, and then modify it to reposition the background graphic to an appropriate spot.

5. Click the **Insert New Title Master** button 🔳 on the Slide Master View toolbar. A title master is added and the view switches to Title Master view.

Next, you'll change the size of the Machu Picchu picture. In the past, when you changed a picture size, you dragged the sizing handles. However, if you want to change the picture to a specific, predetermined size (in this case, two inches in height), you should use the Size tab in the Format Picture dialog box. You'll do that now.

6. Click the **Machu Picchu** image to select it, and then click the **Format Picture** button 🔳 on the Picture toolbar. The Format Picture dialog box opens.

Trouble? If the Picture toolbar does not appear on your screen, click View on the menu bar, point to Toolbars, and then click Picture.

7. Click the **Size** tab, drag to select the value in the Height text box in the Size and rotate section, type **2**, make sure that the **Lock aspect ratio** check box is checked, and then click the **OK** button. The image is resized so that the height is two inches and the width is proportional to the original width.

8. Drag the **Machu Picchu** picture into the title master so it's centered just above the title placeholder text box, as shown in Figure 3-11.

Title master after moving logo   Figure 3-11

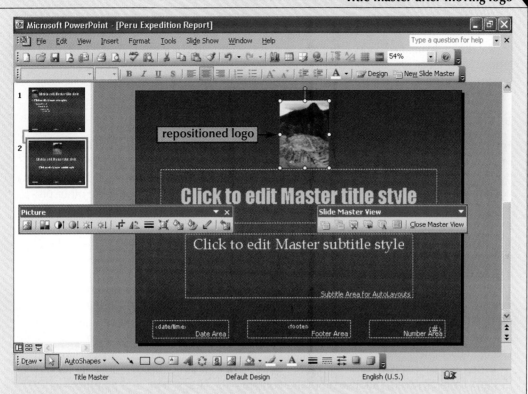

9. Resize the two title placeholders to a little larger than half their original height by selecting each one and dragging a sizing handle, and then drag the picture and the two title place-holders down so they are better centered vertically in the slide, as shown in Figure 3-12.

Title master after moving objects   Figure 3-12

▶ **10.** Click the **Normal View** button 🔲 to return to Normal view, and then save the presentation.

The design template is now complete, with a customized color scheme, gradient background, new fonts, and the picture of Machu Picchu in the background of all the slides. Pablo now asks you to save the custom design template so he can apply it to other presentations.

Saving a Custom Design Template

You used several built-in design templates in earlier tutorials by clicking the Design button on the Formatting toolbar to display the Slide Design task pane, and then clicking the desired design template. What if you want to use a custom design template? That's exactly what Pablo wants. When he creates another expedition plan, report, or some other presentation that would look good using the custom design of the Peru Expedition Report presentation, he wants to be able to select that design from the task pane, just as he would any other design template. Fortunately, PowerPoint allows you to save the design from any PowerPoint presentation as a design template.

The default location for a PowerPoint presentation saved as a design template is the Templates folder. If you save a design template to that folder, then the next time you start PowerPoint, your custom template will appear as one of the templates in the Slide Design task pane. No matter where a template is stored, however, you can create a new presentation based on the template by clicking the Browse link at the bottom of the Slide Design task pane.

When you save a PowerPoint presentation as a design template, not only are all the design elements saved, but also all of the content—the slides, text, and graphics—is saved. Therefore, you usually want to delete all the slides but the title slide, and you even want to delete the text and foreground graphic (if any) from that slide, leaving only the objects on the title master and slide master. This will reduce the file size and conform to the standard of built-in templates. You'll delete the content and then save the custom design template now.

To save a presentation as a design template:

▶ **1.** Click the **Slide Sorter View** button 🔡 to switch to Slide Sorter view, click **Edit** on the menu bar, click **Select All** to select all the slides, press and hold the **Ctrl** key, click **Slide 1** to deselect just that slide, and then release the **Ctrl** key. All the slides except Slide 1 are now selected, as indicated by the thick border around them.

▶ **2.** Press the **Delete** key to delete all the selected slides. Only Slide 1 remains.

▶ **3.** Return to Normal view, and then delete all of the text (but not the placeholder text boxes) on the slide. Only the design and title master graphics and placeholders remain on the slide. See Figure 3-13.

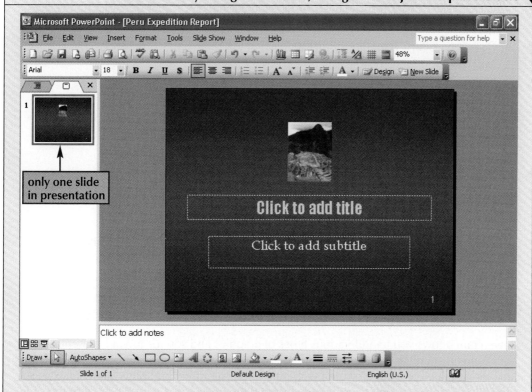

4. Click **File**, click **Save As**, click the **Save as type** list arrow, and then click **Design Template**. The Save in folder changes to Templates. Normally, you would save a design template file in this folder. For the purposes of this tutorial, however, you need to save your template file to the same location where you saved Peru Expedition Report (in the Tutorial.03\Tutorial folder).

5. Click the **Save in** list arrow, and then navigate to the **Tutorial.03\Tutorial** folder included with your Data Files (or to the location where you saved Peru Expedition Report).

6. Replace the text in the File name text box with **Peru Template**, and then click the **Save** button. PowerPoint saves the file as a design template.

7. Click the **Close Window** button ⊠ on the right side of the menu bar. PowerPoint should still be running, but with no file in the presentation window.

You have now created a custom design template that Pablo and others can use with any new presentation.

Using a Custom Design Template

You decide to test your new custom design template on a new presentation.

To apply a custom design template:

1. Click the **New** button 🗋 on the Standard toolbar to open a new presentation.

2. Click the **Design** button on the Formatting toolbar to open the Slide Design task pane. Because you saved your design template in the Tutorial.03\Tutorial folder rather than in the default design template folder, your new template doesn't appear in the task pane, so you need to direct PowerPoint to your folder by clicking the Browse link.

3. Click the **Browse** link at the bottom of the Slide Design task pane, and then change the Look in folder to the **Tutorial.03\Tutorial** folder included with your Data Files (or the location where you saved Peru Template).

4. Double-click **Peru Template** in the list of files in the Tutorial.03\Tutorial folder. As you can see, the new presentation has the design of your custom design template.

5. Click the **New Slide** button on the Formatting toolbar to create a Title and Text slide. Again, you can see the design of your custom design template, with the yellow title text, the picture of Machu Picchu in the upper-left corner, and the yellow diamond bullet in the main text placeholder. If you were actually creating a presentation, you would add text and other objects to the title slide and to the other slides.

6. Click the **Close Window** button ⊠ on the right side of the menu bar, and then click the **No** button in the dialog box that asks if you want to save changes.

You can now report to Pablo that your custom design template works as planned.

Multimedia

Applying Graphics and Sounds to Your Presentation

PowerPoint allows you to add various types of graphics and sounds to your presentation. You're already familiar with adding clip art, drawn images, and digital photos to a slide. In fact, the original PeruPlan file came with images of Paqarimuy and other places and people of Peru. Moreover, you have already inserted the image of Machu Picchu into the slide background, and in Tutorial 2, you inserted a photo, clip art, and drawings you created using the tools on the Drawing toolbar. In addition to still photos and other graphics, you can insert movies and sounds into a presentation.

Reference Window	**Adding Movies and Sounds to a Presentation**

- On the slide to which you want to add a movie or sound, click Insert on the menu bar, point to Movies and Sounds, and then click the desired source (the Clip Organizer or a user-specified file) for the movie or sound.
- Select the movie or sound file from a specified folder and click the OK button, or click the desired movie or sound in the Clip Art task pane.
- When asked whether you want the movie or sound to start automatically or when clicked, click either the Automatically or When Clicked button.

For the presentation on the Peru expedition, you'll use photos, movies, and sound files that are included with your Data Files. In other presentations, you might have to acquire the graphics and sounds in other ways. For example, you can do the following:

- Use a digital camera to take digital photographs.
- Scan prints of photos or slides to create digital images.
- Create images or movies using graphics software.
- Record sound files with a microphone attached to your computer and appropriate software.
- Download images or sound clips from the Internet.
- Insert images or sounds from the PowerPoint Clip Art Organizer.
- Use built-in PowerPoint sound effects (you'll learn about these later in this tutorial).

Pablo asks you to insert a digital image of the village of Paqarimuy into Slide 3, a video clip of the Peruvian altiplano into Slide 5, and sound clips into Slides 2 and 6. All of these files were created by Pablo or other members of the humanitarian expedition.

Adding a Digital Photo to a Slide

In Tutorial 2, you added a photo to the slide master. In a similar way, you can add any photo to a slide as long as it is in, or converted to, a digital format. The procedure for adding a photo to a slide is the same as the procedure for adding a photo to the slide master. You'll begin by adding the digital image to Slide 3.

To add an image to a slide:

▶ 1. Open **Peru Expedition Report** and go to **Slide 3** ("Geography of Paqarimuy").

▶ 2. Make sure the Slide Layout task pane appears on the right side of your screen, and then click the thumbnail for the **Title, Text, and Content** layout (the top-left thumbnail under Text and Content Layouts). The slide layout now includes a title, a placeholder for bulleted text, and a content placeholder on the right side of the slide.

▶ 3. If the bulleted text extends below the bottom of the slide, click anywhere in the body text box, click the **AutoFit Options** button ⬒ located in the slide pane adjacent to the selected text box, and then click the **AutoFit Text to Placeholder** option button. The font size automatically decreases so that all the text fits on the slide. See Figure 3-14.

Slide 3 after changing slide layout ◀ **Figure 3-14**

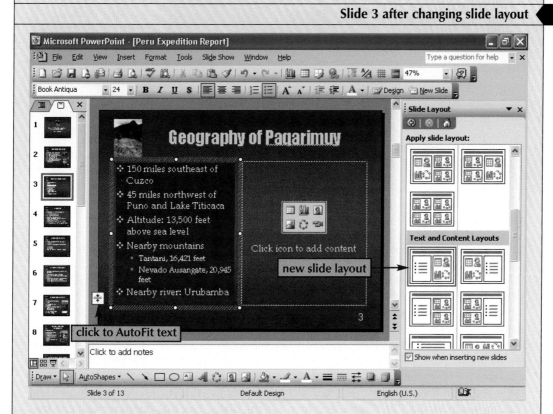

▶ 4. Click the **Insert Picture** button 🖾 in the content placeholder. The Insert Picture dialog box opens.

▶ **5.** If necessary, click the **Look in** list arrow and switch to the **Tutorial.03\Tutorial** folder included with your Data Files, click **PaqaPic** (a digital photograph of the village of Paqarimuy), and then click the **Insert** button. The picture of Paqarimuy is inserted into the slide. See Figure 3-15.

Figure 3-15 | **Slide 3 after adding picture**

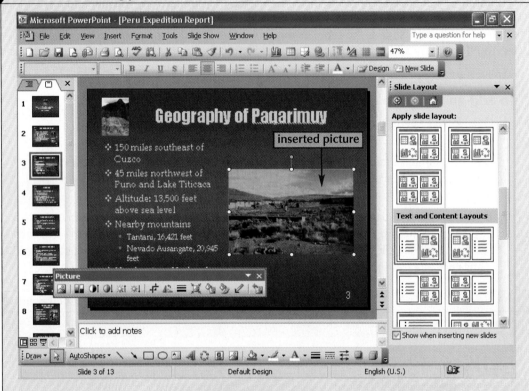

▶ **6.** Click a blank area of the slide to deselect the picture.

You could have moved or resized the picture of Paqarimuy, but its position and size are adequate.

Adding a Movie

A **video clip**, or **digital movie**, is an animated picture file. Files with the filename extension .avi are video clips. Another common video format is an animated GIF. An **animated GIF** file is actually a series of images that are quickly displayed one after another. These files are identified with the file extension .gif.

Pablo wants to give his audience an idea of how barren and desolate the Peruvian altiplano can be, so he asks you to add a video clip to one of the slides. Pablo's video clip shows a 180-degree pan of the land around Paqarimuy. He prepared a simple, low-resolution video clip for this purpose. He made it low resolution to keep the file size smaller so it would load faster into the PowerPoint presentation and take up less disk space.

You can insert a video clip in two ways. You can change the layout to a Content layout, click the Insert Media Clip button, and then use the dialog box that opens, or you can use commands on the menu bar. You'll add the movie now using the Insert Media Clip button in a Content layout.

To add a movie to a slide and view it:

▶ **1.** Go to **Slide 5**, click the **Title, Text and Content** layout, and then close the task pane.

▶ **2.** Click the **Insert Media Clip** button in the content placeholder. The Media Clip dialog box opens, displaying thumbnails of all available media clips, both video and sound, that have been categorized in the Microsoft Clip Organizer. The Clip Organizer lets you add clips to or delete clips from the Clip Art task pane. Video clips are identified by an animation star in the lower-right corner of the thumbnail.

You need to import the video clip that Pablo recorded into the Clip Organizer.

▶ **3.** Click the **Import** button in the Media Clip dialog box, click the **Look in** list arrow, navigate to the **Tutorial.03\Tutorial** folder included with your Data Files, click **PaqMovie**, and then click the **Add** button. The clip appears as the first clip in the Media Clip dialog box.

Trouble? If the clip is already in the Media Clip dialog box, you don't need to add it again, although doing so is not a problem.

▶ **4.** Double-click the **PaqMovie** thumbnail in the Media Clip dialog box. PowerPoint displays a message asking you how you want your movie to start—automatically, or when clicked during the slide show. In other words, do you want the movie to begin automatically as soon as the slide appears during the slide show, or do you want the viewer or presenter to click the movie to play it?

▶ **5.** Click the **Automatically** button to indicate that you want the movie to play automatically. The first frame of the movie appears in the right side of the slide. Now you'll increase the size of the movie picture, but you don't want to make it too big or its low resolution will become a distraction.

▶ **6.** Drag the upper-right sizing handle of the picture until the height is about two inches, move the picture to the right-center of the slide, and then resize the text box so its right edge is near the left edge of the movie picture. Compare your screen to Figure 3-16 and make any necessary adjustments.

Slide 5 after inserting movie ◀ **Figure 3-16**

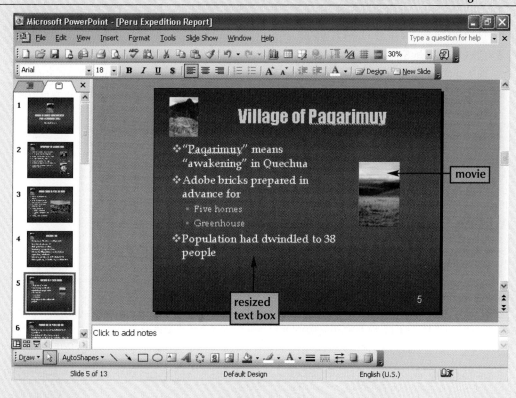

Having inserted the digital movie, you are now ready to view it.

▶ **7.** Double-click the **movie** object. As you can see, the movie shows the rolling hills of the puna grassland and high Andes Mountains, along with alpaca grazing in the foreground. In fact, the video is an animated, wider-angled view of the picture shown in Slide 7.

Because you clicked the Automatically button, the movie will play when Slide 5 appears during the slide show. But Pablo wants the movie to play continuously while Slide 5 is on the screen during the slide show. You'll set the movie so that it loops continuously.

To edit the movie object:

▶ **1.** Right-click the **movie** object, and then click **Edit Movie Object** on the shortcut menu. The Movie Options dialog box opens. This dialog box includes several options for playing and displaying the clip while the slide show is running. See Figure 3-17.

Figure 3-17	▶ Movie Options dialog box

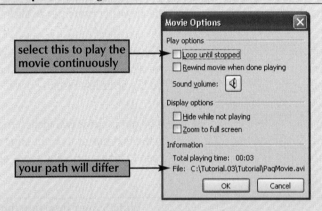

▶ **2.** Click the **Loop until stopped** check box to select it, and then click the **OK** button.

Now you'll test it to see how it works.

▶ **3.** Click the **Slide Show from current slide** button 🖵 to start the slide show from the current slide. Slide 5 appears in Slide Show view and the movie plays continuously.

▶ **4.** Right-click anywhere on the slide, and then click **End Show** on the shortcut menu to return to Normal view.

▶ **5.** Save the presentation.

Next, you'll add sound to your presentation.

Adding Sound Clips

Now that you've added the movie, Pablo wants you to add sound clips of the spoken names of the two villages mentioned in the presentation: Paqarimuy and Taquile. If someone views the presentation without his assistance, the pronunciation of these two names will be available. Pablo's recordings are in .wav files, which is the most common file format for short sound clips.

As with video clips, there are a couple of ways you can add a sound clip to a slide. You can use the Insert Media Clip button in a Content layout, as you did when you inserted the video clip, or you can use menu commands. You'll add the sound files now using menu commands.

To add sound clips to the presentation:

1. Go to **Slide 2**, where the word "Paqarimuy" first appears in the presentation.

2. Click **Insert** on the menu bar, point to **Movies and Sounds**, and then click **Sound from File**. The Insert Sound dialog box opens.

3. Click the **Paq** sound file, located in the **Tutorial.03\Tutorial** folder included with your Data Files, click the **OK** button, and then click the **When Clicked** button to indicate that you don't want the sound to play automatically. PowerPoint inserts a sound icon in the middle of the slide to indicate that a sound clip is available on that slide.

4. Drag the **sound** icon immediately to the right of "Paqarimuy, Peru," and then click a blank area of the slide to deselect the icon. See Figure 3-18.

Slide 2 after inserting sound clip ◀ | Figure 3-18

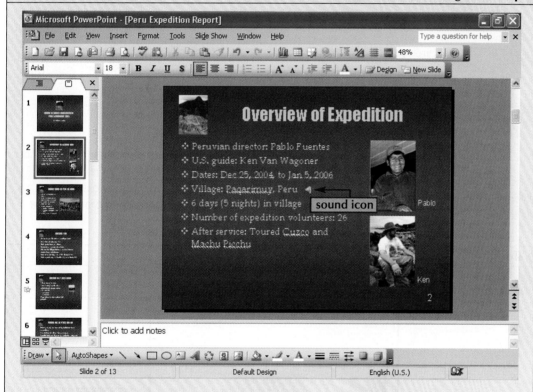

5. Double-click the **sound** icon to play the sound clip.

6. Go to **Slide 6**, where the name of another Peruvian village (Taquile) appears.

7. Using the same method as before, insert the sound clip **Taq** (located in the **Tutorial.03\Tutorial** folder included with your Data Files) into Slide 6, and then drag its **sound** icon to the right of the word "Taquile." Make sure you indicate that you want the sound clip to play when clicked.

8. Double-click the **sound** icon in Slide 6 to hear the pronunciation of "Taquile."

9. Click the **Slide Show from current slide** button 🖵. Slide 6 appears in Slide Show view.

10. Click the **sound** icon on the slide, listen to the sound being played, and then press the **Esc** key to end the slide show and return to Normal view.

11. Save the presentation.

Now, anyone who wants to know how to pronounce the names of the villages can click the sound icons during the slide show.

Adding a Textured Background

Pablo was so pleased with the work of the expedition volunteers that he wants a way to highlight Slide 12, which shows a group photograph of the volunteers. He decides that he wants you to add an appropriate textured background to the slide. You'll do that now.

Reference Window | **Applying a Textured Background**

- Click Format on the menu bar, and then click Background to display the Background dialog box.
- Click the Background fill list arrow, and then click Fill Effects to display the Fill Effects dialog box.
- Click the Texture tab, click the desired texture tile, click the OK button, and then click the Apply or Apply to All button.

To add a textured background:

1. Go to **Slide 12**, click **Format** on the menu bar, click **Background** to display the Background dialog box, click the **Background fill** list arrow, click **Fill Effects** to display the Fill Effects dialog box, and then click the **Texture** tab. As you can see, PowerPoint provides various textures that you can use as slide backgrounds, including green, white, and brown marble. See Figure 3-19.

Figure 3-19 | **Texture tab in Fill Effects dialog box**

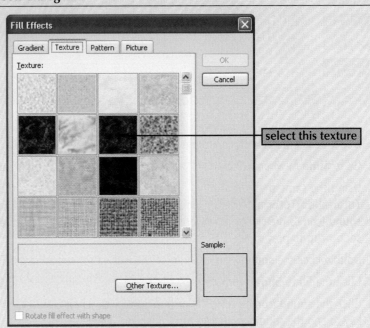

You'll select the brown marble for the background of Slide 12.

▶ **2.** Click the **Brown marble** tile (as indicated in Figure 3-19), click the **OK** button to return to the Background dialog box, and then click the **Apply** button. The brown marble background appears in Slide 12. If you had clicked the Apply to All button, the textured background would have appeared on all the slides. See Figure 3-20.

Slide 12 with textured background ◀ **Figure 3-20**

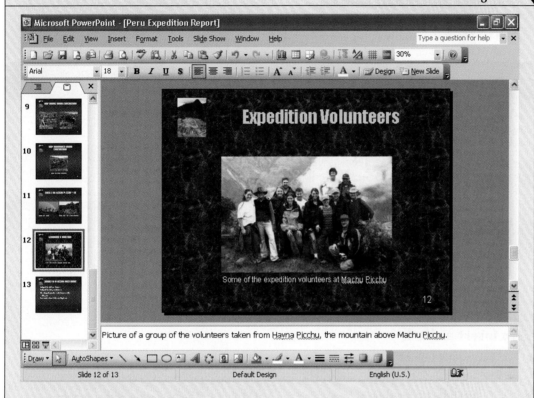

▶ **3.** Save the presentation.

Pablo is pleased with how Slide 12 stands out from the others, and he is happy with the progress you're making on the presentation.

Session 3.1 Quick Check

Review

1. Describe how to insert slides from one presentation into another.
2. What is a color scheme?
3. In creating a custom design template, what are four (or more) elements in your presentation that you might want to change?
4. Define variant as it applies to a gradient fill background.
5. Describe how to save a PowerPoint presentation as a design template.
6. What is a video clip?

Session 3.2

Creating a Chart (Graph)

A **chart**, or **graph**, is a visual depiction of data in a datasheet. The **datasheet** is a grid of cells, similar to a Microsoft Excel worksheet. **Cells** are the boxes that are organized in rows and columns, in which you can add data and labels. The rows are numbered 1, 2, 3, etc., and the columns are labeled A, B, C, etc. You can use a chart to show an audience data trends or to visually compare data.

Reference Window	**Creating a Chart (Graph)**

- Change the slide layout to a Content layout.
- Click the Chart button in the content placeholder.
- Edit the information in the datasheet for the data that you want to plot.
- Modify the chart type, if necessary.
- Modify the chart options, adding titles, modifying the font, and so forth, as desired.
- Click outside the chart area to make the chart inactive.

Pablo feels that the presentation should stress the importance of a village greenhouse by showing the average daytime high and nighttime low temperatures during each month of the year. He asks you, therefore, to add a new slide with a chart showing this relationship. You'll create the chart now.

To insert a chart:

1. If you took a break after the previous session, open the presentation **Peru Expedition Report** located in the **Tutorial.03\Tutorial** folder included with your Data Files.

2. Go to **Slide 10**, the slide before which you want to insert the new slide with a graph.

3. Click the **New Slide** button on the Formatting toolbar to insert a new Slide 11, and then click the **Title and Content** layout in the Slide Layout task pane.

4. Click the title placeholder, and then type **Climate of Paqarimuy**.

5. Close the task pane to provide more space for the slide pane, and then click the **Insert Chart** button 📊 in the content placeholder. PowerPoint inserts a sample chart and datasheet. See Figure 3-21.

New Slide 11 for creating chart ◄ Figure 3-21

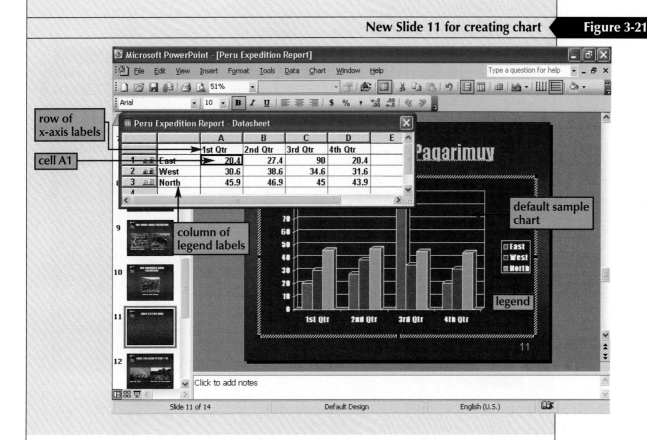

To create the chart for Pablo's presentation, you simply edit the information in the sample datasheet on the screen. When you work with a datasheet, the cell in which you are entering data is the **active cell**. The active cell has a thick border around it. In this chart, you want only two rows: one for the daytime high temperature, and the other for the daytime low temperature. You'll begin by deleting the third row of data on the datasheet.

To modify the chart:

▶ 1. Click the row **3** heading on the left side of the datasheet. The entire row is selected.

▶ 2. Press the **Delete** key to clear the entire row.

▶ 3. Click the first cell in row 1 with the label "East," just to the left of cell A1, type **High** (to indicate the high temperature), and then press the **Enter** key. The label is changed and the active cell moves down to the first cell in row 2. Notice that the legend in the chart also changed to reflect the new row label.

▶ 4. Replace the label "West" with **Low**.

▶ 5. Click the cell with the label "1st Qtr," just above cell A1 in column A, type **J** (for January), and then press the **Tab** key to move to the label for column B.

▶ 6. Type **F** (for February), press the **Tab** key to move to the label for column C, type **M** (for March), press the **Tab** key, type **A** (for April), and then press the **Tab** key. The active cell moves to the top cell in column E and the datasheet scrolls left.

▶ 7. Continue labeling the rest of the columns **M, J, J, A, S, O, N**, and **D** to label columns E through L. Notice that empty columns are added to the chart as you add column labels to the datasheet. See Figure 3-22.

Figure 3-22 ▶ Datasheet for creating a chart

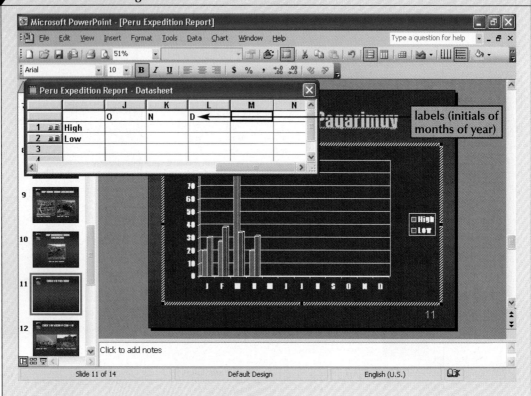

So far, you've created the labels for your chart. Now you'll type the data—the high and low average temperatures for each month in Paqarimuy.

To insert the data into the datasheet:

▶ **1.** Drag the horizontal scroll button on the bottom of the datasheet all the way to the left so that you can see cell A1.

▶ **2.** Click cell **A1** (which currently contains the number 20.4), type **48** (the average high temperature in degrees Fahrenheit during the month of January), press the **Tab** key to go to cell B1, type **50** (the average high during February), press the **Tab** key to go to cell C1, type **49** (the average high during March), and continue in the same way typing the temperatures **45**, **42**, **38**, **36**, **37**, **40**, **43**, **45**, and **48** in cells D1 through L1 for the months of April through December.

▶ **3.** Scroll back to the left to see cell A2, click cell **A2** (which currently contains the number 30.6), and type the following 12 numbers, pressing the **Tab** key between each one, to fill cells A2 through L2 with the nighttime low temperatures for January through December: **25**, **27**, **26**, **23**, **22**, **21**, **21**, **21**, **22**, **23**, **25**, and **26**. Your datasheet is now complete and the chart contains columns to reflect all of the data you entered.

The chart now contains all of the data, but you need to modify the chart to make it more useful to your audience. The chart type is a column chart, but you want to change it to a line chart. You also want to include some additional labels on the chart, and to change the font to make the labels more legible. First, you'll change the chart type.

To change the chart type:

1. Click **Chart** on the menu bar, click **Chart Type** to open the Chart Type dialog box, click the **Standard Types** tab, if necessary, and then click **Line** in the Chart type list box. See Figure 3-23.

Chart Type dialog box ◀ **Figure 3-23**

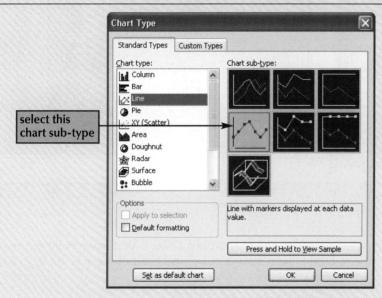

2. If necessary, click the first chart thumbnail in the second row in the Chart sub-type section, as indicated in Figure 3-23, and then click the **OK** button. The chart changes to a line chart. Now that you have entered the desired chart type, you'll add a chart title and an axis label.

3. Click **Chart** on the menu bar, click **Chart Options** to open the Chart Options dialog box, and then click the **Titles** tab, if necessary.

4. Click in the **Chart title** text box, and then type **Average Monthly Temperatures**. After a moment, the chart title you typed appears above the preview of the chart on the right.

5. Click in the **Value (Y) axis** text box, type **Temperature (degrees F)** to indicate that the temperatures are in Fahrenheit, and then click the **OK** button. Your chart should now look like the one shown in Figure 3-24.

Figure 3-24 **Datasheet and chart after adding data**

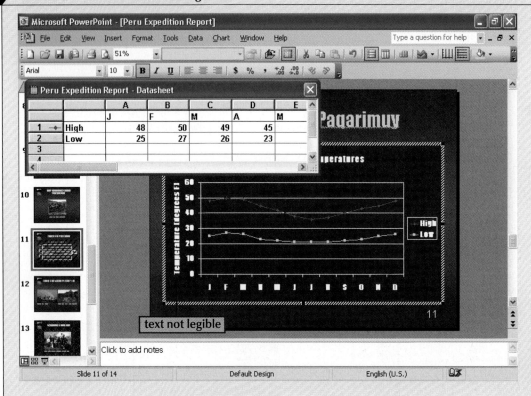

You've almost completed the chart. The only problem now is that PowerPoint automatically uses the title text font, bold Impact, for the chart labels, but this font is not legible in the chart. You'll change all the text in your chart to Arial.

To change the font of the chart labels:

1. Click in the chart area, and then click the **chart title** ("Average Monthly Temperatures") to select the chart title text box.

   Trouble? If you can't see the chart title because the datasheet is in the way, drag the datasheet out of the way by its title bar.

2. Click the **Font** list arrow on the Formatting toolbar, click **Arial**, and then click the **Bold** button **B** on the Formatting toolbar to turn off the bold formatting.

3. Double click the **legend** (which shows the line color and symbols for High and Low) to open the Format Legend dialog box, click the **Font** tab, click **Arial** in the Font list box, click **Regular** in the Font style list box, and then click the **OK** button.

4. Change the font of the **Value axis title** (the title written vertically along the y-axis) to **Arial Regular.**

5. Double-click one of the **Category axis labels** (the labels along the x-axis) to open the Format Axis dialog box. Notice that you can't select this axis as a text box because it's part of the data in the datasheet, not a separate text box.

   Trouble? If the Format Chart Area dialog box opens instead of the Format Axis dialog box, you did not double-click the Category axis. Click the Cancel button, position the pointer over one of the labels on the Category axis so that you see a ScreenTip identifying the Category axis, and then double-click.

▶ **6.** Click the **Font** tab, if necessary, change the font to **Arial** and the font style to **Regular**, and then click the **OK** button.

▶ **7.** Double-click one of the **Value axis labels** (the temperature values along the left edge of the graph), change the font to **Arial Regular**, and then click the **OK** button.

▶ **8.** Click anywhere on the slide outside the chart area to close the datasheet and make the chart inactive, and then click outside the chart again to deselect the chart object. Your completed Slide 11 should look like Figure 3-25.

Slide 11 with completed chart ◀ **Figure 3-25**

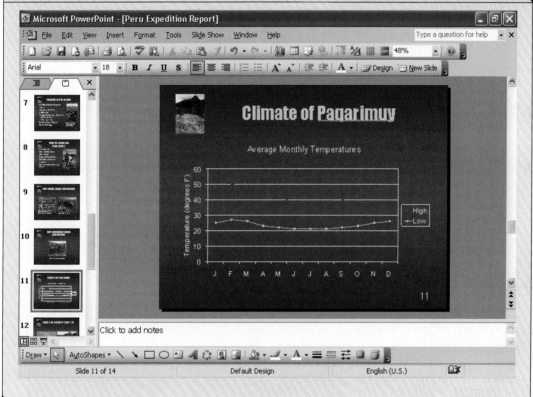

▶ **9.** Save the presentation.

Pablo is pleased with your chart, which graphically shows how cold the climate is in Paqarimuy, and hence the need for a greenhouse to grow certain vegetables.

Building and Modifying an Organization Chart

Because the members of the board of directors and prospective volunteers for future projects like to know how each expedition is organized, Pablo wants you to create an organization chart showing the people involved in the Peru expedition. An **organization chart** is a diagram of boxes connected with lines, showing the hierarchy of positions within an organization. Fortunately, PowerPoint provides a feature for easily creating and modifying an organization chart.

Reference Window	**Creating an Organization Chart**

- Change the slide layout to one of the Content layouts, click the Insert Diagram or Organization Chart button in the content placeholder, click the Organization Chart button, and then click the OK button.
- Type the personnel names, positions, and other information, as desired, into the boxes of the organization chart.
- To add new boxes, click the Insert Shape list arrow on the Organization Chart toolbar, and then click the desired box.
- Select the organization chart boxes and modify the font and fill color if desired.
- Click anywhere outside the organization chart area.

Now you'll insert a new Slide 14 and create an organization chart.

To create an organization chart:

1. Go to **Slide 13** ("Expedition Volunteers"), insert a new Slide 14, give the slide the title **Expedition Organization**, change the slide layout to **Title and Content**, and then close the task pane.

2. Click the **Insert Diagram or Organization Chart** button 🖾 in the content placeholder to open the Diagram Gallery dialog box, click the **Organization Chart** icon (the first icon in the first row), and then click the **OK** button. PowerPoint creates a skeleton of a basic organization chart and displays the Organization Chart toolbar, as shown in Figure 3-26. Now you'll add text to the boxes in the organization chart, delete some boxes, and add new boxes to create the desired chart.

Figure 3-26	New Slide 14 with organization chart

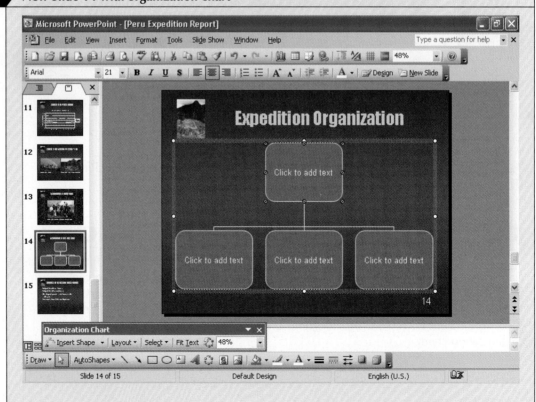

3. Click the **top (level 1)** box of the organization chart. A light-blue insertion point, which might be hard to see, blinks in the center of the box.

4. Type **Pablo Fuentes**, press the **Enter** key, and then type **Expedition Coordinator**. The text you typed replaces the placeholder text in the box. The text overlaps the edges of the box. You'll fix this later.

5. Click outside of the level 1 box, but inside the organization chart area, to deselect the level 1 box but keep the organization chart active.

Now you'll delete all but one of the three boxes on level 2 because only one person, Ken Van Wagoner, is on the level below Pablo in the organization chart.

To modify an organization chart:

1. Click the edge of the first box in level 2. The gray selection handles at the corners of the box indicate that it's been selected. See Figure 3-27.

Preparing to delete an organization chart box ◀ **Figure 3-27**

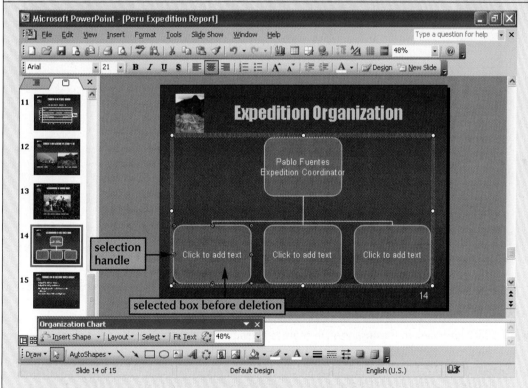

Trouble? If the box has a hatched line around it and no selection handles, click the edge of the box again.

2. Press the **Delete** key to delete the selected box, and when the next box in that row automatically becomes selected, press the **Delete** key again to delete it. Now you should have only one box in level 2.

3. Click in the **level 2** box, type **Ken Van Wagoner**, press the **Enter** key, and then type **Expedition Leader**. Now you're ready to add level 3 boxes below Ken Van Wagoner.

4. Click the **Insert Shape** list arrow on the Organization Chart toolbar, click **Subordinate**, click in the new **level 3** box, and then type **Cultural Team Leader**. You won't type a name associated with the various team leaders because Pablo's audience doesn't know the expedition volunteers, and is interested only in the organization. Now you'll insert a box for another team leader, a co-worker of the cultural team leader.

5. Click the **Insert Shape** list arrow on the Organization Chart toolbar, click **Coworker**, click in the new level 3 box, and then type **Medical Team Leader**.

6. Insert another level 3 co-worker box with the text **Educational Team Leader**, and then click anywhere on the slide outside the organization chart. Compare your Slide 14 to Figure 3-28.

Figure 3-28	Organization chart with first three levels completed

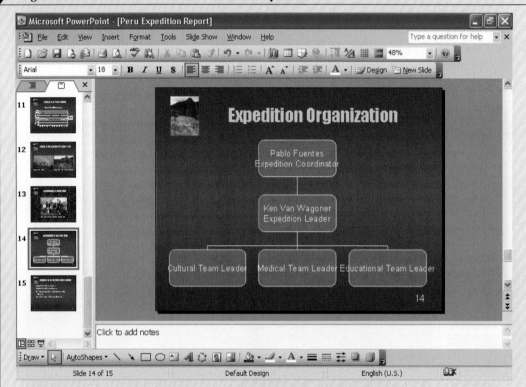

You've made good progress on the organization chart and have to add only three more boxes, subordinates to the Medical Team Leader box.

7. Click anywhere in the organization chart to activate it, and then click the edge of the **Medical Team Leader** box to select it.

8. Click the **Insert Shape** button on the Organization Chart toolbar. You don't have to use the list arrow because the default is to insert a subordinate box. Your chart now has a level 4 box. PowerPoint draws a bent line from the bottom of the Medical Team Leader box to the side of the new subordinate box, but you want a line straight down from the Medical Team Leader box.

9. With the Medical Team Leader box still selected, click **Layout** on the Organization Chart toolbar, and then click **Standard**. Now the subordinate is connected with a straight line to the Medical Team Leader box.

10. Click in the **level 4** box, and then type **Health Team**.

▶ **11.** Insert two more level 4 boxes to the right of the Health Team box, one with the text **Hygiene Team** and the other with the text **Dental Team**, and then click outside the chart area to deselect the organization chart. Your chart should look like Figure 3-29.

Slide 14 with all boxes of organization chart ◀ **Figure 3-29**

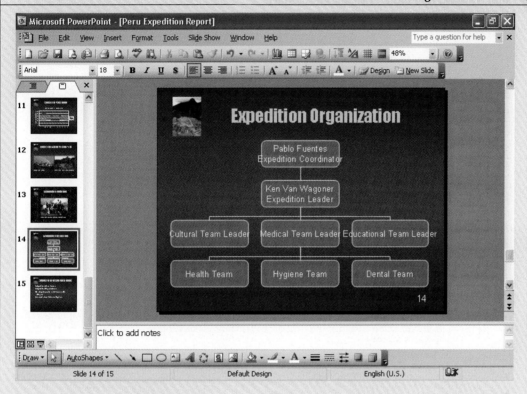

You completed all the organization chart boxes. Pablo looks over this slide and tells you that he thinks yellow text on a dark-brown background would be better for this chart than the default colors of white text on a light-brown background. He also wants you to increase the font size to make the text more legible. Now you'll modify the chart accordingly.

To change font size and color, change the fill color, and make other adjustments:

▶ **1.** Click anywhere in the organization chart to make it active, press and hold the mouse button, drag from the far upper-left corner of the organization chart area to the lower-right corner to select all elements of the chart (so that a dotted-line border surrounds all of the organization chart boxes), and then release the mouse button. Selection handles appear on all the selected boxes of the chart. Make sure all of the boxes are selected.

Trouble? If some of the boxes aren't selected, press and hold the Ctrl key, and then click them.

You'll start by changing the font size and color.

▶ **2.** Click the **Font Size** list arrow on the Formatting toolbar, and then click **16**. The font size of the selected boxes changes to 16 points.

▶ **3.** Click the **Font Color** list arrow A ▾ on the Formatting toolbar, and then click the yellow tile in the color palette. The font color of all the organization chart text changes to yellow.

▶ **4.** Click the **Fill Color** list arrow 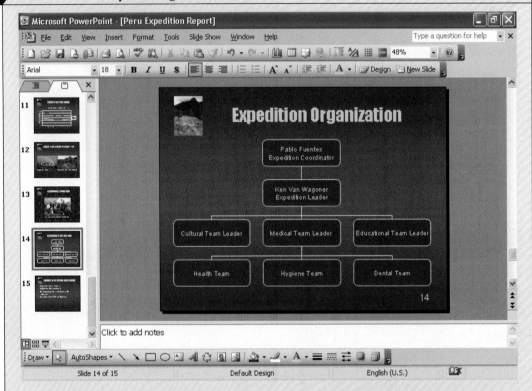 on the Drawing toolbar, and then click the dark-brown tile located on the far left of the color palette. The box fill color changes to dark brown.

▶ **5.** Click a blank area of the slide to deselect the chart. See Figure 3-30.

Figure 3-30 ▶ **Slide 14 with completed organization chart**

Trouble? If the text doesn't fit inside any of the boxes, click the edge of the box to display the selection handles, drag the left-center or right-center selection handle until the box is large enough to contain the text, and then drag the entire box to position it so it doesn't overlap with other boxes.

▶ **6.** Save the presentation.

This completes Slide 14 with its organization chart, and completes the text and content of all the slides in the Peru Expedition Report presentation. The only thing left to do is add some special effects and animations.

Applying Special Effects

Special effects—such as causing one slide to fade out as another slide appears, animated (moving) text, and sound effects—can liven up your presentation, help hold your audience's attention, and emphasize key points. On the other hand, special effects can also distract or even annoy your audience. Your goal is to apply special effects conservatively and tastefully so that, rather than making your presentation look gawky and amateurish, they add a professional look and feel to your slide show.

Using Special Effects

- Don't feel that you must include special effects in your slides. Special effects can distract your audience from the message of the presentation. When in doubt, leave them out.
- If you include transitions, use only one type of transition for all the slides. This will keep your audience from trying to guess what the next transition will be and, instead, will help them stay focused on your message.
- If you include animation, use only one type of animation for all the bulleted lists in the slides. This will keep your presentation consistent and conservative.
- Use sound effects sparingly, just enough to provide emphasis, but not enough to distract the audience from your message.

Pablo wants you to add a few special effects to your presentation. The first special effect that you will add is a slide transition.

Adding Slide Transitions

A slide **transition** is a method of moving one slide off the screen and bringing another slide onto the screen during a slide show. Although applying transitions is usually easier in Slide Sorter view because you can easily select several (or all) slides at once, you can also apply a transition in Normal view.

Adding Slide Transitions

- Switch to Slide Sorter view, and then select the slide(s) to which you want to add a transition.
- Click the Transition button on the Slide Sorter toolbar to display the Slide Transition task pane.
- Click the desired transition effect in the Slide Transition task pane.
- Set the speed, if desired.

You'll add a transition to all the slides in the presentation.

To add a transition effect:

1. Click the **Slide Sorter View** button 🔡 to switch to Slide Sorter view, click the **Zoom** list arrow on the Standard toolbar, and then click a percentage that enables you to see all 15 slides at once. On some screens, no change is needed; on others, the zoom might need to be changed to 50% to make all the slides fit in the window.

2. Click **Edit** on the menu bar, and then click **Select All** (or press the **Ctrl+A** key combination) to select all the slides. Now when you apply a slide transition, all the slides will have that transition.

3. Click the **Transition** button on the Slide Sorter toolbar. The Slide Transition task pane opens.

   Trouble? If the Transition button is not visible on the Slide Sorter toolbar, click the Toolbar Options button 🖫 on the Slide Sorter toolbar to see the rest of the buttons on the Slide Sorter toolbar.

4. Scroll down the **Apply to selected slides** list box in the task pane, and then click **Dissolve**. PowerPoint demonstrates the dissolve transition in the slide thumbnails in the slide sorter pane, and a transition icon appears below the lower-left corner of each slide. See Figure 3-31.

Figure 3-31 ▶ **Completed presentation with Dissolve transition applied to all slides**

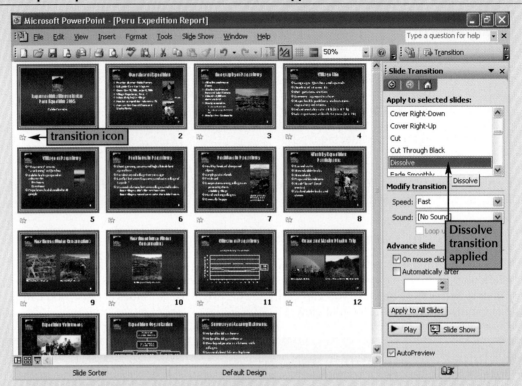

You can change the speed of the dissolve using the Modify transition section of the Slide Transition task pane.

▶ **5.** Click the **Speed** list arrow in the task pane, and then click **Medium**. The transition speed is now set to medium.

▶ **6.** Make sure that the **On mouse click** check box in the task pane is checked, and that the **Automatically after** check box is not.

▶ **7.** Click a blank area of the slide sorter pane to deselect the slides. You'll test the transition by clicking a transition icon.

▶ **8.** Click the **transition** icon below Slide 2. PowerPoint momentarily displays the Slide 1 image at that location, and then performs the dissolve transition to Slide 2. Click any of the transition icons to see how the transition looks for that slide.

When Pablo advances the slide show from one slide to another, each slide will dissolve onto the screen. Now that you've added transitions to the slides, you're ready to add animation.

Applying a Built-In Animation Scheme

An **animation scheme** is a special visual or audio effect applied to an object, such as a graphic or a bulleted list, on a slide. For example, you can add an animation effect to display bulleted items on a slide one item at a time. This process is called **progressive disclosure**. When a slide with a bulleted list has a progressive disclosure animation effect added, only the slide title appears when you first display the slide in your slide show.

Then, when you click the left mouse button (or press the spacebar), the first bulleted item appears. When you click the left mouse button again, the second bulleted item appears, and so on. The advantage of this type of animation effect is that you can focus your audience's attention on one item at a time, without the distractions of items that you haven't discussed yet.

Reference Window

Applying an Animation Scheme

- In Slide Sorter view, select the slide(s) to which you want to add an animation effect.
- Click the Design button on the Slide Sorter toolbar, and then click the Animation Schemes link in the Slide Design task pane.
- Click the desired animation effect displayed in the task pane.

PowerPoint supports three general types of animations: Subtle (the simplest and most conservative animations), Moderate (moderately simple and moderately conservative animations), and Exciting (more complex and less conservative animations). For academic or business presentations, you should generally stick with Subtle or maybe Moderate animations. If you're giving a casual or informal presentation, such as one describing a group game or explaining an exciting travel vacation, you might want to use Exciting animations. For this presentation, you will apply a Moderate animation.

Note that if you apply an animation effect after applying a slide transition, the animation effect will override the transition previously applied. On the other hand, if you apply a transition effect after applying an animation effect, both effects will be applied.

Now you'll add an animation effect to the bulleted lists in Pablo's presentation. For some presentations, you might include only one or two animation effects, but Pablo wants to try various animation effects before he completes his final presentation.

To add an animation scheme:

1. In Slide Sorter view, click **Slide 2**, press and hold the **Shift** key, and then click **Slide 8** to select the first seven slides that have bulleted lists.

2. Click the **Design** button on the Slide Sorter toolbar to display the Slide Design task pane, and then click the **Animation Schemes** link in the task pane. A list of the PowerPoint built-in animations appears in the task pane.

   Trouble? If the Design button is not visible on the Slide Sorter toolbar, click the Toolbar options button ⏷ on the Slide Sorter toolbar to see the rest of the buttons on the Slide Sorter toolbar.

3. Scroll down the **Apply to selected slides** list box until you see the **Moderate** animations, and then click **Ascend**. PowerPoint demonstrates the Ascend animation on each of the selected slides.

   Trouble? If the animation doesn't show automatically, click the AutoPreview check box at the bottom of the task pane to select it.

4. Click **Slide 15**, the only other slide with a bulleted list, to select it, and then apply the **Ascend** animation to it.

5. Close the task pane.

You'll test the transitions and animation effects you applied to the presentation.

To run a slide show with transitions and animation effects:

▶ **1.** Click **Slide 1**, and then click the **Slide Show from current slide** button 🖵. Slide 1 appears in Slide Show view by dissolving onto the screen.

▶ **2.** Click the left mouse button. The title of Slide 2 appears on the screen.

▶ **3.** Click the left mouse button again. The first bulleted item on Slide 2 appears and ascends up the screen to its final location.

▶ **4.** Continue clicking the left mouse button to progress through the slide show, and then return to Slide Sorter view.

▶ **5.** Save the presentation.

Next, you'll apply a custom animation effect to Slide 2.

Applying Custom Animation

The built-in animation schemes offer you many ways to display titles and bulleted items on the screen, but they don't allow you to change the color of previously viewed bulleted items, animate other types of objects (user-added text boxes, sound icons, pictures, and so forth), add sound effects to animations, or change the order of animations. To do these types of things, you have to apply custom animations.

For example, in Slide 2, Pablo wants you to modify the presentation to do the following:

• Add a sound effect to each bulleted item so that it makes a "whooshing" sound when the item appears on the screen during the slide show.
• Dim (change color) each bulleted item after the next bulleted item appears on the screen.
• Animate the sound icon to appear on screen after the bulleted item that contains the word "Paqarimuy."
• Animate the two pictures, along with their captions, so that they appear after the bulleted list.

You'll apply these custom animations to Slide 2 now.

To apply custom animations:

▶ **1.** Double-click **Slide 2** to switch to Normal view with Slide 2 in the slide pane.

▶ **2.** Click **Slide Show** on the menu bar, and then click **Custom Animation**. The Custom Animation task pane opens, and a number appears next to each bulleted item in the slide pane. PowerPoint automatically assigns a number to each animated item in the slide. If you animate additional objects on a slide, PowerPoint will assign them new numbers. You use the numbers to help you customize the animation. These numbers do not appear in Slide Show view. The sound icon has a pointing finger next to it. This indicates that you chose to have the sound played when the mouse is clicked instead of playing automatically when the slide appears during a slide show. See Figure 3-32.

Slide 2 with animated text ◄ **Figure 3-32**

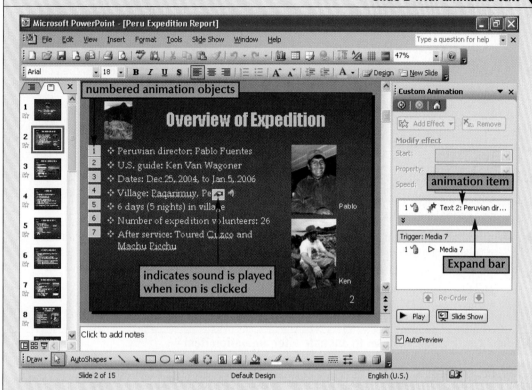

3. Click anywhere within the **bulleted list** text box to select it. This box contains animation items 1 through 7, but only item 1 (called Text 2) appears in the Custom Animation task pane. Because the other items are part of the same text box, PowerPoint doesn't usually display them.

4. In the task pane, click the animation item **1, Text 2: Peruvia...** list arrow, and then click **Effect Options** to display the Ascend dialog box.

5. Click the **Sound** list arrow, drag the scroll bar down to the bottom, and then click **Whoosh** to add this sound effect to the progressive disclosure.

   Trouble? If a message appears telling you that sound effects are not installed, check with your instructor or technical support person if you are working in a lab. If you are working on your own computer, click the Yes button to install the feature now.

6. Click the **After animation** list arrow, and then click the gray tile (the right-most tile in the color palette).

7. Click the **OK** button. The slide automatically animates the progressive disclosure.

   Trouble? If you don't hear anything, you may not have a sound card in your computer system, or you may need to turn up the volume.

You applied custom animation effects to the bulleted list in Slide 2. Next, you'll animate the sound icon so that it appears on the screen along with bulleted item number 4 ("Village: Paqarimuy, Peru") because the sound clip gives the pronunciation of "Paqarimuy."

To animate the sound icon:

▶ 1. Click a blank area of the slide to deselect the text box, and then click the **sound** icon to select it. Sizing handles appear at each corner of the object, and the animation item Media 7 is selected in the task pane.

▶ 2. Click the **Add Effect** button at the top of the task pane, point to **Entrance**, and then click **Fly In**. The sound icon animates by flying in from the bottom, and the icon that indicated the sound is played on a mouse click changes to animation number 8. You'll change the animation so that the icon flies in from the right.

 Trouble? If you don't see Fly In on the Entrance list, click More Effects to open the Add Entrance Effect dialog box, and then click Fly In.

▶ 3. With the sound icon still selected, click the **Direction** list arrow in the task pane, and then click **From Right**. You decide to leave the speed at Very Fast. Now you'll change the animation order by moving the sound icon up just below animation object.

▶ 4. Click the **Expand bar** in the task pane just below animation item 1, Text 2 Peruvian dir... to display all the bulleted items, 1 through 7.

▶ 5. Click animation item **8, Media 7** in the task pane, if necessary, and then click the **Re-Order Up Arrow** button near the bottom of the task pane three times so that animation item Media 7 is just below animation item 4, Village: Paqarim.... See Figure 3-33.

| Figure 3-33 | Slide 2 with sound icon set to animate after animation item 4 |

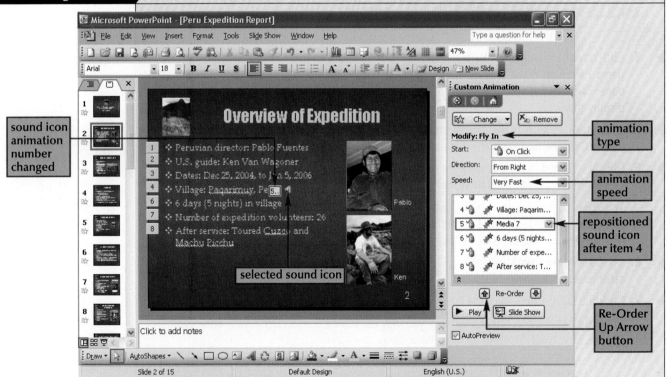

▶ 6. Click the **Play** button at the bottom of the task pane to see and hear the animations in Slide 2.

Your final task in Slide 2 is to animate the two pictures and their captions so they appear on the slide after the bulleted list.

To animate the pictures and their captions:

▶ **1.** Click the picture of Pablo, animate it with the **Entrance** effect to **Fly In**, and then set the Direction to **From Right**.

▶ **2.** Animate the text box "Pablo" with the same animation effect as the photo.

▶ **3.** Animate the picture of Ken and the text box "Ken" so that they also fly in from the right. After you animate these objects, each one will be listed on the task pane. See Figure 3-34.

Slide 2 with picture and caption animation | **Figure 3-34**

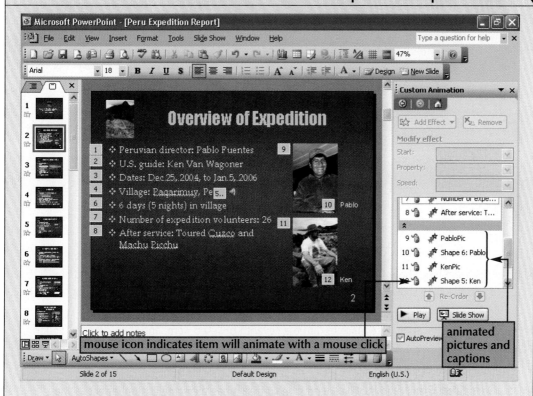

Notice that each animated object listed in the Custom Animation task pane has a mouse icon next to it, as indicated in Figure 3-34. The mouse icon indicates that during the slide show, the animation for that item occurs when someone clicks the left mouse button (or presses the spacebar). Pablo wants the sound icon, the pictures, and the captions to animate automatically, without the presenter clicking the mouse button. You'll set these objects to animate automatically now.

To change how animation occurs during a slide show:

▶ **1.** In the slide pane, click the **sound** icon, press and hold the **Ctrl** key, and then click each of the two pictures and their captions so that animation items 5 and 9 through 12 are selected.

▶ **2.** Click the **Start** list arrow near the top of the task pane, and then click **With Previous**. This means that during the slide show, the animation of these items will start at the same time as the animation of the previous object. In other words, it will animate automatically, without a mouse click. Now all these objects animate automatically. See Figure 3-35.

Figure 3-35 | **Slide 2 after completing custom animation**

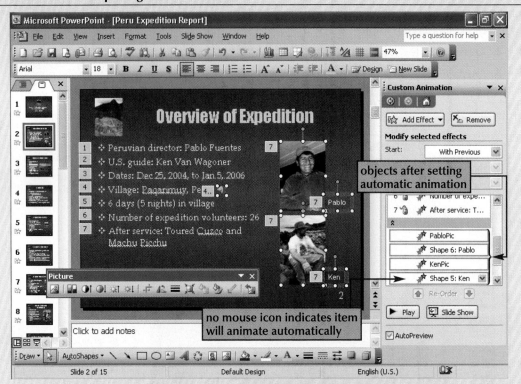

▶ **3.** Click the **Slide Show from current slide** button 🖳 at the bottom of the task pane to begin the slide show with Slide 2, and then press the **spacebar** seven times to display each of the seven bulleted items.

▶ **4.** Press the **spacebar** once more to dim the seventh bulleted item, and then click the **sound** icon to hear the pronunciation of "Paqarimuy."

▶ **5.** Press the **Esc** key to return to Normal view rather than going on to the other slides.

▶ **6.** Go to **Slide 6** and animate the sound icon so that it has the same custom effect as the sound icon in Slide 2 (fly in from the right), and then set it to appear at the same time as the third bulleted item by repositioning it in the animation items list in the task pane so that it is listed immediately after the third bulleted item, and then setting its Start option to With Previous.

▶ **7.** Start the slide show from Slide 6 and test the animation to make sure that the sound icon flies automatically from the right at the same time as the third bulleted item, and then end the slide show.

▶ **8.** Close the task pane, and then save the presentation.

This completes the presentation. You could edit each slide, one at a time, with custom animations to focus on key information or to add interest and excitement to the slide. But Pablo feels that the presentation has enough animation.

Now you'll run through the entire slide show to see how all the animation effects, transitions, the video clip, and so on will appear.

To run through the entire slide show:

1. Go to **Slide 1**, and then click the **Slide Show from current slide** button ⬛. The slide show starts with Slide 1 dissolving onto the screen. This is the transition effect you added.

2. Click the left mouse button or press the **spacebar** to move to Slide 2, advance through the animation of the bulleted list, and then click the **sound** icon on the slide after you dim the seventh bulleted item.

3. Continue through the slide show until the title of Slide 5 ("Village of Paqarimuy") appears on the screen, click the left mouse button or press the **spacebar** three more times to display the three bulleted items. The movie starts after the last bulleted item appears on screen, and plays continuously.

4. Advance to **Slide 6** ("Problems in Paqarimuy"), click the **sound** icon on this slide at the appropriate time, and then continue advancing through the slide show.

5. When you have finished viewing the slide show, go to **Slide 1**, replace Pablo's name in the subtitle with your name, and then save the presentation.

6. Print the presentation in grayscale as handouts, with six slides per page.

Pablo now wants to practice his presentation, including marking slides with the pointer pen.

Using the Pointer Pen to Mark Slides During a Slide Show

The **pointer pen** is a PowerPoint mouse pointer icon that allows you to draw lines on the screen during a slide show. For example, you might use it to underline a word or phrase that you want to emphasize, or to circle a graphic that you want to point out. After you go through a presentation and mark it, PowerPoint gives you the choice of keeping the markings or discarding them. Now you'll show Pablo how to use the pointer pen.

To use the pointer pen during a slide show:

1. Go to **Slide 3** and start the slide show.

2. Press the **spacebar** five times to display the last bulleted item ("Nearby river: Urubamba") in Slide 3. You want to underline the phrase "13,500 feet" to emphasize that Paqarimuy is a very high-altitude village.

3. Move the mouse until you see the mouse pointer, and then click the **Pen** icon ✏, located in the lower-left corner of the screen to open a menu. The Pen icon and others appear only when you move the mouse, and they appear as transparent until you position the pointer over them.

4. Click **Felt Tip Pen**, which changes the mouse pointer to a red-filled circle. By clicking and dragging the pen on the screen, you can draw lines.

5. Move the pointer below the "1" in "13,500," press and hold the left mouse button, and then drag the pointer from left to right to draw a line below "13,500 feet." See Figure 3-36.

Figure 3-36 ▶ Slide 3 with ink mark

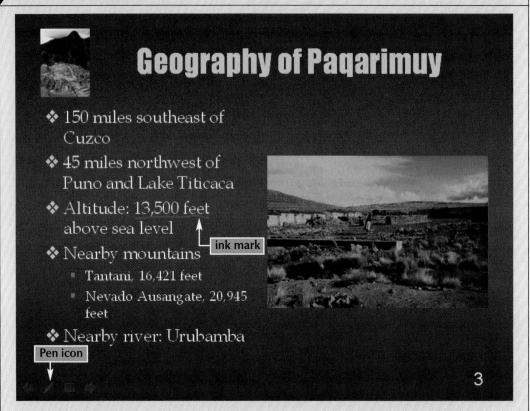

6. Press the **spacebar** to move to the next slide. Note that you cannot click the left mouse button to proceed through the slide show while a pointer pen is selected.

7. Click the **Pen** icon ✎ in the lower-left corner, and then click **Arrow**. The mouse pointer changes back to the ordinary arrow pointer.

8. Press the **Esc** key to terminate the slide show. A dialog box appears asking if you want to keep your annotations.

9. Click the **Discard** button. Slide 4 appears in the slide pane in Normal view.

As you can see, the pointer pen is a powerful tool for highlighting and pointing out information during a slide show.

Hiding Slides

Pablo decides that he can also use most of the slides in this presentation for prospective expedition volunteers; however, all of the slides are not appropriate for the volunteers. For example, he doesn't feel that Slide 11 ("Climate of Paqarimuy") with its temperature chart, will be of interest to most potential expedition volunteers. One solution is to temporarily hide that slide so it won't show up during the presentation.

You'll demonstrate how to hide and unhide a slide.

To hide and unhide a slide:

▶ **1.** Go to **Slide 11**, click **Slide Show** on the menu bar, and then click **Hide Slide**. The slide remains in the slide pane in Normal view, but PowerPoint marks the slide number in the Slides tab so that you know the slide will be hidden during the slide show. See Figure 3-37. Now you'll see your slides in Slide Show view.

Slide 11 after hiding slide ◄ | **Figure 3-37**

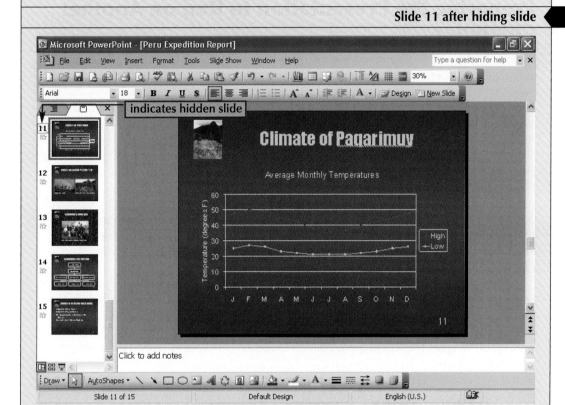

▶ **2.** Go to **Slide 10**, and then click the **Slide Show from current slide** button 🖳.

▶ **3.** Press the **spacebar** or click the left mouse button. Slide 12 ("Cuzco and Machu Picchu Trip") appears on the screen. The slide show skips Slide 11 ("Climate of Paqarimuy") as you intended.

▶ **4.** Press the **Esc** key to end the slide show. Slide 12 appears in the slide pane in Normal view.

Now that you've seen how to hide a slide, you should go back and "unhide" it so it will be available for Pablo's presentation to the board of directors.

To unhide a slide:

▶ **1.** Go to **Slide 11**, click **Slide Show** on the menu bar, and then click **Hide Slide**. This toggles the Hide Slide effect off for Slide 11. The hidden slide icon disappears from the Slides tab.

▶ **2.** Go to **Slide 10**, switch to Slide Show view, and then press the **spacebar** to view Slide 11, verifying that it does indeed show up in the slide show now.

▶ **3.** Return to Normal view, and then save the presentation.

Pablo is now confident that his presentation will go smoothly, providing the needed information to his audiences in an engaging manner. Your final tasks are to help him prepare the materials to run not only on his computer, but also on the computers in the rooms where he'll give his presentations.

Preparing the Presentation to Run on Another Computer

Pablo will present the electronic (on-screen) slide show to the board of directors in a suitably equipped conference room at Global Humanitarian; however, he might be using computers without PowerPoint to give presentations to potential volunteers. He knows that he doesn't need PowerPoint installed because he can use PowerPoint Viewer. **PowerPoint Viewer** is a separate program that you can use to give your slide show on any Windows 95/98/2000/NT/XP computer. The Microsoft PowerPoint license allows you to create a Viewer disk and install the Viewer program on other computers without additional charge. Pablo asks you to use the Package for CD feature to create a CD that contains the PowerPoint Viewer files and a copy of his presentation. **Package for CD** places the entire presentation on a CD so you can take the presentation and show it on any computer with the Viewer program. Pablo can then use this CD to install PowerPoint Viewer and run the presentation file on any computer. Although Pablo can't modify any of the slides using PowerPoint Viewer, he can review the entire slide show, including special effects, and he can use the pen pointer during the slide show.

Pablo wants to make sure that whatever computer he uses, the fonts (Impact and Book Antiqua) are available, so he'll save the presentation with embedded fonts. With embedded fonts, the presentation will always have the desired fonts, regardless of whether they are installed on the computer where you give the slide show. Be aware, however, that embedding fonts increases the size of the presentation file, so you want to embed fonts only if necessary.

Before completing the following steps, consult with your instructor. You'll need a computer with a CD writer (often called a "CD burner") and a blank, unused, writable CD.

To save a file with embedded fonts, and use Package for CD:

1. Click **File** on the menu bar, and then click **Save As** to display the Save As dialog box.

2. Click **Tools** on the dialog box toolbar, and then click **Save Options**. The Save Options dialog box opens.

3. Click the **Embed TrueType fonts** check box to select it, and then click the **OK** button. (In some cases, you might want to select the Embed characters in use only check box to save disk space, but the risk in this is that if you need to add text to your presentation, you might not find the needed characters.)

4. Click the **Save** button in the dialog box, and then click the **Yes** button when you're asked if you want to replace the existing file. The **Peru Expedition Report** file is now saved with the fonts embedded so it will have the same appearance on computers that might not have those fonts.

5. Click **File** on the menu bar, and then click **Package for CD**. The Package for CD dialog box opens.

   Trouble? If the Package for CD feature isn't installed, PowerPoint will ask you if you want to install it now. If you are working in a lab, ask your instructor or technical support person for assistance; if you are working on your own computer, click the Yes button.

6. Type **Peru Expedition** in the Name the CD text box. See Figure 3-38.

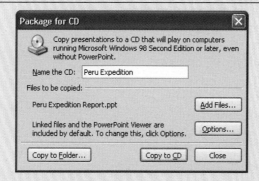

7. Click the **Copy to CD** button. The CD drive drawer on your computer automatically opens, and a message appears asking you to insert a blank CD into the drive.

8. Place a blank, writable CD in the CD drive and close the drawer, and then click the **Retry** button. PowerPoint copies the presentation files and PowerPoint Viewer to the CD. This might take a minute or so. When the copying is complete, the CD drawer opens again, and PowerPoint asks if you want to make another copy.

9. Click the **No** button in the dialog box, and then click the **Close** button in the Package for CD dialog box.

10. Close the PowerPoint program window without saving any changes to the presentation.

11. Remove the CD from the CD drive.

You can now test the CD with your PowerPoint presentation.

To run the PowerPoint presentation from a CD:

1. Insert the CD that you just created into the CD drive and close the drawer. A dialog box appears containing the PowerPoint Viewer license agreement.

2. Click the **Accept** button. The dialog box closes and the slide show starts automatically.

3. Go through the slide show.

Trouble? If the movie does not play automatically on Slide 5, click it to play it, and then click it again to stop it. Sometimes, media clips do not play automatically when you use the Viewer.

Trouble? If the presentation doesn't work exactly as you prepared it, don't worry. Some features don't translate to the CD exactly.

4. After the blank screen appears at the end of the presentation, click the left mouse button or press the **spacebar** to end the presentation.

You give the CD to Pablo so he can show his presentation on any computer that has a CD drive.

You've completed Pablo's presentation. He believes that the graphics, sound, and special effects for the on-screen slide show will help his audience stay focused on his presentation. He thanks you for your help.

Review

Session 3.2 Quick Check

1. Describe how to insert a chart into a slide.
2. What is an organization chart?
3. How do you insert an organization chart into a slide?
4. Define the following terms:
   a. transition effect
   b. animation effect
   c. progressive disclosure
   d. sound effect
   e. pointer pen
5. Describe how to add a transition effect to a slide.
6. What is PowerPoint Viewer?

Review

Tutorial Summary

In this tutorial, you learned how to insert slides from another presentation and create a design template by creating a custom color scheme and background and by changing the typeface and color of the font. You also learned how to add a background image, apply graphics and sound in the form of digital images, video clips, and audio clips, and add a textured background. You learned how to create a chart (graph) and an organization chart, and how to apply special effects such as slide transitions and animations. Finally, you learned how to use the pointer pen to mark slides during a slide show, hide a slide, and prepare a presentation to run on another computer.

Key Terms

active cell	digital movie	progressive disclosure
animated GIF	gradient fill	shading style
animation scheme	graph	special effect
cell	organization chart	transition
chart	Package for CD	variant
color scheme	pointer pen	video clip
datasheet	PowerPoint Viewer	

Practice

Get hands-on practice of the skills you learned in the tutorial using the same case scenario.

Review Assignments

Data Files needed for the Review Assignments: CuzcTour.ppt, PeruLogo.jpg, PeruExp.ppt, Cuzco.wav, SacsSnd.avi, MachPicc.wav, HuaynaP.wav, SacsMov.wav

A key attraction to potential volunteers of the humanitarian expeditions is the tour of Peru after the service project. Pablo wants to create a PowerPoint presentation that focuses on the tourism part of the Peru expedition. He wants to provide prices, dates, pictures, and other details about the tour of the Cuzco and Machu Picchu areas of Peru. He asks you to help him create the presentation.

1. Open the presentation file **CuzcTour** from the Tutorial.03\Review folder included with your Data Files, change the name on Slide 1 from Pablo Fuentes to your name, and then save the presentation as **Cuzco Machu Picchu Tour** to your high-capacity disk (your hard disk or a Zip disk).
2. Apply the built-in color scheme for the Default Design template that has a black background and white text.

3. Change the background of all the slides to a two-color gradient fill using the default colors (Color 1 set to black and Color 2 set to green), with the Horizontal shading style and the variant with black on top and green on the bottom.

4. In the slide master, change the title text to left-aligned yellow and bold, leaving the title font at 44-point Arial. Change the main text (bulleted list text) to Times New Roman and leave it white.

5. In the slide master, change the first-level bullets to yellow squares, and the second-level bullets to medium-blue circles.

6. Also in the slide master, resize the width of the title text box about an inch smaller so that you can insert a logo to the left of the title, and then insert the graphic file **PeruLogo** (in the Tutorial.03\Review folder) and position it to the left of the title text box. Adjust the graphic size and the title text box so they look good together at the top of the slide.

7. Add a title master, and then reposition the logo on the title master so it's centered above the title text box.

8. In Normal view, change the background texture of Slide 1 (only) to Medium Wood.

9. Save the current version of the presentation as a normal presentation file, and then save it as a custom design template to the Tutorial.03\Review folder using the file-name **Cuzco Machu Picchu Template**. Make sure you delete any unnecessary slides and text from the template file.

10. Close the design template file, reopen the **Cuzco Machu Picchu Tour** file, and then insert Slide 8, "Expedition Costs (Per Person)," from the presentation file **PeruExp** located in the Tutorial.03\Review folder at the end of the presentation, after Slide 8 ("Organization of Tour Company").

11. In Slide 2, insert the sound file **Cuzco**, located in the Tutorial.03\Review folder, set the sound to play automatically during the slide show, and position the sound icon to the right of the title.

12. Repeat the procedure of the previous step, except insert the sound file **SacsSnd** into Slide 4, the sound file **MachPicc** into Slide 6, and the sound file **HuaynaP** into Slide 7.

13. In Slide 4, insert the movie file **SacsMov**, located in the Tutorial.03\Review folder, and set it to play automatically during the slide show. Resize the movie object to make it easier to see, and set it to loop continuously. (*Hint*: If the sound icon moves, drag it back to its position next to the slide title. If the Title, Text, and Content layout does not apply to the slide, click Insert on the menu bar, point to Movies and Sounds, and then click Movie from File.)

14. In Slide 3, create a chart of the monthly rainfall in Cuzco. Use the following data (month, rainfall in inches): J, 6.0; F, 4.2; M, 4.0; A, 1.8; M, 0.5; J, 0.2; J, 0.1; A, 0.1; S, 0.7; O, 2.2; N, 2.8; D, 4.5. Make sure the Chart type is Column, and set the Chart sub-type to Clustered Column (the first chart sub-type in the first row). Add the Value (Y) axis label "Rainfall (inches)." Don't include a title or a label for the months.

15. Click the legend that PowerPoint automatically inserts to the right of the bar graph to select it, and then press the Delete key. (*Hint*: If the chart is no longer active, double-click it.)

16. In the graph, change the font size of the labels on the Value (Y) axis and the Category (X) axis to 24 points.

17. In Slide 8, create an organization chart. Make a single box at level 1 with the text "U.S. Expedition Head," a single box at level 2 with the text "Local Leader," and three boxes at level 3 with the text "Cuzco Tour Director," "Machu Picchu Tour Director," and "Lima Tour Director." Decrease the font size to 18 points to fit the text in the boxes.

18. Add the Push Up slide transition to all the slides, change the speed to Medium, and add the Camera sound effect to the slide transition.

19. Apply the Moderate animation scheme called Elegant to Slides 2, 4, 6, and 9 (those with bulleted lists). (*Hint*: Press and hold the Ctrl key while you click the slides to select them.)

20. In all the slides with photographs and captions (but not in the slide with the movie), set the pictures to have the Entrance animation called Zoom, set the captions to have the Entrance animation called Appear, and set the photographs to enter after the bulleted list (if any) on a mouse click, and set the caption to appear immediately, without a mouse click, after the picture is on the screen (After Previous).

21. In Slide 6, set the bulleted items to dim after animation. Set the dim color to black.

22. Hide Slide 3, and then go through the slide show. Use the pointer pen to mark words, phrases, pictures, or other objects in the slides. At the end of the show, keep the pen marks.

23. Save the presentation. (Don't unhide Slide 3.)

24. Package the presentation for a CD, and embed the fonts. Name the CD **Cuz-MP Tour**.

25. Print the presentation in grayscale as handouts with six slides per page.

Case Problem 1

Data Files needed for this Case Problem: **GeNetics.ppt, Bonnie.jpg, Atorv.jpg, Drugs.jpg, Applause.wav**

GeNetics Research Labs Dr. Bonnie Ornatowski, who received her Ph.D. in biochemistry from Bryn Mawr College, is a chief scientist for GeNetics Research Labs, a company based in Cambridge, Massachusetts. GeNetics takes drug formulations developed at university laboratories, tests the drugs, develops the delivery systems, gets approval for sale of the drugs from the Federal Drug Administration (FDA), sells the drugs, and then pays the university and its discoverers a royalty from the profits. Over the past six years, Bonnie has supervised the clinical testing, FDA approval, production, and marketing of a new statin drug, which lowers blood cholesterol, triglycerides (fats), and low-density lipoproteins (LDLs). Recently, Bonnie was selected as Honored Alumni from the College of Science at her alma mater, and was invited to give a presentation on some aspect of her career. She wants you to help her prepare a presentation that explains her career and her work with the new statin drug. Remember to change the slide layouts as needed when you complete the following:

1. Open the presentation file **GeNetics** from the Tutorial.03\Cases folder included with your Data Files, change the name on Slide 1 from Bonnie Ornatowski to your name, and save the presentation to a high-capacity disk using the filename **GeNetics Research Labs**.

2. Apply the design template called Digital Dots, which has a light-blue background and white text.

3. In the slide master, change the title text to light yellow, which is not one of the color scheme colors, but which you can find on the Standard tab of the Colors dialog box.

4. Change the second-level bullet to the same yellow color as you did the title text. Leave it the same character.

5. In the slide master and title master, change the slide number text box to 20-point Arial, switch to Normal view, open the Header and Footer dialog box, and display only the slide number on all of the slides (except the title slide).

6. In Slide 2, change the layout, and then add the digital image of Bonnie, which is the file **Bonnie** in the Tutorial.03\Cases folder. Position the picture to the right side of the slide, and then increase the size of the bulleted list text box so that the first two bulleted paragraphs fit on two lines each. The third one will then fit on three lines. Change the white background of the image to transparent.

7. In Slide 4, add an organization chart. In each box, include a person's name, and below the name, his or her position in the company. Don't include any punctuation in the boxes. In the top-level box, add "Karen Lamb, R&D Vice President." In the second-level boxes, add "Bonnie Ornatowski, Senior Scientist" on the left and "Alberto Thurston, Senior Scientist" on the right. Keep only two boxes on the second level. Below Bonnie, add three boxes: "James Jordan, Team 1A Leader," "Daniel Kelsch, Team 2A Leader," and "Kennedy Guisman, Team 3A Leader."

8. In Slide 7, change the slide layout to Title and Content over Text, and in the content placeholder, add the chemical structure of atorvastatin, located in the file **Atorv**. Make the size of the structure as large as possible while still fitting between the title text and the bulleted list.

9. In Slide 8, add a bar chart based on the data in the following table:

	Tot Chol	LDL-C	HDL-C	Trigly
Placebo	3	4	-2	9
Zocor	-43	-33	8	-24

10. Change the chart type to clustered column (no 3-D effect), and then add a Value (Y) axis label of "Percent Change."

Explore

11. Change the slide background of Slide 8 to only one color, bright blue (one of the color scheme colors).

12. In Slide 10, add the digital image **Drugs**, located in the Tutorial.03\Cases folder. Change the white background of the image to transparent, and then resize and reposition it to make the slide look attractive.

13. In Slide 11, add the sound clip **Applause**. Set it to play automatically in the slide show. Position the sound icon to the right of "Career" in the title.

14. Set the slide transition for all the slides to Cover Left-Down. Set its speed to Slow. Set its sound to Click.

15. In Slides 3, 9, and 10, set the text to enter by fading in one by one.

16. In Slide 9, set the bulleted items to dim to bright blue after the next item appears on the screen.

17. In Slide 10, set the image to enter using Center Revolve (under Moderate).

18. Hide Slide 4, and then go through the slide show. Use the pointer pen to make marks on some of the slides as you go through. Keep the pen marks once you're done.

19. Unhide the slide, and save the presentation.

20. Print the presentation in grayscale as handouts with six slides per page.

Case Problem 2

Challenge

Explore additional PowerPoint features that are associated with the skills you learned in this tutorial to complete a presentation for a small business.

Data Files needed for this Case Problem: Alaskan.ppt, ACWBus.ppt, Totem.jpg, Bowls.jpg

Alaskan Creative Woodworks Bobette Perkins of Anchorage, Alaska, has what she thinks is a winning business idea, but she needs money to start a company that will lead from ideas to profits. She has an appointment with the Alaska State Economic Development Agency (ASEDA), which provides small-business loans for promising new businesses and allocates grants for new businesses in economically depressed areas of Alaska. Bobette asks you to help her prepare the presentation of her business plan to the ASEDA. She has supplied information for two short presentations, but now wants you to combine the information and create an attractive, interesting slide show. Complete the following:

1. Open the presentation file **Alaskan**, located in the Tutorial.03\Cases folder included with your Data Files, change the name in Slide 1 from Bobette Perkins to your name, and save the presentation to a high-capacity disk as **Alaskan Creative Woodworks**.

2. Go to Slide 4. After Slide 4 in the current presentation, insert Slides 2, 3, and 4 from the beginning of Bobette's business plan presentation for Alaskan Creative Woodworks, located in the file **ACWBus** in the Tutorial.03\Cases folder.

3. Edit the color scheme according to the following directions: change the Background to a dark brown, Text and lines to white, Shadows to a dark green, Title text to yellow, Fills to a light brown, Accent to a light green, Accent and hyperlink to black, and Accent and followed hyperlink to medium green. Apply the new color scheme to all the slides.

4. Change the background to a two-color gradient fill, with the dark brown Background color in the upper-left corner of the slide, and the light brown Fills color in the bottom-right corner.

5. Change the title text font to 44-point bold Tahoma, if necessary. If your system doesn't have the Tahoma font, select any other TrueType sans serif font except Arial.

6. Change the body text font to Garamond, leaving other font attributes unchanged. If your computer doesn't have the Garamond font, select any other TrueType serif font except Times New Roman or any other Times font.

7. Change the first-level bullets to a yellow square.

8. Change the second-level bullets to a light green filled circle.

9. Save the presentation, and then save it as a design template with only necessary slides and content. Name the template file **Alaskan Creative Woodworks Template** and save it to the same location as your presentation. Close the template file and then reopen the presentation file.

Explore

10. In Slide 3, add an organization chart. In the top box, type "Bobette Perkins" on the first line, "President" on the second line, and "12 Years' Experience" on the third line. Add two second-level boxes, each with three lines; for the one on the left, type the text "Jianyin Shao," "V.P. Marketing," and "8 Years' Experience"; for the one on the right, type the text "Miwako Turley," "V.P. Operations," and "14 Years' Experience." Add two third-level boxes below Jianyin Shao, each with only two lines of text; for the one on the left, type "Karl Jorgensen" and "Advertising Director," and for the one on the right, type "Melissa Platt" and "Marketing Director." Add three subordinates below Miwako Turley, each box with only two lines of text; for the one on the left, type "Paulette Torre" and "Human Resources Director," for the one in the middle, type "Seymour Cleveland" and "Manufacturing Director," and for the one on the right, type "Paul Robertson" and "Executive Secretary."

Explore

11. Change the organization chart style to Bookend Fills. Click the AutoFormat button on the Organization Chart toolbar, click Bookend Fills, and then click the OK button. Insert hard returns, if necessary, in the text lines that don't fit within their boxes so that the text spans two lines.

12. In Slide 6, add a picture of a wooden totem pole, using the file **Totem**. Adjust, as desired, the slide layout, the size and position of the image, and the size of the bulleted list text box to maximize the readability and appearance of the slide. Set the picture to animate onto the screen (immediately, without a mouse click) using the Entrance effect Center Revolve.

13. In Slide 10, add a picture of wooden bowls, using the file **Bowls**. Adjust, as desired, the slide layout, the size and position of the image, and the size of the bulleted list text box to maximize the readability and appearance of the slide. Set the picture to animate in the same way as the one in Slide 6.

14. In Slide 5, add a line chart showing the trend in tourism in Alaska. Set the Chart type to Line with markers displayed at each data value (the first sub-type in the second row). In the datasheet, use the following labels in the top row: "2002," "2003," "2004," and "2005." Use the label "Tourists" in the cell to the left of cell A1. For the number of tourists in each of the above years, type (respectively) "1.25," "1.47," "1.28," and "1.42."
15. Add the Value (Y) axis label "Number of Tourists (in millions)."

Explore
16. In the chart, click the legend to select it, and then press the Delete key to delete the legend.

Explore
17. Change the thickness of the line and the size and color of the markers on the line in the chart. Click the line to select it, right-click it, click Format Data Series on the shortcut menu, and then click the Patterns tab. In the Line section, click the Weight list arrow, and then click the thickest line in the list. In the Marker section, change the size to 15 points, and then change the foreground and background colors of the marker to yellow.
18. Add the Moderate Entrance effect Zoom to the chart. Have the chart appear automatically.

Explore
19. Add the Wipe Left slide transition to Slides 4 through 9. Set the speed to Medium and the sound to Click for that transition effect.
20. Set all the slides with multiple bullets, except those with picture images, to progressive disclosure using the Moderate effect Descend with a dimming color set to a light brown-orange.
21. Go through the presentation in Slide Show view. Use the pointer pen to underline keywords. Keep the marks when you are finished.
22. Save the presentation, and then print the presentation in grayscale as handouts with six slides per page.
23. Package the presentation for a CD.

Create

Create slides for a presentation about a rental property company by using the skills you learned in this tutorial.

Case Problem 3

Data Files needed for this Case Problem: bedrm1.jpg, bedrm2.jpg, cabinfnt.jpg, fireplac.jpg, fitness.jpg, kitchen.jpg, livingrm.jpg

Recreation Rentals, Inc. Linda Halgren is a property agent for Recreation Rentals, Inc. (RRI) of Las Vegas, Nevada. RRI specializes in renting cabins and condos on behalf of their owners. She contacts owners who rent their properties, encourages them to list their properties with her, and then rents the properties to interested vacationers. Recently, Linda signed an agreement with an owner of a cabin located near one of the ski resorts at Lake Tahoe, Nevada. She wrote the text of a PowerPoint presentation and took digital photographs of the property, but she needs your help in creating an exciting presentation to show to potential renters. Create a presentation that looks like Figure 3-39. Select colors, fonts, bullets, and other elements as close to those in Figure 3-39 as you can.

Figure 3-39

Lake Tahoe Rental Cabin

Linda Halgren
Recreation Rentals, Inc
Las Vegas, Nevada
www.recreation-rentals.com
702-555-RENT (702 555-7368)

Bed and Bath

- 3 bedrooms
- 2 full bathrooms
- Walkout decks
- Jetted tub in master bedroom
- Linens and towels provided

2

Living Room

- Fireplace
- All-leather furniture
- Entertainment center
  - 27" color TV
  - Digital cable (HBO, Showtime, ESPN, etc.)
  - 200-watt stereo with 50 CDs
  - VHS and DVD player
- Reading library

3

Kitchen/Dining

- Farm table seats for 8
- Refrigerator
- Dishwasher
- Microwave oven
- Conventional oven
- "Flat-top" range
- Blender and mixer
- Coffee maker
- Telephone

4

Beech Mountain Club

- Free guest membership
- Golf
- Tennis
- Swimming
- Fitness room
- Recreation areas

5

Nearby Activities

- Biking (mountain)
- Bird Watching
- Bowling
- Canoeing
- Golf
- Hiking
- Historic Sites
- Ice Waking
- Miniature golf
- Movies

- Museums
- Rafting
- Rock Climbing
- Site Seeing
- Skiing
- Sledding
- Swimming
- Tennis
- Theatre
- Water sports

6

Average Snow Depth

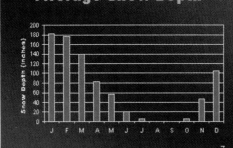

7

Cabin Rates

- Peak seasons (Winter and Summer)
  - $250 per night
  - $800 per week
- Off season (Spring and Fall)
  - $175 per night
  - $650 per week
- Deposit and cleaning fee required
- No smoking, no pets

8

To help you complete the presentation, do the following:

1. Use a color scheme of mostly earth tones—browns, tans, black, white, and grays.
2. Change the background to a two-color gradient fill.
3. Add the digital images provided in the Tutorial.03\Cases folder included with your Data Files to the appropriate slides. Resize the images and the text boxes to maximize readability and appearance. (*Hint*: For slides with two pictures, change the slide layout to Title, Text, and 2 Content.)
4. In the slide on average snow depth, for the average depth from January through December, respectively, use these values: 182, 176, 140, 82, 56, 20, 5, 0, 0, 5, 47, 105.
5. In Slide 1 (only), add the textured background as shown.
6. Add the Newsflash slide transition to all the slides.
7. Customize the animation so that the images animate onto the screen. Once you pick an animation effect, apply the same effect to all the images.
8. Use an animation scheme to set all the slides with multiple bullets to progressive disclosure, with dimming color set to a yellowish color in the color palette.
9. Replace Linda Halgren's name on Slide 1 with your name, save the presentation with the filename **RRI Tahoe Cabin**, and then print the presentation in grayscale as handouts with four slides per page.

Research

Use the Internet to research restaurants in your area and compile the data in a presentation.

Case Problem 4

There are no Data Files needed for this Case Problem.

Comparison of Local Restaurants Students spend a lot of money on food, and new students are always interested in which local restaurants provide the best food and service at a reasonable price. Your task is to conduct a study and compare the prices of at least three restaurants in your area, and then create a PowerPoint presentation to present your results. Do the following:

1. Connect to the Internet and then go to the Web sites of at least three local restaurants of the same general type that have menus posted. Note the prices of similar menu items. Include at least three categories (appetizers, salads, entrees, desserts, breads or baked goods, drinks, and so forth), and in each category, include at least three items.
2. Open a new PowerPoint presentation titled "Comparison of . . ." and list the names of the restaurants that you studied. Add your name as the presenter. Save it using the filename **Local Restaurant Comparison**.
3. Include at least one slide explaining your methodology—how you conducted your study.
4. Include at least one table or chart comparing the relative costs of the restaurants. You'll probably want to organize the presentation with one category per slide.
5. In your presentation, include at least three pictures or clip-art images. You can acquire the pictures from the Internet, scan pictures from magazines, or take your own digital photographs.
6. Include a slide with an organization chart of a typical or representative management structure of a restaurant. Show that organization with positions (but not necessarily names). You might want to send an e-mail to one of the restaurants in your comparison asking how the store's management is set up.
7. Apply an appropriate built-in design template.
8. Apply appropriate slide transitions and custom animations to make your presentation interesting and attractive.

9. Search for sound clips on the Internet and add one or more to your presentation. Try searching for clips of money being counted or a cash register being opened.
10. Select one of the slides that you think your audience might be least interested in, and hide that slide.
11. Save the presentation using the default filename, and then print it as handouts with four or six slides per page.

Research

Go to the Web to find information you can use to create presentations.

Internet Assignments

The purpose of the Internet Assignments is to challenge you to find information on the Internet that you can use to work effectively with this software. The actual assignments are updated and maintained on the Course Technology Web site. Log on to the Internet and use your Web browser to go to the Student Online Companion for New Perspectives Office 2003 at **www.course.com/np/office2003**. Click the Internet Assignments link, and then navigate to the assignments for this tutorial.

Reinforce

Multimedia

Lab Assignments

The New Perspectives Labs are designed to help you master some of the key concepts and skills presented in this text. The steps for completing this Lab are located on the Course Technology Web site. Log on to the Internet and use your Web browser to go to the Student Online Companion for New Perspectives Office 2003 at **www.course.com/np/office2003**. Click the Lab Assignments link, and then navigate to the assignments for this tutorial.

Assess

SAM Assessment and Training

If you have a SAM user profile, you may have access to hands-on instruction, practice, and assessment of the skills covered in this tutorial. Log in to your SAM account and go to your assignments page to see what your instructor has assigned.

Review

Quick Check Answers

Session 3.1

1. Click Insert on the menu bar, click Slides from File to open the Slide Finder dialog box, select the desired PowerPoint file, click the desired slides, and then click the Insert button.
2. the set of matching colors that makes up the background, fonts, and other elements of the presentation
3. background, fonts, font sizes, font colors, bullets, and background graphics
4. a variation of a particular shading style
5. Delete all the slides but one, delete the text and graphics from that slide, click File, click Save As, change the file type to Design Template, and then select the desired filename and folder location.
6. an animated picture file, usually with the filename extension .avi

Session 3.2

1. Change the slide layout to one of the Content layouts, click the Chart button in the content placeholder, edit the datasheet, and then change other chart options as desired.

2. a diagram of boxes, connected with lines, showing the hierarchy of positions within an organization

3. Change the slide layout to one of the Content layouts, click the Diagram button in the content placeholder, select the organization chart, click the OK button, type text into the boxes, and then add and remove organization chart boxes as desired.

4. Definitions:
   a. transition effect: a method of moving one slide off the screen and bringing another slide onto the screen during a slide show
   b. animation effect: a special visual or audio effect applied to an object (such as graphics or bulleted text)
   c. sound effect: a sound that takes place during a slide show
   d. pointer pen: a PowerPoint mouse pointer that allows you to draw lines on the screen during a slide show

5. Select the slide in Slide Sorter view, click the Slide Transition button, and then select a slide transition.

6. PowerPoint Viewer is a separate program that you can use to present your slide show on any Windows 95/98/2000/NT computer.

Objectives

Session 4.1
- Apply a template from another presentation
- Import, modify, and export a Word outline
- Import graphics into a presentation
- Embed and modify a table from Word
- Link and modify an Excel chart

Session 4.2
- Add links to slides within a presentation and to other presentations
- Add action buttons to a presentation
- View a slide show with embedded or linked objects
- Publish a presentation as a Web page
- Learn how to collaborate with workgroups

Labs

The Internet: World Wide Web

Student Data Files

Integrating PowerPoint with Other Programs and Collaborating with Workgroups

Presenting Information About an Annual Banquet

Case

Global Humanitarian, Fundraising

Fundraising is a major activity of Global Humanitarian. Funds are needed to help finance the following: service expeditions; village development projects (build water catchment systems, wells, irrigation systems, culinary water systems, Lorena stoves, greenhouses, schoolhouses, and clinics); student internships; and business mentoring projects. In addition, funds are needed to pay for the necessary administration costs of running this large organization.

▼ **Tutorial.04**

▽ **Tutorial folder**

Gala.ppt
GalaOutl.doc
GalaTabl.doc
Gala03.jpg
Gala06.jpg
Gala08.jpg
Gala09.jpg
Gala11.jpg
Gala12.jpg
GHChart.xls
GHMission.ppt

▽ **Review folder**

Chicken.jpg
Crafts.jpg
Dolls.jpg
Guide.jpg
Herd.jpg
Loan.ppt
LoanOtln.doc
Loans.xls
Mentor.jpg
ProjTabl.doc
Taxi.jpg
Weave.jpg

▽ **Cases folder**

GCChat.jpg   HeadQ.jpg
GCDes.ppt   Music.ppt
GCGroup.jpg   PPCData.xls
GCOtln.doc   PPCDes.ppt
HAOHikes.doc   PPCOtln.doc
HAOServ.ppt   PPCTbl.doc
HAOTempl.ppt   Temp.jpg

Global Humanitarian raises funds in the following ways:

- **Direct appeal to individuals and companies.** Development officers meet personally with potential benefactors and follow up with mailings and telephone calls.
- **Web presence.** Global Humanitarian maintains a Web site, and they include a link on the site for people to use to make a donation.
- **Annual Global Humanitarian gala.** The gala is an annual dinner, and it is the biggest fundraising event of the year.

The Global Humanitarian administrators who oversee the annual gala are the top administrators—Norma Flores, president of Global Humanitarian; Miriam Schwartz, managing director of the Austin office; and Pablo Fuentes, managing director of the Lima office. One of their first tasks for organizing the gala is to prepare a presentation for the other administrators and volunteers who will help with the event. Norma asks you to bring together several pieces of previously prepared materials to create an effective PowerPoint presentation about the gala.

In this tutorial, you'll import, modify, and export a Microsoft Word outline to and from your presentation, and you'll import a digital photograph. You will embed and modify a Word table in your presentation and link and modify an Excel chart. You will also create and edit hyperlinks, add action buttons, create and customize a toolbar, and publish a presentation on the World Wide Web.

Session 4.1

Planning the Presentation

Before you begin to create Norma's slide show, she discusses with you her plans for the presentation.

- **Purpose of the presentation**: to present an overview of the fundraising gala and assign responsibilities
- **Type of presentation**: training
- **Audience for the presentation**: Global Humanitarian's employees and volunteers
- **Audience needs**: an overview of the gala and specific task assignments
- **Location of the presentation**: meeting rooms at Global Humanitarian headquarters
- **Format**: on-screen slide show

With the above general plan for the presentation, Norma, Miriam, and Pablo prepare the outline of the presentation, as well as some of the key information about the gala.

Applying a Template from Another Presentation

You already know how to apply a design template from a design template file. You can use a similar method to apply a design from any other presentation file.

For the gala presentation, Norma wants you to use the design template from a presentation she recently prepared about Global Humanitarian's mission and purpose. You'll apply that design template now.

To apply a design template from another presentation:

▶ 1. Open the file **Gala** from the **Tutorial.04\Tutorial** folder included with your Data Files, and then save the file with the new filename **Gala Planning** to the same folder. The title slide appears on the screen with the name of the two principal presenters, Norma Flores and Miriam Schwartz, listed. The presentation has the Curtain Call design template applied. Notice that this presentation includes only this one slide. See Figure 4-1. You'll add additional slides later.

Title page of new presentation with the Curtain Call design template applied ◀ **Figure 4-1**

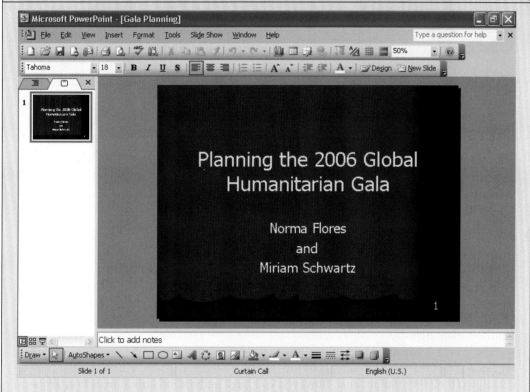

Trouble? If you're using a floppy disk for your Data Files, you won't have enough space to save all of the files you create in this tutorial. If you don't have access to a hard disk or some other high-capacity disk, skip those steps in which you're asked to create a Web page (in the "Publishing Presentations on the World Wide Web" section).

▶ 2. Click the **Design** button on the Formatting toolbar to display the Slide Design task pane. You won't use one of these built-in template files or a custom slide design, but rather a slide design already created in another presentation file.

▶ 3. Click the **Browse** link at the bottom of the task pane. The Apply Design Template dialog box opens.

▶ 4. Click the **Look in** list arrow, navigate to the **Tutorial.04\Tutorial** folder included with your Data Files, and then, if necessary, change the **Files of type** list box to **All PowerPoint Files**. The dialog box displays all the presentation files within the folder. Now you'll select the presentation Norma prepared earlier.

▶ **5.** Click **GHMission**, and then click the **Apply** button. The design template from the presentation GHMission is applied to the Gala Planning presentation. See Figure 4-2.

Figure 4-2 ▶ **Presentation with new design template**

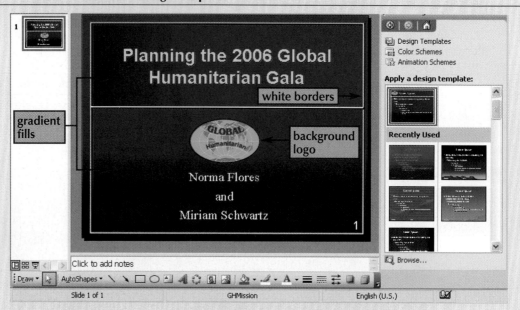

▶ **6.** Close the task pane, and then save the file with its new design using the default filename.

In Figure 4-2, you can see some of the design elements that Norma created in her original presentation, including the color scheme with a blue-to-black gradient background, yellow title text, white body text, a background graphic of white borders, and the Global Humanitarian logo.

Now you're ready to add additional slides to your presentation. All the slides you will add exist in some format already; your job will be to integrate files created in other programs into the presentation. First, however, you must understand about importing, embedding, and linking objects.

Using Integration Techniques: Importing, Embedding, and Linking

As you learned in Tutorial 1, an **object** is anything in a presentation that you can manipulate as a whole. This includes clip art, photos, and text boxes, as well as other graphics, diagrams, and charts that you've already worked with. In addition, you can insert objects, such as a word-processing document or a spreadsheet chart, that were created in other Office programs. The program in which the objects are created is the **source file**; the program into which the objects are inserted is the **destination file**.

When you insert objects, you either import, embed, or link them. Refer to Figure 4-3 as you read the definitions of each of these following terms.

Integration techniques   **Figure 4-3**

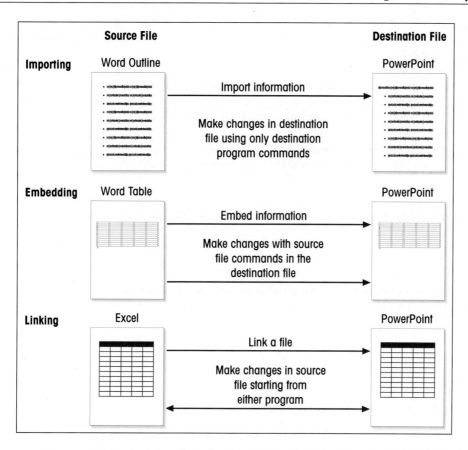

Importing an object means simply copying a file that was created using one program into another program's file. For example, when you insert graphics and sounds into a presentation, you actually import them. Imported objects become part of the PowerPoint presentation. When you import a file, the source program and the destination program don't communicate with each other in any way, as illustrated in Figure 4-3. For example, if you want to modify a graphic (such as change its size or colors) after importing it into PowerPoint, you make these changes in PowerPoint rather than in the graphics program. If you want to access the source program's commands to modify the object, you need to start the source program and then open and modify the file in the source program. To see the changes you made to the object in the destination program, you need to import the object again.

Embedding is similar to importing but allows a one-way connection to be maintained with the source program, not the source file. For example, if you embed a Word table in a PowerPoint presentation and then double-click the table, you will be able to access and use Word commands to edit the table while still in PowerPoint. When you finish editing the embedded table and return to PowerPoint, the changes you made to the table will appear in the object in PowerPoint only; the changes do not appear in the original Word file that you used to create the table. This is because the embedded object is a copy of the original Word file, not the Word file itself. Therefore, if you make subsequent changes to the original Word file using Word, the changes will not be reflected in the embedded Word table in PowerPoint. In other words, an embedded object has no relationship to the original source file, but it does maintain a connection to the source program.

When you **link** an object, you create a connection between the source file and the linked object. You do not place a copy of the source file in the destination file; instead, you place a representation of the actual source file in the destination file. When an object is linked, you can make changes to the source file, and those changes are reflected in the representation of the linked object in the destination program. When you link, for example, an Excel spreadsheet to a PowerPoint slide, the spreadsheet file must be available to the PowerPoint presentation file if you want to edit the file; otherwise, PowerPoint treats the spreadsheet as an embedded file.

You should be aware that not all software allows you to embed or link objects. Only those programs that support **object linking and embedding** (or **OLE**, pronounced oh-LAY) let you embed or link objects from one program to another. Fortunately, sophisticated programs, such as PowerPoint, Word, and Excel, are all OLE-enabled programs and fully support object linking and embedding.

Norma has created an outline in Word listing the text of many of the slides she wants to include in her presentation. Your next task is to import the Word outline into the presentation.

Importing and Exporting a Word Outline

If your presentation contains quite a bit of text, it might be easier to create the outline of your presentation in Word, so that you can take advantage of the extensive text-editing features available in that program. Fortunately, if you create an outline in a Word document, you don't need to retype it in PowerPoint. You can import it directly into your presentation.

Although you can create handouts in PowerPoint, if you want to enhance the handouts using Word's formatting commands to make it easier to read, or use the presentation of the outline as the outline for a more detailed document, you can export the outline to a Word document.

First, you'll import an outline into your presentation.

Importing the Word Outline

As you know, when you work in the Outline tab in PowerPoint, each level-one heading (also called Heading 1 or A head) automatically becomes a slide title; each level-two heading (also called Heading 2 or B head) automatically becomes a level-one bulleted paragraph; each level-three heading (also called Heading 3 or C head) automatically becomes a level-two bulleted paragraph, and so forth. Similarly, Word has an outline mode in which you can create outline text that automatically becomes level-one text, level-two text, and so forth, in the Word document. The level-one text becomes a built-in Heading 1 style; level-two text becomes a built-in Heading 2 style, and so forth. So Norma created a Word document using the outline mode (alternatively, she could have simply applied the built-in headings to the outline text). Your next task, then, is to import her outline into PowerPoint.

To import a Word outline:

1. Click **Insert** on the menu bar, and then click **Slides from Outline**. The Insert Outline dialog box opens.

2. Change the Look in folder to the **Tutorial.04\Tutorial** folder included with your Data Files, click **GalaOutl**, and then click the **Insert** button. The Word outline is inserted as new slides after the current slide in the PowerPoint presentation, with all the level-one text becoming new slide titles. See Figure 4-4. No matter what the font and font sizes of the text in the Word document were, the text is formatted with the default font and sizes of the PowerPoint presentation.

Presentation with imported Word outline | **Figure 4-4**

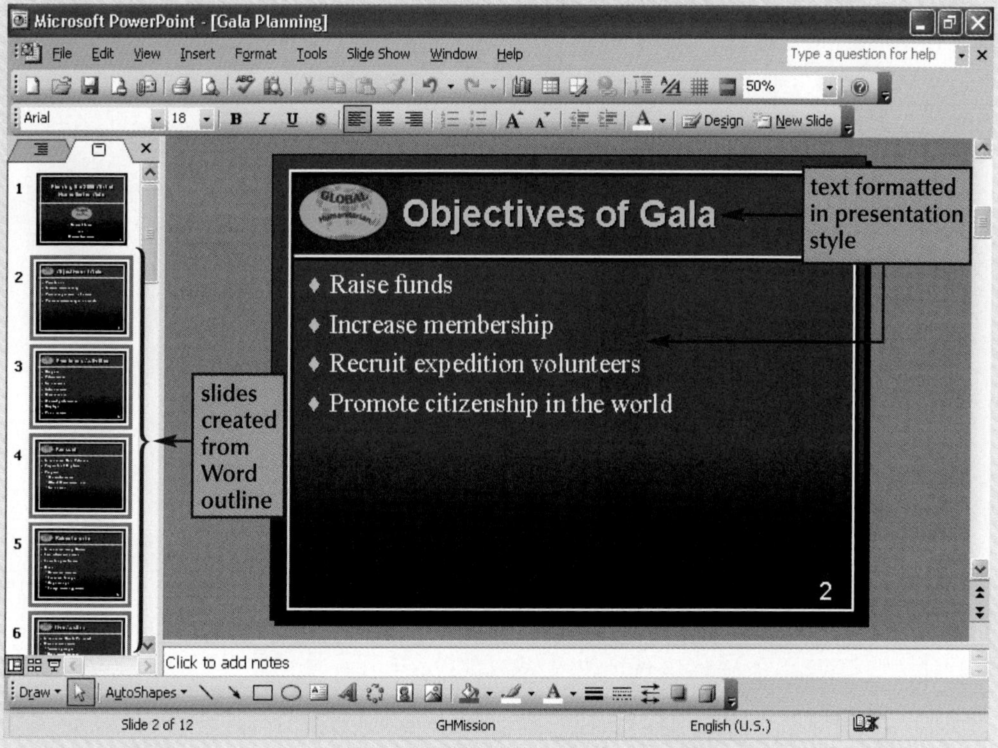

Because you imported the outline, the text is now part of PowerPoint and has no relationship with the Word file GalaOutl. Any changes you make to the PowerPoint text will have no effect on the GalaOutl file.

Exporting the Outline to Word

After looking over the presentation, Norma wants you to move the information on fundraising sources so that it appears earlier in the presentation, and then export the revised text as a Word outline so that she can create assignment sheets based on the revised outline. You'll do this now.

To modify the outline:

1. Switch to Slide Sorter view. Norma wants you to move Slide 12 ("Fundraising Sources") so that it appears earlier in the presentation.

2. Drag **Slide 12** to the left of Slide 3. The Fundraising Sources slide becomes the new Slide 3. The old Slide 3 ("Events and Activities") becomes the new Slide 4, and all the other slides similarly change their slide numbers.

3. Double-click **Slide 3** to return to Normal view, and then click the **Outline** tab so you can see the text of the outline. By changing the order of the slides, you changed the outline. See Figure 4-5.

Figure 4-5 Presentation with modified outline

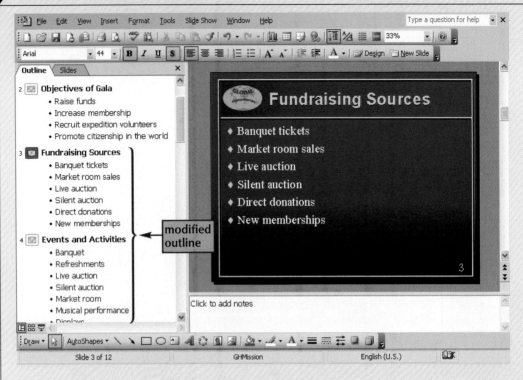

Now you'll export the revised outline to a Word file.

To export the outline to Word:

1. Click **File** on the menu bar, point to **Send to**, and then click **Microsoft Office Word**. The Send To Microsoft Office Word dialog box opens. See Figure 4-6.

Figure 4-6 Send To Microsoft Office Word dialog box

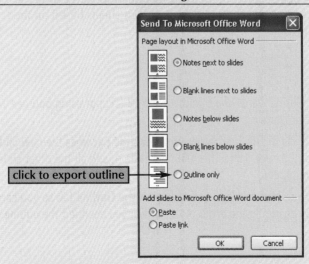

You could export the presentation in a variety of ways, but for this presentation, you'll choose to export only the outline.

2. Click the **Outline only** option button, and then click the **OK** button. Word automatically starts and opens a new Word document containing the PowerPoint text. See Figure 4-7. Notice that the process of exporting the outline preserves the font, font styles, and bullets of the PowerPoint presentation. Also notice that the text on the PowerPoint title slide becomes the title and subtitle in the Word document.

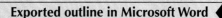

Exported outline in Microsoft Word | Figure 4-7

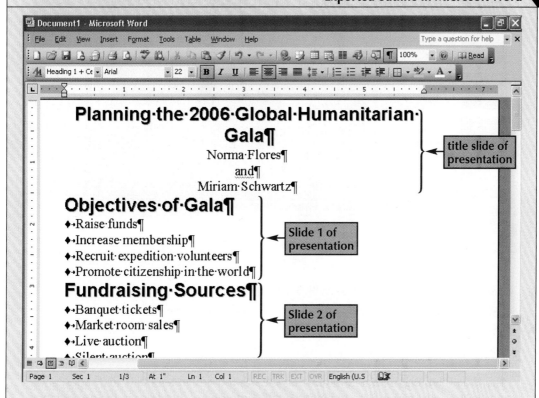

3. Save the Word document to the **Tutorial.04\Tutorial** folder using the filename **Gala Outline**, and then exit Word.

Now, Norma wants you to add digital photographs to the presentation. You'll do this next.

Importing Graphics

You already know how to import graphics, as you have inserted digital images and clip art into earlier presentations. Now, to make the Gala Planning presentation more attractive, you'll import digital photographs of last year's gala to give the Global Humanitarian personnel a better idea of some of the events.

To import (insert) graphics into the presentation:

1. Click the **Slides** tab so you don't see the outline, but rather the slide thumbnails.

2. With Slide 3 ("Fundraising Sources") in the slide pane, use the **Insert Picture** button on the Drawing toolbar to insert the file **Gala03**, located in the **Tutorial.04\Tutorial** folder. A photo of people preparing for last year's gala appears in Slide 3.

▶ **3.** Reposition the picture so that it's centered between the top and bottom of the slide and aligned to the right of the bulleted text. See Figure 4-8.

Figure 4-8	▶ Slide 3 after importing graphic

▶ **4.** Repeat the above step for Slides 6, 8, 9 (put this picture below the bulleted list), 11, and 12 using the picture files **Gala06**, **Gala08**, **Gala09**, **Gala11**, and **Gala12**.

▶ **5.** Save the presentation file using the default filename.

The Gala Planning presentation now has the desired design template, text slides, and graphics. Your next task will be to embed a table into one of the slides in the presentation.

Embedding and Modifying a Word Table

You know how to use PowerPoint commands to create a table in a slide, but what if you've already created a table using Word? You don't have to re-create it in PowerPoint; instead, you can copy the table and place it in a slide. If you embed the table instead of importing it, you can then edit it using Word's table commands.

Reference Window	**Embedding a Word Table**

- In Normal view, click Insert on the menu bar, and then click Object to open the Insert Object dialog box.
- Click the Create from file option button to select it, click the Browse button, navigate to the location of the file you want to insert, click it, and then click the OK button.
- Make sure the Link check box is not selected.
- Click the OK button.

Now you're ready to embed the Word table. Keep in mind that Norma created the table with a black font on a white background, so it is legible in a Word document. But as you'll see, it's not legible in the PowerPoint presentation, with its dark background.

To embed a Word file in a presentation:

1. Insert a new Slide 13 into the presentation, change its slide layout to **Title Only**, close the task pane, and then type the text **Gala Personnel** in the title placeholder.

2. Click **Insert** on the menu bar, and then click **Object**. The Insert Object dialog box opens. You can now create a new embedded file or use an existing one. You'll use an existing file.

3. Click the **Create from file** option button, click the **Browse** button to open the Browse dialog box, change the Look in folder to the **Tutorial.04\Tutorial** folder included with your Data Files, click the Word filename **GalaTabl**, and then click the **OK** button. See Figure 4-9.

Insert Object dialog box ◀ **Figure 4-9**

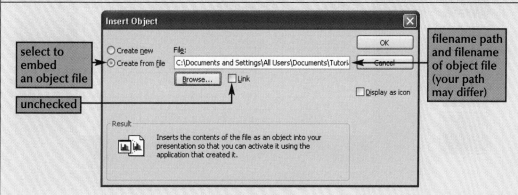

In Figure 4-9, the path and name of the file appear in the File text box. (Note that the path shown on your computer might be different.)

4. Make sure the **Link** check box is not selected, as shown in Figure 4-9, and then click the **OK** button. The embedded table appears in Slide 13.

5. Resize the table by dragging the corner sizing handles so that the table is as large as possible and still fits on the slide below the slide title, and then click a blank area of the slide, outside the table, to deselect it. You can barely read the table with its current colors, so you fix the colors next.

6. Save the presentation.

Norma asks you to modify the embedded table by changing the table color scheme. Because you embedded the table, you will use the program that created the object (in this case, Word) to make this change.

To modify an embedded object:

▶ **1.** Double-click anywhere in the table in Slide 13. The embedded table object becomes active in Word; the Word ruler appears above and to the left of the table, and the Word menu bar and toolbars replace the PowerPoint menu bar and toolbars. See Figure 4-10.

| Figure 4-10 | Slide 13 with embedded Word table made active |

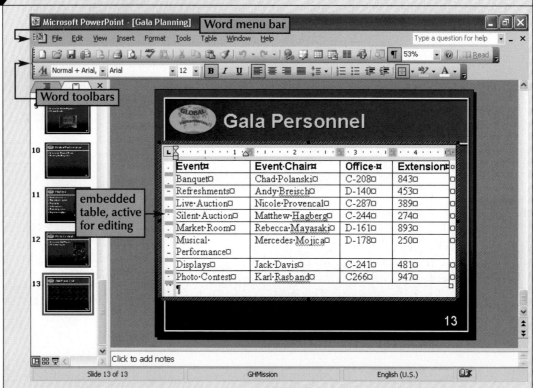

▶ **2.** Click **Table** on the menu bar (which is now Word's menu bar), click **Table AutoFormat** to open the Table AutoFormat dialog box, click **Table Colorful 1** in the Table styles list, and then click the **Apply** button. The table color scheme changes so that the table text will be legible and attractive on the PowerPoint slide.

▶ **3.** Click a blank area of the slide, outside the table, to return to PowerPoint with the object selected.

▶ **4.** Click a blank area of the slide again to deselect the object. Now you'll see how the table looks in Slide Show view.

▶ **5.** Switch to Slide Show view. As you can see, the table is attractive and legible. See Figure 4-11.

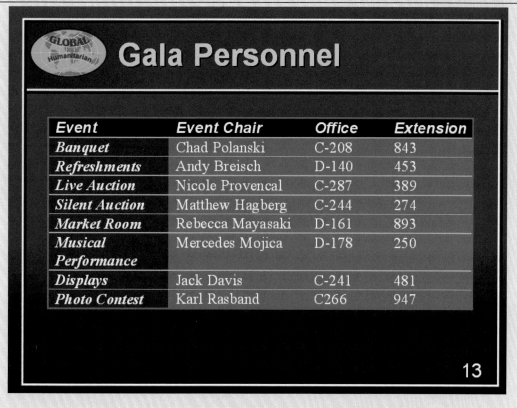

6. Press the **Esc** key to return to Normal view, and then save the presentation using the default filename.

You have now completed Slide 13, which contains the embedded object. Next, you'll link an Excel chart to the presentation.

Linking and Modifying an Excel Chart

Now you know how to insert objects into a PowerPoint slide by importing them and by embedding them. What if you needed to include in your presentation data that might change? For example, you might need to include data from an Excel worksheet, but you know that the final numbers won't be available for a while or that the numbers will change over time. In this case, you can link the data. Then, when the source file is updated, you can automatically update the linked object in the destination file so that it reflects the changes made to the source file.

Linking an Object	Reference Window

- In Normal view, click Insert on the menu bar, and then click Object to open the Insert Object dialog box.
- Click the Create from file option button, click the Browse button, navigate to the location of the file you want to insert, click it, and then click the OK button.
- Click the Link check box.
- Click the OK button.

Norma decides to include a bar graph of past and projected income and expenses from the fundraising activities at the gala. She chooses a bar graph because it emphasizes the earnings over the designated time period (the past five years), and shows trends that might help project income from this year's gala.

Miriam Schwartz already created a chart showing this data in an Excel workbook. Norma anticipates that she might have to modify Miriam's workbook after she creates the PowerPoint presentation. For example, the estimates for costs of the current gala might change as more exact values on rental fees, setup costs, celebrity appearance honoraria, auctioneer fees, and other expenses become available. Norma wants any changes made to the workbook to be reflected in the PowerPoint file, so rather than retype or import the data into a PowerPoint chart, she asks you to link Miriam's Excel workbook to the PowerPoint presentation.

You'll link Miriam's Excel graph of income and expenses to a new Slide 14 in Norma's presentation now.

To insert the chart and link the Excel worksheet:

1. With Slide 13 in the slide pane, insert a new Slide 14, set the layout to **Title Only**, and then type **Projected Income** as the slide title. (Remember to close the task pane.)

2. Click **Insert** on the menu bar, click **Object**, click the **Create from file** option button, click the **Browse** button, and then change the Look in folder to the **Tutorial.04\Tutorial** folder included with your Data Files.

   Ordinarily, you would now simply select the Excel file you want to link; however, because in this instance you'll be modifying a Data File, you'll first make a copy in case you make a mistake, or in case you or others want to go through the tutorial again.

3. Right-click the filename **GHChart**, then click **Copy** on the shortcut menu.

4. Right-click a blank area of the file list in the Browse dialog box to bring up another shortcut menu, and then click **Paste** on this shortcut menu. A copy of the income and expenses worksheet, with the filename **Copy of GHChart**, appears in the filename list.

   Because "Copy of GHChart" isn't a particularly descriptive filename, you'll change the file-name to Gala Projected Income.

5. Right-click the filename **Copy of GHChart**, and then click **Rename** on the shortcut menu.

6. Type **Gala Projected Income**, and then press the **Enter** key. The copy is renamed.

   Trouble? If you get an error message that you're changing the filename extension, click the No button, repeat Step 5, type "Gala Projected Income.xls," and then press the Enter key.

7. Make sure **Gala Projected Income** is highlighted, and then click the **OK** button. The path and filename of the selected file appears in the File text box of the Insert Object dialog box. You need to select the Link check box in order to link, rather than embed, the file.

8. Click the **Link** check box to select it, and then click the **OK** button. After a few moments, the chart appears in Slide 14. You have linked the Excel workbook to the PowerPoint presentation.

9. Click anywhere in the slide outside the chart to deselect the object. See Figure 4-12. Some of the text on the chart is barely legible, but you'll soon fix that.

Slide 14 with linked Excel chart | **Figure 4-12**

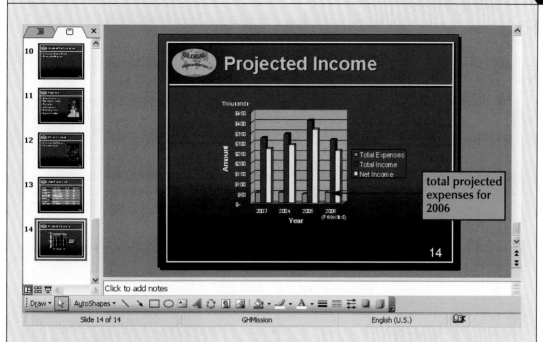

▶ **10.** Save the presentation using the default filename.

Another method for linking a file to a PowerPoint presentation is to use the Paste Special command on the Edit menu in PowerPoint. You select the object in the source file that you want to link, and then click the Copy button on the Standard toolbar in the source program. Then you switch to the destination file in PowerPoint, and use the Paste Special command on the Edit menu. In the Paste Special dialog box that opens, you can choose to paste the copied object as a link. The Paste Special method is especially handy when you don't want to link an entire file to a PowerPoint presentation.

After you linked the chart, Norma received new information about the projected expenses of the gala. She asks you to make changes to the worksheet data, which will then be reflected in the chart.

To modify the linked chart:

▶ **1.** Notice on the chart that the Total Expenses for 2006 (Projected) is approximately $50 thousand, and then double-click anywhere on the chart. Excel starts and opens the Gala Projected Income workbook.

▶ **2.** Click the **Maximize** button ▣ on the Excel window so that Excel fills the entire screen.

▶ **3.** Click the **Income Data** sheet tab near the bottom of the Excel window to display the data on the income and expenses of the gala.

▶ **4.** Click cell **F4**, which currently contains the number $22,558, type **34,684**, which is the newly projected administrative salary, and press the **Enter** key. The new value is now $34,684, and the total expenses for 2006, in cell F19, changes from $54,614 to $66,740.

▶ **5.** Click the **Chart** sheet tab near the bottom of the Excel window, save the worksheet using the default filename, and then exit Excel. The change you made in the chart in Excel is automatically reflected in the increased height of the Total Expenses column for the year 2006 in the PowerPoint slide.

▶ **6.** Resize the chart as large as possible on the slide, and then click a blank area of the slide to deselect the chart.

▶ **7.** Click the **Slide Show from current slide** button 🖵 to see how the chart looks in full-screen view. See Figure 4-13.

Figure 4-13 ▶ Linked and modified chart in Slide Show view

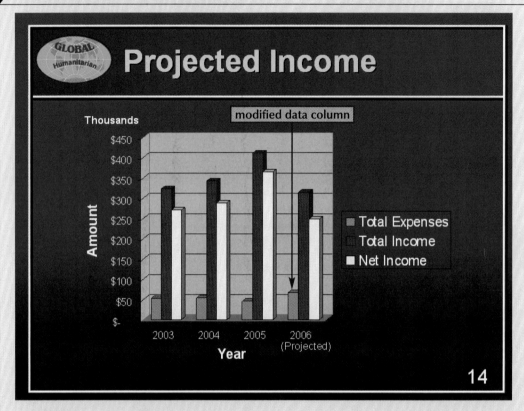

Trouble? If your chart doesn't have the approximate size and position of the chart shown in Figure 4-13, press the Esc key to return to Normal view, adjust the size or position of the chart, and then return to Slide Show view.

▶ **8.** Press the **Esc** key to exit Slide Show view and return to Normal view.

▶ **9.** Save the presentation using the default filename.

You have now linked and edited an Excel chart from PowerPoint. If you decide later to make further changes to the data in the workbook, you can do so either by directly starting Excel and opening Gala Projected Income or by double-clicking the chart in PowerPoint. Either way, any changes made to the workbook will be reflected in the linked object in the PowerPoint slide.

If you close and then reopen the presentation, you will see a message telling you that the presentation contains links, and asking you if you want to update them. To have PowerPoint update the links for the latest version of the source files, click the Update Links button. To have PowerPoint use the information currently in the destination file, click the Cancel button.

Session 4.1 Quick Check

1. How does applying a design template from another presentation differ from applying a design template from the Templates folder?
2. Describe how you use a Word outline to create slides in PowerPoint.
3. How do you save the text of a PowerPoint presentation in the form of a Word outline?
4. Define or describe:
   a. import
   b. embed
   c. link
   d. OLE
5. If you modify the source file of a linked object, such as an Excel chart linked to a PowerPoint slide, what happens to the linked object in the PowerPoint slide?
6. If you insert a picture created with scanning software and hardware, is the picture file imported, embedded, or linked?
7. Why would you link an object rather than embed it?

Session 4.2

Creating and Editing Hyperlinks

As you know, a **hyperlink** (or **link**) is a word, phrase, or graphic image that you click to "jump to" (or display) another location, called the **target**. The target of a link can be a location within the document (presentation), a different document, or a page on the World Wide Web. Graphic hyperlinks are visually indistinguishable from graphics that are not hyperlinks. The mouse pointer changes to a hand with a pointing finger when it is positioned over a link. In a presentation, text links are underlined and are a different color than the rest of the text, unless you have made a change to the color scheme. Once you've click a text link during a slide show, the link changes to another color to reflect the fact that it has been clicked, or **followed**.

Norma wants to easily move from Slide 4, which lists the major events and activities of the Global Humanitarian gala, to any slide dealing with a particular activity. Therefore, she asks you to create hyperlinks between each item in Slide 4 and the corresponding slides in the presentation, and then to create hyperlinks from each slide back to Slide 4.

To create a hyperlink to another slide in the presentation:

1. If you took a break after the last session, open the **Gala Planning** presentation located in the **Tutorial.04\Tutorial** folder included with your Data Files, and then switch to Normal view and close the task pane, if necessary.

2. Go to **Slide 4**.

   First, you'll link the text "Banquet" with the slide that describes the banquet.

3. Double-click the word **Banquet** to select the entire word, and then click the **Insert Hyperlink** button 🖳 on the Standard toolbar. The Insert Hyperlink dialog box opens. See Figure 4-14.

Figure 4-14 ▶ **Insert Hyperlink dialog box**

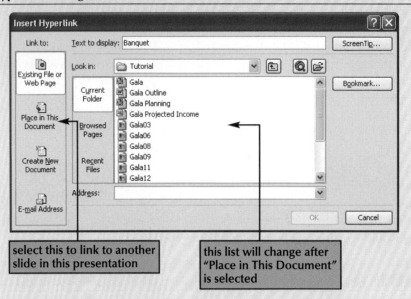

select this to link to another slide in this presentation

this list will change after "Place in This Document" is selected

You need to identify the file or location to which you want to link. Clicking each of the buttons in the Link to panel on the left side of the dialog box changes the rest of the dialog box so that you can then specify the exact location to jump to. For example, as you can see in Figure 4-14, the current item selected in the Link to panel is Existing File or Web Page. But in this presentation, you want to link to another location within the presentation, that is, within the current document.

▶ 4. Click the **Place in This Document** button in the Link to panel on the left side of the dialog box. The dialog box changes to list all of the slides in the presentation.

▶ 5. Click **5. Banquet** in the Select a place in this document list. The Slide preview area on the right side of the dialog box shows Slide 5. See Figure 4-15.

Figure 4-15 ▶ **Insert Hyperlink dialog box after selecting a slide in current document**

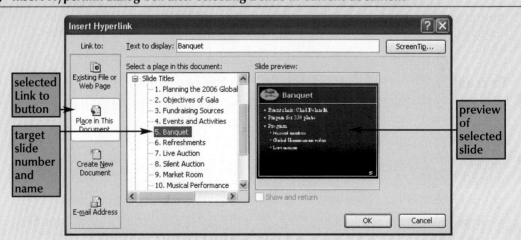

selected Link to button

target slide number and name

preview of selected slide

▶ 6. Click the **OK** button in the Insert Hyperlink dialog box. The word "Banquet" remains selected in the slide pane, but it is now underlined.

▶ 7. Click a blank area of the slide to deselect the text. The word "Banquet" now appears as light-blue, underlined text, indicating that the word is a hyperlink. (Recall that you can specify the hyperlink color when you set the presentation color scheme.)

8. Repeat this procedure to add hyperlinks for each of the other bulleted items in Slide 4 so that each item is a hyperlink to its corresponding slide. Slide 4 should then look like Figure 4-16.

Slide 4 after inserting hyperlinks 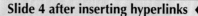 **Figure 4-16**

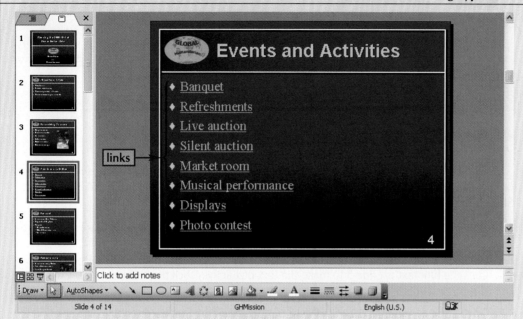

Trouble? If you make a mistake, repeat the procedure. The Edit Hyperlink dialog box will open in place of the Insert Hyperlink dialog box. You can then change the target of the hyperlink.

9. Save the presentation.

Now that you have added hyperlinks from the text in Slide 4 to the corresponding slides, you need hyperlinks from all the other slides back to Slide 4. This way, Norma can easily jump to an event slide, jump back to Slide 4, and then jump to another event slide. To create a link back to Slide 4, you will insert text on the target slide that will become the hyperlink.

To create hyperlinks from the slides back to Slide 4:

1. Go to **Slide 5**, click the **Text Box** button on the Drawing toolbar, click the text pointer ↓ near the lower-right corner of the slide (just to the left of the slide number), click the **Align Right** button on the Formatting toolbar, and then type **Return to Event List**. Clicking the Align Right button causes the text to move to the left instead of to the right, so the text won't cover the slide number.

2. Select the text **Return to Event List**, click the **Insert Hyperlink** button , set the hyperlink target to Slide 4 ("Events and Activities"), and then click the **OK** button to return to Slide 5.

3. Click the slanted-line border of the text box to select the entire text box object, drag the text box by its border to position it as shown in Figure 4-17, if necessary, and then deselect the text box.

Figure 4-17 ▶ **Slide with new link text added**

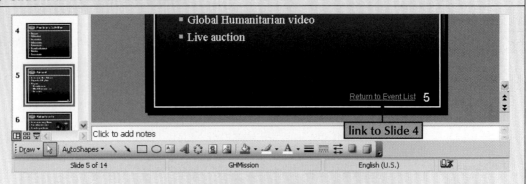

Now you'll add the links back to Slide 4 from the rest of the slides. Because all of the links will jump to the same slide, you can copy the text box and the link you created on Slide 5 to the other slides.

To copy a link:

▶ 1. Click the **link** text in Slide 5 to make the text box active, click the text box border to select the entire text box object, and then click the **Copy** button 📋 on the Standard toolbar.

▶ 2. Go to **Slide 6**, and then click the **Paste** button 📋 on the Standard toolbar. The link text is copied to the same position on Slide 6 as it was on Slide 5. Now you'll verify that the pasted link on Slide 6 has the same target as the original link on Slide 5.

▶ 3. Right-click the newly pasted link text, click **Edit Hyperlink** on the shortcut menu to open the Edit Hyperlink dialog box, verify that **4. Events and Activities** is selected in the Select a place in this document list, and then click the **Cancel** button.

Trouble? If you don't see Edit Hyperlink on the shortcut menu, you clicked the text box border instead of the link text. Repeat Step 3, but make sure you right-click the link text.

▶ 4. Repeat Step 2 to paste the link text to Slides 7 through 12 (that is, all the slides that are targets of the hyperlinks on Slide 4).

▶ 5. Save the presentation.

With all the items on Slide 4 hyperlinked to the other slides and then back again, you're ready to test the results.

To use a hyperlink to jump to a specific slide:

▶ 1. Go to **Slide 4**, and then click the **Slide Show from current slide** button 🖥.

▶ 2. Click the **Refreshments** hyperlink. PowerPoint immediately displays Slide 6 ("Refreshments").

▶ 3. Click the **Return to Event List** hyperlink. PowerPoint again displays Slide 4. See Figure 4-18. The Refreshments link text is now light yellow, indicating that the hyperlink was followed.

Slide Show view of slide with followed hyperlink ◀ **Figure 4-18**

Events and Activities

- ◆ Banquet
- ◆ Refreshments ← followed link
- ◆ Live auction

> **4.** Try all the other hyperlinks to make sure they work, and then return to Slide 4 in Normal view.

In addition to creating hyperlinks among the slides, you can add action buttons that have essentially the same effect. For Norma's presentation, you'll insert an action button that will add a link to another presentation.

Adding Action Buttons

An **action button** is a ready-made icon for which you can easily define a hyperlink to other slides or documents, as well as several other actions. You can use one of the 12 action buttons in PowerPoint, such as Action Button: Sound.

Reference Window

Adding an Action Button as a Link to Another Presentation

- In Normal view, click Slide Show on the menu bar, point to Action Buttons, and then click the desired button.
- Click the pointer at the location on the slide where you want the action button to appear.
- In the Action Settings dialog box, click the Hyperlink to option button, click the Hyperlink to list arrow, and then click Other PowerPoint Presentation to open the Hyperlink to Other PowerPoint Presentation dialog box.
- Select the presentation to which you want to jump, and then click the OK button.
- Click the OK button in the Action Settings dialog box.
- Resize and reposition the action button icon as desired.

Norma wants you to add a link between her presentation and the **GHMission** presentation, which gives the objectives and mission of Global Humanitarian. You'll create a hyperlink to that presentation by adding an action button.

To add an action button to link to another presentation:

> **1.** Go to **Slide 2** ("Objectives of Gala").
> **2.** Click **Slide Show** on the menu bar, point to **Action Buttons**, and then click the **Action Button: Document** button ☐ (the second button in the third row). The pointer changes to ┼.

▶ **3.** Click ┼ roughly centered between the last bulleted item in Slide 2 and the bottom of the slide. A button appears on the slide and the Action Settings dialog box opens with the Mouse Click tab on top. (The dialog box covers the button.) See Figure 4-19. You can choose one of five actions to occur when you click the action button, or you can switch to the Mouse Over tab and choose an action to occur when you position the mouse pointer over the button. You will set the button so that you jump to another presentation when you click the button.

| Figure 4-19 | **Action Settings dialog box** |

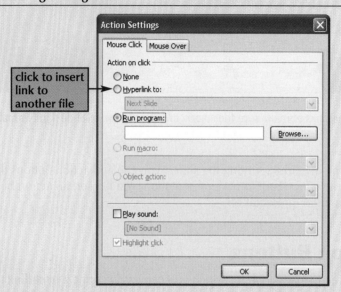

▶ **4.** Click the **Hyperlink to** option button, click the **Hyperlink to** list arrow, scroll down, and then click **Other PowerPoint Presentation**. The Hyperlink to Other PowerPoint Presentation dialog box opens. It is similar to the Open dialog box.

▶ **5.** Change the Look in folder, if necessary, to the **Tutorial.04\Tutorial** folder included with your Data Files, click **GHMission**, and then click the **OK** button.

▶ **6.** Make sure **Global Humanitarian: Our Objectives and Mission** is selected in the Hyperlink to Slide dialog box, and then click the **OK** button. The path and filename of the file you selected appear in the Hyperlink to text box.

▶ **7.** Click the **OK** button to close the Action Settings dialog box.

▶ **8.** If necessary, drag the action button to the location shown in Figure 4-20, and then deselect the button.

| Figure 4-20 | **Slide 2 with action button** |

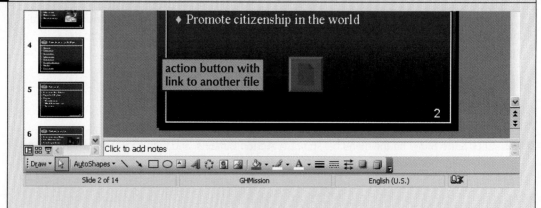

9. Switch to Slide Show view with Slide 2 ("Objectives of Gala"), on the screen, and then click the action button. Slide 1 of the GHMission presentation appears on the screen.

   Trouble? If a warning appears telling you that hyperlinks can be harmful to your computer and asking if you want to continue, click the Yes button.

10. Go through the entire GHMission presentation until you reach the blank slide at the end, and then press the **spacebar** once more. (You could also press the Esc key or right-click any slide followed by clicking End Show, and PowerPoint would return to the original presentation.) PowerPoint returns to Slide 2 of the Gala Planning presentation.

11. Return to Normal view, and then save the presentation using the default filename.

Norma looks at your work so far and is pleased with your progress. The presentation now includes an imported table from Word, an Excel chart, text links to other slides in the presentation, and an action button with a link to another presentation. In the next session, you'll help Norma ensure that her presentation will run smoothly and be available to all of her intended audience.

Viewing a Slide Show with Embedded or Linked Objects

When you present a slide show using a presentation with linked files, those files must be available on a disk so that PowerPoint can access them; and when you embed a file, the source program must be available if you want to edit the embedded object. This is because a copy of the linked file or source program for an embedded file is not included within the PowerPoint file itself; only the path and filename for accessing the linked file are there. Therefore, you should view the presentation on the system that will be used for running the slide show to make sure it has the necessary files. If embedded or linked objects don't work when you run the slide show, you'll have to edit the object path so that PowerPoint can find the objects on your disk.

To view the slide show:

1. Go to **Slide 1**, and then click the **Slide Show from current slide** button. Slide 1 appears in Slide Show view.

2. Click the **left mouse button** (or press the **spacebar**) to go to Slide 2, and then click the action button to jump to the other slide show.

3. Press the **Esc** key to return to the Gala Planning presentation.

4. Advance to **Slide 4** ("Events and Activities") and test some of the hyperlinks, using the "Return to Event List" link on each linked slide to jump back to Slide 4.

5. After viewing all the slides and testing the hyperlinks, return to Slide 1 in Normal view.

Norma is pleased with how well the embedded and linked objects work in her slide show. She now asks you to print a hard copy of the slides.

To print the presentation:

1. Switch to Print Preview and preview the slides in grayscale. The slide title is difficult to read.

2. Click the **Options** button on the Preview toolbar, point to **Color/Grayscale**, and then click **Pure Black and White**. The slide title is now legible.

3. Scroll through the slides to make sure that all the slides are legible, and stop at Slide 14. The labels on the Excel chart on Slide 14 are hidden. This is because they were formatted with white text to make them visible on the blue presentation background.

4. Click the **Close** button on the Preview toolbar, make sure Slide 14 is in the slide pane, click the **Color/Grayscale** button 🖼 on the Standard toolbar, and then click **Pure Black and White**. The slide changes to black and white and the Grayscale View toolbar opens.

5. Click the **Setting** button on the Grayscale View toolbar, and then click **Light Grayscale**. The labels are now legible. See Figure 4-21.

Figure 4-21 | **Slide 14 in Print Preview with grayscale settings applied**

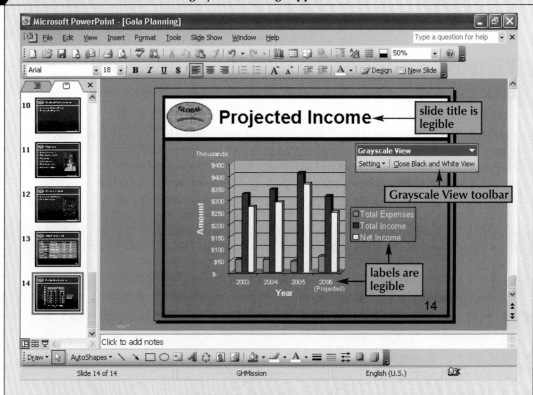

6. Click the **Close Black and White View** button on the Grayscale View toolbar, switch back to Print Preview, and then go to **Slide 14**. The grayscale settings you set in Normal view are applied in Print Preview as well.

7. Close Print Preview, go to **Slide 1**, change the subtitle to your name, and then save the presentation.

8. Print the slides as handouts, six slides per page.

9. Switch to Slide Sorter view, and then change the zoom, if necessary, to **50%** so you can see all the slides on your screen at once. See Figure 4-22.

Completed presentation in Slide Sorter view   **Figure 4-22**

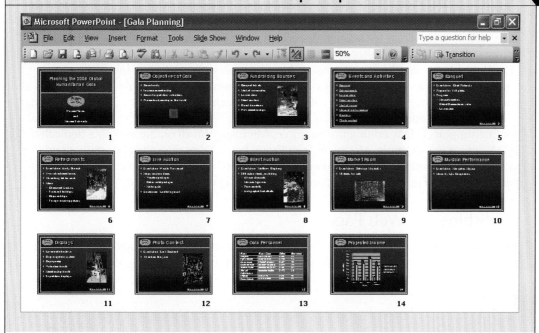

Publishing Presentations on the World Wide Web

The Internet: World Wide Web

As you probably know, the **Internet** is the largest and most widely used computer network in the world. In fact, it's really a network of thousands of smaller networks, all joined together electronically. Part of the Internet is a global information-sharing system called the **World Wide Web** (also called the Web or WWW). The Web allows you to find and view electronic documents called **Web pages**. Organizations and individuals make their Web pages available by placing them on a **Web server**, a dedicated network computer with high-capacity hard disks. The Web, then, is a connected network of these Web servers. The location of a particular set of Web pages on a server is called a **Web site**. You can access a particular Web site by specifying its address, also called its **Uniform Resource Locator** (**URL**). To specify URLs and to view Web pages, you use a **Web browser**, a software program that sends requests for Web pages, retrieves them, and then interprets them for display on the computer screen. Two of the most popular browsers are Microsoft Internet Explorer and Netscape Navigator.

Most Web sites contain a **home page**, a Web page that contains general information about the site. Home pages are like "home base"—they are starting points for online viewers. They usually contain links to the rest of the pages in the Web site.

Publishing a Web page usually means copying HTML files to a Web server so that others can view the Web page. In PowerPoint, however, the Publish command opens a dialog box in which you can customize the Web page you are saving.

Normally, you and the organization for which you work would create Web pages using a **Web page editor**, software specifically designed for this purpose, such as Microsoft FrontPage. But sometimes you want to publish a PowerPoint presentation, for example, as a link from the organization's home page. Global Humanitarian, similar to most large organizations, has its own Web site, but Norma thinks the pictures and information in the Gala Planning presentation would make an excellent resource for all those who help organize the gala.

To prepare Norma's PowerPoint presentation (or any presentation) for viewing on the World Wide Web, first you have to convert it to a file format called HTML, with the filename extension .htm or .html. **HTML** stands for **Hypertext Markup Language**, a special language for describing the format of a Web page so that Web browsers can interpret and display the page. The HTML markings in a file tell the browser how to format the text, graphics, tables, and other objects. Fortunately, you don't have to learn Hypertext Markup Language to create HTML documents; PowerPoint does the work for you. You can easily save any PowerPoint presentation as an HTML (or related) document using PowerPoint's Publish as Web Page command. This command allows you to create a set of HTML documents (or pages)—one HTML page (with the filename extension .htm) for each slide, various graphics files, an index page, and other supporting files—or to create a single Web page file (with the file-name extension .mht) that includes within it all the supporting documents and information.

If you want to edit a resulting .htm document, you'll have to use either a word processor that supports HTML editing (for example, Microsoft Word) or, better still, a dedicated HTML editor (for example, Microsoft FrontPage). PowerPoint doesn't support direct editing of HTML documents. If you want to edit a resulting .mht file, you'll have to edit the original presentation file in PowerPoint, and then save it again as a .mht file.

Publishing the Web Pages

Norma wants you to save the Gala Planning presentation as a Web page so that she can copy it to the company's Web site. You remember that you added an action button to link to the GHMission presentation, so that presentation will need to be saved as a Web page as well. You'll do this first.

To save a presentation as a Web page:

1. Open **GHMission** from the **Tutorial.04\Tutorial** folder included with your Data Files, click **File** on the menu bar, and then click **Save as Web Page**. The Save As dialog box opens, with the Save as type automatically set to Single File Web Page. See Figure 4-23.

Figure 4-23	Save As dialog box for saving a single file Web page

2. Change the filename in the File name text box to **GlobalHumanitarianMission** (all one word, no spaces).

3. Click the **Save** button. PowerPoint creates the Web page file GlobalHumanitarianMission in the default (Tutorial.04\Tutorial) folder.

4. Close the **GlobalHumanitarianMission** presentation without saving changes.

Having saved GlobalHumanitarianMission (from GHMission) as a Web page file, you now need to fix the hyperlinked action button in the Gala Planning presentation so that its target is the Web page file GlobalHumanitarianMission rather than the presentation file GHMission. You need to do this before you save Gala Planning as a Web page because you cannot edit Web page files within PowerPoint.

To change the hyperlink target and save the presentation as a Web page:

▶ **1.** With Gala Planning in the PowerPoint window, go to **Slide 2** in Normal view.

▶ **2.** Right-click the **action button**, and then click **Edit Hyperlink** on the shortcut menu. The Action Settings dialog box appears on the screen with the Mouse Click tab on top. Now you want to change the target file from GHMission to the Web page GlobalHumanitarianMission.

▶ **3.** Click the **Hyperlink to** list arrow, click **Other File**, change the Look in location to the **Tutorial.04\Tutorial** folder (if necessary), click **GlobalHumanitarianMission**, and then click the **OK** button.

▶ **4.** Click the **OK** button in the Action Settings dialog box. Now you're ready to save Gala Planning as a Web page.

▶ **5.** Publish the Gala Planning presentation as a single file Web page, using the procedure previously described, except in the Save As dialog box, change the filename from Gala Planning (with a space) to **GalaPlanning** (without a space). This ensures that any type of browser can open the file, even browsers that don't accept spaces in the filenames.

Now that you saved the presentation as a single Web page, you're ready to see how it looks in a Web browser.

Viewing a Presentation in a Web Browser

It's always a good idea to see exactly what the presentation looks like in a browser before you actually publish it to a Web server. You can, of course, start your browser and then open the Web page, but you can also do this from within PowerPoint. You'll do this now.

To view the presentation in a Web browser from within PowerPoint:

▶ **1.** With GalaPlanning still open in the PowerPoint window, click **File** on the menu bar, and then click **Web Page Preview**. PowerPoint starts your browser with the Web page open in the browser window. (In this book, we used Internet Explorer 6.0.)

Trouble? If your computer uses a version of Internet Explorer other than 6.0, your pages will look slightly different than those shown here. If your computer uses Netscape Navigator, you will not be able to view the Web page because Navigator does not support single file Web pages at this time.

▶ **2.** If necessary, maximize the browser window so it fills the screen. See Figure 4-24.

Figure 4-24 Presentation Web page in browser

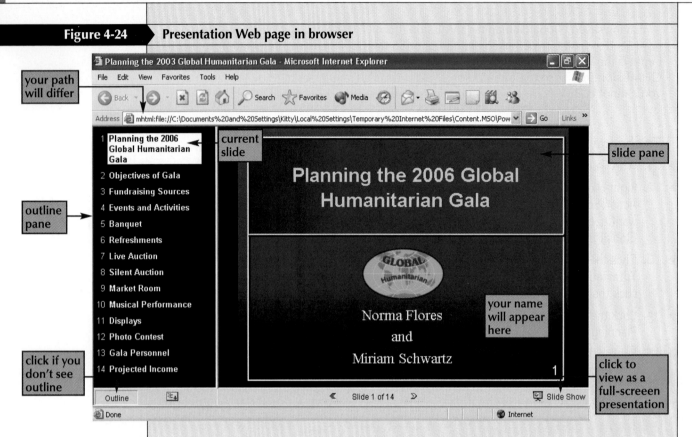

As you can see, the first slide of your presentation appears in the main frame of the browser, and an outline of the slides appears along the left edge of the outline pane. Each outline item is a hyperlink to its corresponding slide. Also, a navigation toolbar appears at the bottom of the window. These hyperlinks and the toolbar help you navigate through the presentation. Now you'll see how the navigation works.

Trouble? If you don't see the outline, click the Outline button at the bottom of the screen.

▶ 3. Click the **Next Slide** button 〉 on the navigation toolbar at the bottom of the Web page. The slide pane now displays Slide 2 of the presentation.

▶ 4. Click **4 Events and Activities** in the outline pane of the Web preview. The slide pane now displays Slide 4 ("Events and Activities").

▶ 5. Click the **Silent auction** hyperlink in Slide 4 in the contents pane. The slide pane now displays Slide 8.

▶ 6. Click the **Previous Slide** button 〈 on the browser toolbar. Slide 7 ("Live Auction") appears on the screen. As you can see, the navigation buttons help you easily move one slide forward or backward, whereas the outline hyperlinks allow you to jump from one slide to any other—in any order.

▶ 7. Click **2 Objectives of Gala** in the outline pane, and then click the **action button** on the slide. Slide 1 of the GlobalHumanitarianMission Web page appears in the browser window, or in a new window of the browser.

Trouble? If Slide 1 of the GlobalHumanitarianMission Web page does not appear, start Internet Explorer, click File on the menu bar, click Open to open the Open dialog box, browse to the file GalaPlanning, click the OK button in the Open dialog box, and then repeat Step 7.

▶ 8. Go through the slides of GlobalHumanitarianMission as desired.

▶ **9.** After going through GlobalHumanitarianMission in your browser, click the **Back** button [🔙 Back] on the browser toolbar as many times as necessary to return to Slide 2 of the GalaPlanning presentation. (You can't just press Esc to exit the GlobalHumanitarianMission Web page and return to the GalaPlanning Web page.)

▶ **10.** Look through the GalaPlanning Web page as you desire, and then exit your Web browser.

  Trouble? If you had to start Internet Explorer to use the action button on Slide 2, close both Internet Explorer windows.

▶ **11.** Close the presentation without saving any changes.

Norma is pleased with how the presentation looks in the browser and sends the files to the company's technical support person to publish to the Global Humanitarian Web site. Next, she wants to schedule a specific time to broadcast her presentation over the Internet to get feedback from others.

Sharing and Collaborating with Others

PowerPoint provides a wide variety of methods for delivering your presentations and collaborating with others, including sending presentations via e-mail, broadcasting a presentation over the Internet, and making a presentation available on the World Wide Web. You're probably already familiar with e-mail, and you just learned about publishing a presentation as a Web page. This section will focus on holding online meetings and broadcasting a presentation.

An **online meeting** is a method of sharing and exchanging information with people at different locations in real time (the actual time during which an event takes place) as if all the participants are together in the same room. To hold an online meeting, you can use Microsoft NetMeeting, which is installed as part of Office 2003 and is accessible within the Office 2003 programs. **NetMeeting** is a program that manages online meetings. It allows participants to write notes on an electronic "whiteboard," send and receive typed messages, and exchange files. You can also record the results of your meeting, archive the results, and put them on a Web server so that those who missed the meeting can "replay" it at a later time.

An **online broadcast** is a method for showing a PowerPoint presentation online. It may or may not include an online meeting. A broadcast in its simplest form is analogous to the broadcast of a television show: The presentation is sent electronically to all the participants at a prearranged time. To run an online broadcast in PowerPoint 2003, you need to download the presentation broadcast feature from the Microsoft Office Online Web site.

Scheduling and Hosting an Online Meeting

Reference Window

- As the presenter, click Tools, point to Online Collaboration, click Schedule Meeting, and then enter the appropriate information in the NetMeeting dialog box, including your first and last name, your e-mail address, your physical location, and the URL of the Web server you will use to host the meeting.
- Click the OK button to close the NetMeeting dialog box and open the Outlook 2003 Meeting window.
- Schedule the meeting and choose the meeting participants using the Outlook 2003 Meeting window, and then click the Send button on the Meeting window toolbar.
- Click the View This NetShow button, when, as the presenter using Outlook, an Outlook Reminder window will open a few minutes before the meeting.
- Type in the chat area or draw on the whiteboard.
- End the online meeting by clicking the End Meeting button.

Reference Window	**Setting Up and Running an Online Broadcast**
	• If necessary, download and install the Microsoft PowerPoint 2003 broadcast feature from the Microsoft Office Online Web site. • As presenter, schedule an online meeting with the people who you want to view the online broadcast. • At the designated time, open the presentation you want to broadcast, click Slide Show on the menu bar, point to Online Broadcast, and then click Begin Broadcast. Your presentation is automatically saved as a Web page, and then appears in the Web browsers of the participants. • Run the slide show as you normally would, typing notes in the chat and whiteboard areas to communicate points to the viewers.

Norma decides to arrange an online broadcast of her presentation for the people in the Peru office. Then, she and Miriam, along with the help of their staff and many volunteers, successfully plan and carry out the Global Humanitarian gala, which is a huge success.

Review	# Session 4.2 Quick Check

1. What is a hyperlink?
2. What are two examples of hyperlink targets?
3. What is an action button?
4. How do you save a presentation as a single Web page?
5. Describe what a presentation looks like in your browser.
6. Describe how to broadcast a presentation over the Internet.

Review	# Tutorial Summary

In this tutorial, you learned how to import, modify, and export a Microsoft Word outline to your presentation and import a digital photograph. You learned how to embed and modify a Word table in your presentation and link and modify an Excel chart. You also learned how to create and edit hyperlinks, add action buttons, create and customize a toolbar, and publish a presentation on the World Wide Web.

Key Terms

action button	link	target
destination file	NetMeeting	Uniform Resource Locator
embed	object	(URL)
follow	object linking and	Web browser
home page	embedding (OLE)	Web page
hyperlink	online broadcast	Web page editor
HTML (Hypertext Markup	online meeting	Web server
Language)	publish	Web site
import	source file	World Wide Web
Internet		

Practice

Get hands-on practice of the skills you learned in this tutorial using the same case scenario.

Review Assignments

Data Files needed for the Review Assignments: LoanOtln.doc, Loan.ppt, Mentor.jpg, ProjTabl.doc, Chicken.jpg, Crafts.jpg, Dolls.jpg, Guide.jpg, Herd.jpg, Taxi.jpg, Weave.jpg, and Loans.xls

Norma and Miriam earmarked about $50,000 of the over $400,000 raised during the Global Humanitarian gala for the Global Humanitarian Entrepreneurial Support Program. This program provides small, low-interest loans and assistance for home and family businesses in less developed countries. It also provides training and mentoring in basic business practices. Norma and Miriam want you to help prepare a presentation reporting on recent entrepreneurial projects in Peru. Complete the following:

1. Open a new, blank presentation, and then import the Word outline **LoanOtln** located in the Tutorial.04\Review folder included with your Data Files.
2. Type "Entrepreneurial Support Programs in Peru" as the title in the title slide, and type your name as the subtitle in the title slide.
3. Apply the design template from the presentation file **Loan**, located in the Tutorial.04\Review folder.
4. Turn on slide numbering in the Header and Footer dialog box.
5. Save the presentation to the Tutorial.04\Review folder using the filename **Entrepreneurial Support Programs**.
6. Switch to Slide Sorter view, select Slides 4 through 10, and then apply the Title, Text, and Content layout to the selected slides.
7. In Slide 2, change the slide layout so an object will appear below the bulleted list, and then import the digital image **Mentor**, located in the Tutorial.04\Review folder. Resize the picture so it's as large as possible without covering the slide border lines or slide number.
8. In Slide 3, embed the Word table from the file **ProjTabl**, located in the Tutorial.04\Review folder, and then resize the table so it appears as large as possible without covering the brown border lines of the slide.
9. Import the appropriate pictures from the Tutorial.04\Review folder to Slides 4 through 10.
10. In Slide 5, set the white background of the Dolls picture to be transparent.
11. In the Tutorial.04\Review folder, make a copy of the Excel file **Loans**, change the name of the copy to **Loans Chart**, and then link it to Slide 11.
12. Double-click the chart on Slide 11, edit the number of loans given in 2005 to 48, edit the number successful to 29, switch back to the worksheet containing the chart, save and close the file and exit Excel. Make sure the chart was updated on Slide 11. (Resize the chart on Slide 11 if necessary.)
13. In Slide 3, below the table, create a text box and type "[Chicken] [Dolls] [Guide] [Herd] [Crafts] [Taxi] [Weaves]," including the brackets and a space between each bracketed word. Each bracketed word corresponds to one of the entrepreneurial projects covered in the presentation. Position the text box so it's centered below the table.
14. Select "Chicken" (but not the brackets around it) and make it a link to Slide 4, select "Dolls" and make it a link to Slide 5, and so forth for the other five words in the text box so that each word is a hyperlink to the corresponding project.
15. In Slides 4 through 10, create a text hyperlink "Return to Projects List" back to Slide 3. Position the hyperlink text box in the lower-left corner of each slide, and adjust the position of the text box or the graphic so they don't overlap. (*Hint*: Remember that you can copy the hyperlink from Slide 4 to the other slides.)
16. Add a document action button to Slide 11 in the lower-left corner of the slide, and link it to Slide 3. (*Hint*: Click the Hyperlink to list arrow in the Action Settings dialog box, and then click Slides.) Add an action button to Slide 3 to jump to Slide 11.

17. After completing the slide show, save the presentation.

18. Switch to Slide Show view and test the links you added.

19. View the presentation in grayscale, make any adjustments necessary so that all the elements are legible, then print the presentation as handouts with four slides per page.

20. Save the presentation as a single Web Page named **EntrepreneurialSupportPrograms** (no spaces). Test the Web page in your browser, and then close your browser.

Apply

Apply the skills you learned in this tutorial to modify a presentation for a national programming consulting firm.

Case Problem 1

Data Files needed for this Case Problem: PPCOtln.doc, PPCDes.ppt, PPCTbl.doc, PPCData.xls, Temp.jpg, and HeadQ.jpg

Programming-Plus Corporation Donald Van Pelt of Chicago is CEO of a large national consulting firm called Programming-Plus Corporation (P+C). P+C provides freelance programming in C++, Java, and other languages; supplies temporary employees with expertise in programming; and trains corporate programmers in advanced programming techniques. Donald asks you to help prepare a PowerPoint presentation to give to sales personnel so they can present information about P+C services. Compplete the following:

1. Open a new, blank presentation, type "Programming Plus Corp." as the title in the title slide, and then type your name as the subtitle in the title slide.

2. Import the Word outline **PPCOtln**, located in the Tutorial.04\Cases folder included with your Data Files.

3. Apply the design template from the presentation file **PPCDes**, located in the Tutorial.04\Cases folder.

4. Reapply the Title and Text Slide layout to all the slides with bulleted lists. (*Hint*: Switch to Slide Sorter view, select Slides 2 through 9, open the Slide Layout task pane, click the Slide Layout list arrow for the desired layout, and then click Reapply Layout.)

5. Save the presentation to the Tutorial.04\Cases folder using the filename **PPCServices**. (You won't include any spaces in the filename in anticipation of creating a Web page because some browsers don't accept spaces in filenames.)

6. In Slide 3, embed a Word table from the file **PPCTbl**, located in the Tutorial.04\Cases folder. Resize the table so it appears as large as possible.

7. In Slide 4, change the slide layout to Title and Content, and then click the Insert Chart button to create a chart.

Explore

8. Import data from an Excel file to the chart. Click the gray square in the upper-left corner of the datasheet to select all the cells, and then press the Delete key to delete all the current data. Start Microsoft Excel, open the Excel file **PPCData**, located in the Tutorial.04\Cases folder, select all the data in the spreadsheet, click the Copy button, and then exit Excel. Return to Slide 4 in the presentation, click the cell above the unlabeled column—the cell above and to the left of cell A1—and then click the Paste button on the Standard toolbar.

9. Click Chart on the menu bar, click Chart Options, click the Titles tab, type "Amount in $Millions" as the Value (Z) axis title, click the OK button, and then deselect the chart.

10. In Slide 7, import the digital image **Temp**, located in the Tutorial.04\Cases folder. Position the image to the right of the bulleted list.

11. In Slide 2, import the digital image **HeadQ**, located in the Tutorial.04\Cases folder. Position the image below the bulleted list.

12. Still in Slide 2, insert a text box to the right of the image with the text "Contact Us" with 24-point Arial font, and then make that text a hyperlink to Slide 9.

13. In Slide 9, insert the action button titled Home and make it a hyperlink to the first slide. This will allow Donald to easily jump from the end to the beginning of the slide show.
14. After completing the slide show, save the presentation using the default filename.
15. View the slide show in Slide Show view and test the links that you inserted.
16. Omit the background graphics from the master, preview the presentation in grayscale, make any adjustments necessary, and then print the presentation as handouts with six slides per page.
17. Save the presentation as a Web page, and then view the slide show in your browser.

Apply

Use your PowerPoint skills to create a presentation for a small Internet discussion management company.

Case Problem 2

Data Files needed for this Case Problem: GCDes.ppt, GCOtln.doc, GCChat.jpg, and GCGroup.jpg

GlobalChat Crystal Bennett of Columbus, Ohio, is president of GlobalChat, a small but growing company that specializes in managing Internet discussion groups. The company sells software to individuals, families, schools, companies, and other organizations to help them set up and conduct electronic chat rooms and other types of discussion groups. Crystal asks you to help her prepare and publish a presentation on the services offered by her company. Complete the following:

1. Open a new, blank presentation, type "GlobalChat" on the first line of the title in the title placeholder, type "Bringing the World Together" on the second line in the title placeholder, and then type your name in the subtitle placeholder.
2. Apply the design template **GCDes**, located in the Tutorial.04\Cases folder included with your Data Files.
3. Select "GlobalChat" in Slide 1, increase the font size to 72 points, and change the font color to the blue color in the color scheme.
4. Import the Word outline in the file **GCOtln**, located in the Tutorial.04\Cases folder.
5. Save the presentation as **GlobalChat** in the Tutorial.04\Cases folder.
6. In Slide 2, change the slide layout to Title and Text over Content, and then import the clip art **GCChat**, located in the Tutorial.04\Cases folder.
7. Also in Slide 2, make each of the software names a hyperlink to the corresponding slide that describes the software feature.
8. On each of the three slides that describe software features, import the clip art **GCGroup**, change the slide layout to Title and Text over Content, change the size of the clip art to a height of one inch, move the clip art to the lower-right corner of the screen, and then increase the size of the bulleted list text box so it fills the remaining blank area.

Explore

9. Select the GCGroup clip art on each of the three slides, and make it a hyperlink back to Slide 2.
10. In Slide 7, insert Action Button - Home, and then set its hyperlink target to the first slide.

Explore

11. Change the color of the action button in Slide 7 to the bright-blue Follow Shadows Scheme Color. (*Hint*: Right-click the action button, and click Format AutoShape.)
12. Check all the hyperlinks in Slide Show view.
13. Set the slide transition for all the slides to Comb Horizontal.
14. Give Slides 2 through 7 the Exciting animation scheme called Float.
15. Start with Slide 1 and run the presentation in Slide Show view.
16. Save the presentation using the default filename, and then print the presentation as handouts with four slides per page.
17. Save the completed presentation as a single file Web page, and then view the slide show in your browser.

Create

Create a presentation using the skills you learned in this tutorial for a company selling products and services for outdoor activities.

Case Problem 3

Data Files needed for this Case Problem: HAOServ.ppt, HAOTempl.ppt, and HAOHikes.doc

High Adventure Outfitters   High Adventure Outfitters (HAO) is a small business in Jackson, Wyoming, a center for many types of outdoor activities, including hiking, backpacking, camping, canoeing, hunting, and river running. The owner and president of HAO, Matthew Steinberg, provides guided tours for various types of activities in western Wyoming. Matthew asks you to set up a PowerPoint presentation on his company's supplies and services. Create the finished presentation as shown in Figure 4-25, and then create a Web page of the presentation.

Figure 4-25

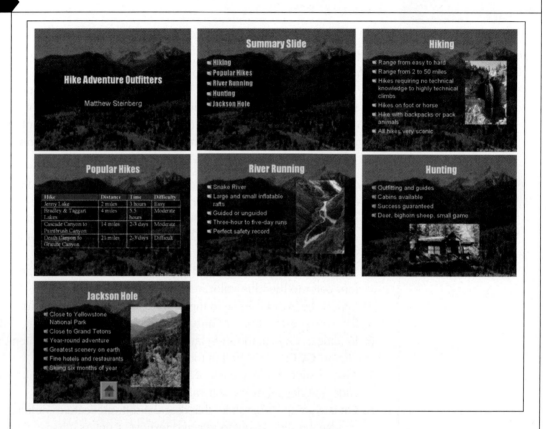

Read all the steps before you start creating your presentation.

1. The presentation is created from **HAOServ**, located in the Tutorial.04\Cases folder included with your Data Files. Change the name "Matthew Steinberg" on Slide 1 to your name, and save it as **HAOServices**.
2. The presentation uses the design template from the file **HAOTempl**, located in the Tutorial.04\Cases folder.
3. The information for the table of hikes on Slide 4 comes from the file **HAOHikes**, located in the Tutorial.04\Cases folder. You will have to modify the table later so that its size, fonts, and borders are legible and attractive. Keep this in mind and decide whether to embed or link the table.
4. Slide 2 is a summary slide featuring all the slides except the first one.
5. Slide 2 has hyperlinks from each of the bulleted items to the other slides (except Slide 1).
6. Slides 3 through 7 have a text hyperlink called "Return to Summary Slide" that links back to Slide 2.
7. Slide 7 includes an Action Button - Home, with a hyperlink to the first slide.
8. Save your final presentation, and then save it as a Web page using the filename **HAOServices**.

Research

Use the Internet to collect information about your favorite music and prepare a presentation on the topic.

Explore

Case Problem 4

Data File needed for this Case Problem: Music.ppt

My Favorite Music   Prepare a presentation to your classmates on your favorite type of music, whether it's classical or popular, rhythm and blues or Broadway, jazz or rap. Do the following:

1. Using Microsoft Word, create an outline of your presentation on your favorite music. Include at least six titles, which will become slide titles. (Remember to switch to Outline view in Word to type your slide titles.) Use books and magazines from your college library, encyclopedia, the Internet, CD slipcovers and booklets, or other sources of information to get backgrounds, biographies, lyrics, reviews, and analyses on your chosen topic. If you haven't covered Microsoft Word in your courses and don't know how to create an outline with heading styles, use the Help feature of Word.
2. Save the Word file using the filename **My Music Outline** to a high-capacity disk.
3. In another Word document, create a table. Your table might list the names of musical compositions, their composers, their performers, the types of music, the years of release, or other information.
4. Save the Word file with the table using the filename **My Music Table** to the Tutorial.04\Cases folder included with your Data Files.
5. Open a new, blank presentation, and include an appropriate title of your choosing and a subtitle with your name as the presenter.
6. Import the Word outline into PowerPoint.
7. Apply the design template from the presentation file **Music**, located in the Tutorial.04\Cases folder.
8. Reapply the slide layouts to each slide, as needed, so it uses the proper font and has the proper format. (*Hint*: Switch to Slide Sorter view, select the relevant slides, open the Slide Layout task pane, click the Slide Layout list arrow for the desired layout, and then click Reapply Layout.)
9. Embed your table into a slide of your presentation. Resize and reposition it as needed to maximize its readability.
10. Insert at least two action buttons into your presentation with links to other slides within your presentation.
11. Include at least one text hyperlink in your presentation, with a link to another slide. The text of the hyperlink can be a bulleted item, the text in a table cell, or a text box.
12. Add graphics, sound effects, slide transitions, and animations to the slide show, as desired.
13. Save your presentation using the filename **MyMusic**, and print the presentation as handouts with four slides per page.
14. Save your presentation as a single file Web page and then view the slide show in your browser.

Research

Go to the Web to find information you can use to create presentations.

Internet Assignments

The purpose of the Internet Assignments is to challenge you to find information on the Internet that you can use to work effectively with this software. The actual assignments are updated and maintained on the Course Technology Web site. Log on to the Internet and use your Web browser to go to the Student Online Companion for New Perspectives Office 2003 at **www.course.com/np/office2003**. Click the Internet Assignments link, and then navigate to the assignments for this tutorial.

Assess

SAM Assessment and Training

If you have a SAM user profile, you may have access to hands-on instruction, practice, and assessment of the skills covered in this tutorial. Log in to your SAM account and go to your assignments page to see what your instructor has assigned.

Reinforce

The Internet: World Wide Web

Lab Assignments

The New Perspectives Labs are designed to help you master some of the key concepts and skills presented in this text. The steps for completing this Lab are located on the Course Technology Web site. Log on to the Internet and use your Web browser to go to the Student Online Companion for New Perspectives Office 2003 at **www.course.com/np/office2003**. Click the Lab Assignments link, and then navigate to the assignments for this tutorial.

Review

Quick Check Answers

Session 4.1

1. They are the same, except that the presentation file will usually not be found in the Templates folder, whereas the design template file will be.
2. In PowerPoint, click Insert on the menu bar, click Slides from Outline, select the Word file with the outline, and then click the Insert button.
3. Click File on the menu bar, point to Send To, click Microsoft Word, select the desired Word page layout, click the OK button, specify the filename, and then click the OK button.
4. a. Import means to insert a file that was created using one program into another program's file.
   b. Embed means to insert a file so that a connection with the source program is maintained.
   c. Link means to insert a file so that a connection between the source file and the destination file is maintained, and changes made to the source file are reflected in the linked object in the destination file.
   d. OLE means object linking and embedding.
5. The object is updated to reflect the changes made to the source file.
6. imported
7. so that modifications you make to the source file are reflected in the destination file

Session 4.2

1. A hyperlink is a word, phrase, or graphic that you click to display an object at another location.
2. Hyperlink targets can be other slides within the presentation or other presentations.
3. An action button is a ready-made icon for which you can easily define hyperlinks to other slides or documents.
4. Click File, and then click Save as Web Page.
5. A frame on the left contains an outline of the slides, the slide itself appears in a frame on the right, and navigation buttons appear at the bottom of the slide.
6. Announce to the participant the time and place of the broadcast, open the presentation that you will broadcast, click Slide Show, point to Online Broadcast, and then click Begin Broadcast.

Glossary/Index

Task Reference

TASK	PAGE #	RECOMMENDED METHOD
Action button, insert	PPT 169	In Normal view, click Slide Show, point to Action Buttons, click a button, click at the desired location in the slide, select the action setting (for example, hyperlink or sound), click OK
Animation, custom, apply	PPT 128	In Normal view, click Slide Show, click Custom Animation, click object that you want to animate in slide pane, click Add Effects list arrow, point to animation category, click desired animation, select desired direction of animation; set animation order, set animation timing, specify animation path, add sound effects, or make other modifications as desired
Animation Scheme, built-in, apply	PPT 127	See Reference Window: Applying an Animation Scheme
AutoContent Wizard, run	PPT 10	Click File, click New, click From AutoContent Wizard on New Presentation task pane, follow instructions
Background, gradient, create	PPT 98	Click Format, click Background, click Background fill list arrow, click Fill Effects, click Gradient tab, set the desired gradient effects, click OK, click Apply or Apply to All
Background, texture, add	PPT 112	See Reference Window: Applying a Textured Background
Border of table, draw	PPT 68	Click 🖊, set desired border style and border width on Tables and Borders toolbar, drag 🖊 along border
Bullet style, modify	PPT 99	Click in text of bulleted item, click Format, click Bullets and Numbering, select desired bullet (including color and size), click OK
Chart, insert	PPT 114	See Reference Window: Creating a Chart (Graph)
Clip Art, insert	PPT 16	Change slide layout to a Content layout, click 🖼 in content placeholder, click clipart image, click OK
Clip Art, recolor	PPT 47	Click clipart image, click 🎨, click color list arrow of color to change, click desired color, click OK
Color Scheme, create	PPT 96	Click the Design button, click Color Schemes, click Edit Color Schemes, click Custom tab, change color of elements as desired, click Apply
Design Template, apply	PPT 43	Click the Design button, click design thumbnail in task pane
Design Template, apply from other presentation	PPT 151	Click the Design button, click Design Templates, click Browse, select folder and presentation filename, click Apply
Design Template, apply to one slide or selected slides	PPT 58	Click the Design button, select slide(s), click design thumbnail list arrow, click Apply to Selected Slides
Diagram, create	PPT 70	Change slide layout to a Content layout, click 🔄, click desired diagram type, click OK, modify diagram as desired
Fill color, change	PPT 73	Click object to select it, click 🎨▾, select desired color
Font, modify	PPT 56	Click edge of text box, click Font list arrow, click font
Font color, modify	PPT 56	Click edge of text box, click 🅰▾, click color (or click More Colors and click color, click OK)
Footers, create	PPT 62	Click View, click Header and Footer, make sure there is a check mark in the Footer Check box, click Ⅰ in Footer text box, type text, click Apply to All
Graph, insert		See Chart, insert
Graphics, import		See Picture, insert
Grayscale, preview presentation in	PPT 30	Click 🖥, click Grayscale

TASK	PAGE #	RECOMMENDED METHOD
Handouts, print	PPT 31	Click File, click Print, click Print what list arrow, click Handouts, click Slides per page list arrow, click number, click OK
Hyperlink, create	PPT 165	Select phrase or object, click ⬛, click desired Link to button, select the desired slide in this presentation or select a folder and file or a URL, click OK
Layout, slide, change	PPT 46	Click Format, click Slide Layout, click desired layout
Master, slide or title, modify	PPT 51	Shift-click ⬛, make modifications, click ⬛
Movie clip, insert	PPT 109	Click Insert, point to Movies and Sounds, click Movie from File, select folder and movie file (video clip) filename, click OK, choose to play automatically or on mouse click
Notes, create	PPT 29	Click ⌶ in Notes pane, type text
Notes, print	PPT 31	Click File, click Print, click Print what list arrow, click Notes Pages, click OK
Numbering, slide	PPT 62	Click View, click Header and Footer, click Slide Number check box, click Apply or Apply to All
Object, change order	PPT 54	Click object, click the Draw button, point to Order, click desired layering order
Object, embed	PPT 159	Click Insert, click Object, click Create from file option button, make sure Link check box is not selected, select folder and filename, click OK
Object, link	PPT 161	See Reference Window: Linking an Object
Object, resize	PPT 47	Click object, drag sizing handle
Object, rotate	PPT 76	Click object to select it, drag rotate handle with ↻
Organization chart, insert	PPT 120	See Reference Window: Creating an Organization Chart
Outline text, demote	PPT 23	Click Outline tab (if necessary), click paragraph, click ⬛
Outline text, promote	PPT 21	Click Outline tab (if necessary), click paragraph, click ⬛
Outline, export	PPT 156	Click File, point to Send to, click Microsoft Office Word, click Outline only (or select other option), click OK
Picture, insert	PPT 107	Click ⬛, change to desired folder, click picture filename, click Insert
Pointer pen, mark slides during slide show with	PPT 133	Click ⬛, click desired pen type, draw lines with pen pointer
PowerPoint, exit	PPT 12	Click ⬛ on PowerPoint window
PowerPoint, start	PPT 4	Click Start button, point to All Programs, point to Microsoft Office, click Microsoft Office PowerPoint 2003
Presentation, close	PPT 9	Click ⬛ on presentation window
Presentation, open	PPT 5	Click ⬛, select disk and folder, click filename, click Open
Presentation, print	PPT 30	Click File, click Print, select options, click OK
Ruler, view (or hide)	PPT 60	Click View, click Ruler
Shape, create	PPT 72	Click the AutoShapes button, point to shape type, click desired shape, drag ╋ in slide
Slide Show, view	PPT 8	Click ⬛
Slide Sorter View, switch to	PPT 7	Click ⬛
Slide, add new	PPT 19	Click the New Slide button
Slide, delete	PPT 17	In Slide Pane, click Edit, click Delete Slide. In Outline tab, click ⬛, press Delete. In Slide tab, click slide, press Delete
Slide, go to next	PPT 6	Click ⬛
Slide, go to previous	PPT 6	Click ⬛
Slides, hide	PPT 135	In Normal view, click (or Ctrl-click) slides in Slide tab to select one or more slides, click Slide Show, click Hide Slide

TASK	PAGE #	RECOMMENDED METHOD
Slides, unhide	PPT 135	In Normal view, click (or Ctrl-click) hidden slide(s) in Slide tab to select one or more slides, click Slide Show, click Hide Slide
Slides, insert from other presentation	PPT 92	See Reference Window: Inserting Slides from Another Presentation
Slide Transitions, apply	PPT 125	See Reference Window: Applying Slide Transitions
Sound clip, insert	PPT 111	Click Insert, point to Movies and Sounds, click Sound from File, select folder and sound filename, click OK
Speaker Notes, create	PPT 29	Click Ⅰ in Notes Pane, type text
Style Checker, fix style problem	PPT 26	Click light bulb, click option to fix style problem
Style Checker, set options	PPT 25	Click Tools, click Options, click Spelling and Style tab, click Style Options, set options, click OK, click OK
Style Checker, turn on	PPT 25	Click Tools, click Options, click Spelling and Style tab, select Check style check box, click OK
Summary Slide, add	PPT 77	Switch to Slide Sorter view, select desired slides, click 🗗
Tab stop, add	PPT 61	Select text box, click View, click Ruler, click tab stop alignment selector button to select desired tab stop style, click location on ruler
Tab stop, delete	PPT 62	Drag the tab stop off the ruler
Tab stop, move	PPT 62	Select text box, click View, click Ruler, drag tab stop to new location on ruler
Table, create	PPT 66	Change slide layout to a Content layout, click 🖽, set number of columns and rows, fill in and format cells as desired
Text box, add	PPT 74	Click 🄰, click ↓ in slide, type text
Text box, move	PPT 76	Click text box, drag edge (not sizing handle) of text box
Text box, resize	PPT 75	Click text box, drag sizing handle
Transparent color, picture, set	PPT 54	Click picture, click ✎, click color in picture
Video clip, insert		See Movie clip, insert
Web page, publish	PPT 174	Click File, click Save as Web Page, select Save as type, click Save
Word Outline, import	PPT 154	Click Insert, click Slides from Outline, select folder and Word document filename, click Insert